THROUGH THE MAGIC DOOR

Ursula Moray Williams, Gobbolino
and the Little Wooden Horse

THROUGH THE MAGIC DOOR

Ursula Moray Williams, Gobbolino and the Little Wooden Horse

An official biography by Colin Davison

northumbria | press

Published by Northumbria Press
Trinity Building, Newcastle upon Tyne NE1 8ST

First published 2011
© Colin Davison 2011

A catalogue record for this work is available from the British Library.

ISBN: 978-0-857160-06-5

Designed by Northumbria Graphics, Northumbria University
Printed by Short Run Press

CONTENTS

Acknowledgements

I wish to thank members of Ursula's immediate family for their help, encouragement and advice, particularly her sons Andrew and James John, in the preparation of this biography, for permission to quote from works and letters, to reproduce illustrations, and for correcting many inaccuracies. Responsibility for remaining errors and for comments not attributed to others remains my own. Other members of the John family trusted me with memories and correspondence, for which I am deeply grateful, and hope that they will feel repaid to some degree by what they read. They include Elizabeth, Eve, Jeremy, Peter, Robin and Susan John, Elizabeth Beckett, Alexandra Butler, Alison Crowther and Sophie Richmond.

Erkel Moray Williams kindly allowed publication of Ursula's many letters to her late husband Alan, which she went to great pains to date, and with her children Nicholas, Ella and Aleksander warmly welcomed me in Denmark. In England and New Zealand, many Unwins provided extensive information about the family's distinguished and fascinating history. My thanks go to Richard Calver, David, Martin, Diana, William, Carol, Brigit, and Christine Unwin, to Merlin Unwin for permission to quote from family correspondence, and to Michael Brodrick, Joy London, Judith and Ruth Miller, Basil Nolan, Frances Pra-Lopez, Sue Studholme and Lynette Turberville Smith. Most letters between Ursula and her twin sister Barbara were destroyed, apparently by mutual arrangement, but Vifill Magnússon and Ágústa Sigfusdottir in Iceland kindly supplied surviving examples and their own recollections.

Much of Ursula's archive is held at Seven Stories, the Centre for Children's Books at Newcastle upon Tyne, with publisher-related and educational material also available at the universities of Reading, Bristol, Exeter and Roehampton. Staff at all centres have cheerfully supplied information and documents, often beyond the call of duty. Record offices including Hampshire, Surrey, Worcestershire, Buckinghamshire, Gloucestershire and Warwickshire, the Bodleian, Oxford University, plus numerous libraries, museums, schools, charities, public bodies, publishers, newspapers and voluntary groups in the UK and abroad responded to sometimes vague enquiries with impressive precision and speed. It was cheering that so many replied with an aside about having loved *Gobbolino* or the *Little Wooden Horse* since childhood.

Dennis Archer, Harold Barstow, Hannah Green, Ralph Hallett, Robert Howe, Paul Langton, Anthea Morton-Saner, Brian Ryder and Harry Willis Fleming have generously shared their enthusiasm and knowledge of their special fields for considerable periods, sometimes I fear at the expense of more valuable claims on their time. David Rymill has worked splendidly to put together a touring exhibition and has helped in numerous other ways. My thanks go also to Glenys Ambrus, Alastair Arnott, Sid Atkins, Penny Barfield, Jill Barker, Dr Robert Bearman, Evelyne Berlioz, Sylvia Blanche, Peter Bloor, Wendy Bowen, Victoria Bryant, Carol Burdekin, Austin Burn, Lesley Caine, Kornelia Cepok, Sarah Charlton, John Clark, Gill Clarke, Philip Clifford, Dr Neil Cocks, Belinda Copson, John Coulter, Margaret Courtney, Elizabeth Crowley, Trevor Cunnick, Claire Davies, Christopher Dawkins, Sally Day, Pennie Denton, the Rev. John Dickson, Anne Dinan, Gunvor Edwards, Mike Eglington, Peter Elliott, the Rt Rev. David Evans, Matthew Eve, John Eyre, Chris Farara, Des Farnham, Christine Faunch, Christian Fernandes, Susan Fogarty, Geoff Fox, Donald Gimson, Michael Good, Stephen Govier, Linda Graham, Chris Green, Mary Greensted, Heather Hailey, Shelagh Hancox, Anne Harvey, Rachel Hassall, Susan Hayes, Terry Heard, Gerald Heath, Susan Hetherington, Angela Hicken, Syd Hill, Steve Hird, Arthur Holden, Steve Holland, Julie Hooker, Martin Horrox, Paul Howard, Barbara Innes, Arthur Jenkins, Claire Jones, Daniel Lawson, Caroline Liggett, Hannah Lowery, Jette Lund, Mairi Macdonald, Howard Mallinson, Patricia Maguire, Margaret Mahy, Sally Martin, Linda Merman, Bob Miles, Duncan Mirylees, Graeme Moir, Virginie Morand, Tor Morisse, Nicky Morris, Elaine Moss, Paul Moynihan, Dr. Cordelia Moyse, Carol Mullins, Kenia Munoz, Linda Newington, Emily Oldfield, Father David O'Malley, Deborah Overton, Frances Owen, Caroline Owens, Nick Park, Neil Parkinson, Hugh Petrie, Catherine Polley, Mike Pryce, Helen Pugh, John Pulford, Mary Ray, Prof. Kim Reynolds, Fran Ricketts, Jean Rose, Norman Rosser, Sara Sadler, Mike Shaw, Father Patrick Sherlock, Robert Simonson, Di Stiff, Nigel Sutcliffe, Tony Sutherland, Christine Taylor, Sandra Theaker-Elliott, Fiona Thomas, Jill Thompson-Lewis, Colin Thornton, Louise Trevelyan, Gina Turner, Tania Vian-Smith, Claire Weatherhead, Charles Webb, Yasmine Webb, Stephen Webbe, Patrick White, Alan Williams, Dame Jacqueline Wilson, Anne Wood, Sue Woolgar, Katherine Wootton, Gina Worboys, Sophie Workman, Kate Wright, Jen Young and Margaret Young.

Lyricist Sidney Clare cannot have endeared himself to writers of biography with his advice not to talk about the departed "if you can't say anything real nice." Yet this one would not have been possible without the cooperation of hundreds of people who knew Ursula Moray Williams or those close to her, and almost without exception they expressed profound admiration for a woman of tremendous energy and innumerable acts of kindness. I am most indebted to so many who rummaged through attics and memories to help. They include: Jessie Alexander, Sandra Andrews, Charles Archer, Antoinette Bachmann, Sheila Bangs, Chris Barnett, Gerry

Barnett, Gill Barrett, Ann and David Battersby, Joanne and John Bell, Mavis and David Bell, Father Bill Bergin, Rosamund Berry, Diana Birch, Nancy and Michael Blinkhorn, Alexander Boyd, Doreen, Martin and Andrew Buckley, Shirley Bulpitt, Amanda Bunbury, Douglas Bunce, Jean and Julian Burgess, Ursula Burlingham, Jessie and Maurice Chambers, Anita Cheney, Ann and Nicholas Clark, Bridget and David Cooper, Christopher Cordingly, Lord Cottesloe, John Darlington, Tom Davies, Rosalyn Deakin, Rod Duncan, Margaret Feeney, Jenny and Michael Fuller, Marthe Gardner, James Gilchrist, Helen Gooding, Inge Gosney, Janna and Justin Gowthorpe, Simon Griffin, Doreen Harris, Jill Harris, Joy Hawker, Susan Hawkins, Jo Heydon, Roy Higgins, Dagny Holland-Martin, Shirley Hughes, Barbara Innes, Joyce Jacobs, Stuart James, the Rev. Basil Jenkyns, Father Brian Jerstice, John Johnson, Sue Kearnan, Janet Knott, Werner Krauskopf, Tony Larkham, Alison and Christopher Laughton, Clive Lawrence, John Leahy, Sir Michael Leighton, Sue Lindsay, Anne Liversidge, Rosamund Long, Sheila McCook-Weir, Lord Malmesbury, Barbara Marsh, Emlyn Matthews, Belinda McEvoy, Ted McWhirter, Andy Moore, Sarah Mordant-Smith, Graham "Psyche" Morgan, Elizabeth Nixon, Dennis Oxley, Py Paavolainen, Beatrice Paine, Clive Pearce, Elaine Pearse, Alain and François Perrelet, Pamela and the Rev. Horace Phillips, Simon Phillips, Barbara Phipps, Fiona Podd, Gillian Pole-Carew, Wendy Porteus, Rene Ratkovic, Louise and Paul Reynolds, Nicola Rhodes, Jane Rørdam, Robert Rowland, Pauline Rowson, Katrin Rutter, Gillian Shute, Lesley and Graham Slater, Margaret Smallwood, Carol Smith, David Smith, Philip Smith, Elizabeth Stirling-Lee, Nick Tait, Roger and Stephen Tandy, Ruth Taylor, David Tew, Joanna Tucker, Marjorie Vincent, Catherine Wallace, Arthur Watkins, Rosalind Watt, Emlyn Williams, Anne Wood, Bruce, Rosie Woodward and Alison Young.

Extracts from Puffin Post and letters of Eleanor Graham are reproduced by permission of Penguin Books Ltd. Comments by George Anderson, Ian and Walter Harrap are reproduced with permission by Chambers Harrap Publishers Ltd.

I thank Shirley Hughes and John Rowe Townsend for permission to quote from letters and published works. Extracts of letters from Kaye Webb are quoted by permission of Kate and John Searle. I am grateful to Curtis Brown and Bedales School for permission to reproduce extracts from their archives.

The cover picture of Ursula is by Inge Gosney, by whose kind permission it is reproduced. The photograph of Bradley's bookshop is reproduced by permission of Petersfield Museum, and that taken at Hurn Court by permission of the Red Cross Balfour Museum, Winchester.

Every effort has been made to trace copyright holders. The publishers will happily rectify in future editions any omissions or errors of which they are made aware.

Finally, because lengthy acknowledgements are often read from the end, I thank my wonderful wife Maggie for tolerating three years of neglect during which I chased after an older woman and for her frequent wise advice about dealing with the outcome of that infatuation.

Colin Davison

Preface

"Writers for children must still be children themselves."
A.S. Byatt, *The Children's Book*, Vintage (2010)

Ursula Moray Williams, ninety-five, blind and nearly deaf, clamped on the red earphones and settled back to listen. The story was about a Little Wooden Horse. On other days it might be about a cat: Gobbolino, or Jeffy, or one called Mackenzie. There were stories about ponies and hobby horses, about toymakers or funny Bogwoppits, or about a Good Little Christmas Tree. The words were her own, but some had been written sixty or more years earlier. Ursula had forgotten her heroes and like successive generations of her own readers listened to their adventures as if for the first time.

There were many stories to choose from, for she had enjoyed one of the longest and most prolific publishing careers of the twentieth century. From 1931, when just twenty years old, until the appearance of *Paddy on the Island* in 1987 when she was seventy-six, Ursula Moray Williams published sixty-eight books including bestsellers like *Adventures of the Little Wooden Horse* which remained in print for seven decades. Another, *Gobbolino the Witch's Cat*, became even more popular, although it so nearly disappeared from circulation. If one includes short stories, plays, poetry and unpublished works, the list of her titles approaches two hundred. That would be a noteworthy record in itself, but in addition she provided admirable illustrations for thirty of her own books, including two complete sets for *Gobbolino*, plus some for other authors. But as remarkable as her output as a children's author was the background that produced it, in particular the extraordinary, fantastical world in which she grew up and which shaped her imagination.

Ursula was born in Petersfield, Hampshire, on Wednesday, 19 April 1911 – ten minutes after her identical twin Barbara. Their father Arthur Moray Williams gave both girls his second Christian name. He was at the time a Classics teacher at a public school where he had met his wife Mabel. They came from clever but different family backgrounds: his a mixture of Anglican clerics, adventurers and industrialists; hers merchants, educationalists and strict Nonconformists. Mabel's brother, Stanley (later Sir Stanley) Unwin, was to become one of the world's most influential publishers and although he published only one of his niece's books, he played a key role in her early career.

My children grew up with some of Ursula's classic titles. "Just one more chapter," they begged at bedtime. "Just one more page ... just one more paragraph." "Just one more LINE," if earlier pleas failed. By chance, our family moved to a village close to hers, but even then I knew little about the author. I wondered about the kind of person that could write stories with the power to captivate our seven- or eight-year-olds like no others – absurd yet utterly credible, exciting, funny, inspiring in their slightly old-fashioned way, but not out of date and never overtly moralistic. I had not the least idea that they were interconnected with the writer's own upbringing to an astonishing degree. That discovery led me to write this biography.

Until 2002, when she was ninety-one, Ursula had regularly flown over the Cotswold and Malvern hills in her son's flimsy microlight aircraft and used earphones to hear what he was saying from the pilot's seat. The receivers, as big as coconut shells, fitted tightly, blocking out all sound except the voice that talked into the microphone. So later, as her hearing declined, she used them from her armchair for communication with a wonderful world that was otherwise shut off from her senses. It was her son's idea to use the system in her living room, and so, as he recited her stories, Ursula could reflect upon a remarkable life, for the adventures included frequent references to identical twins, to horses, to mountains, to ideals of virtue and courage, and to the extraordinary, grandiose and dilapidated house of childhood fantasy in which she grew up. When she died on 17 October 2006 she had in a sense never left it.

Colin Davison

Chapter 1

"The house was the biggest he had ever seen, and the oldest and most tumbledown."

– *A Castle for John-Peter,* Ursula Moray Williams[1]

The old car crunched to a halt and three children peered out into the rain. Their father got out to open two worn, white, metal gates before the vehicle lumbered on through the ruts and puddles of the muddy road which lay between large fields dotted with elms. On they drove, past a saw mill where a clanking traction engine blew up the smell of freshly cut timber, and through another gateway as the lane curved to the left. Then appeared a tall brick wall overgrown with creepers, hiding what looked to be a secret garden just like the one in the children's favourite book.[2]

It was hard to see ahead. The drive was largely enclosed by dense greenery, tall tangles of laurel and lilacs, limes, beeches and sycamore, flecked with the purple blooms of bushy rhododendrons and the stalks of red campion arching from the woodland fringe. Suddenly, through an opening in the trees, the children caught a glimpse of the extraordinary house they had been told about.

Beyond an allotment garden was the rough, unadorned, almost windowless rear wall of a building with a peculiar octagonal turret, as tall again as the lower storeys. The building disappeared behind another high wall, momentarily out of the children's view until their father swung the car around a wide semicircle onto the front drive to reveal the house itself. It seemed ancient, enormous, and abandoned. Yet this was to be the home where Ursula Moray Williams would write her first ten published books by the age of twenty-four, and which she would use as a source of inspiration in another fifteen.[3]

It was the summer of 1922. Ursula and her identical twin Barbara were eleven, four years older than their brother Alan. They had been living in Petersfield, Hampshire, where the girls had joined the Brownies and learnt to ride. So when their father had been asked to run a convalescent home in Stoneham Park, near Southampton,[4] they were sorry to leave. Half a mile away from the Home of Recovery, across once elegant grounds laid out by Capability Brown, stood an even larger mansion: North Stoneham House. Built over a century earlier, but never completed, it had been damaged by fire in 1831. Since that date, and possibly before, the gradually crumbling building lay unoccupied until it was requisitioned during the First World War for wounded Belgian officers. A colonial judge had then briefly rented the habitable rooms and when he left Arthur Moray Williams and his wife Mabel decided to move in. They were all going to live, he proudly told the children, in "a folly deep in the woods."

The house needed substantial repairs to make it suitable for long-term occupation. So to allow time for these to be carried out and for their rooms to be decorated, it was decided that the children should spend a few weeks with Mabel's father at Bromley. When all was in order, they travelled back by train to Eastleigh railway station where their father helped them to load their bags, and themselves, into the back of his second-hand Studebaker. Its canvas top gave limited protection against the rain that August afternoon, but if its young occupants were dampened during the three-mile journey to North Stoneham, their curiosity was not.

The turret that could be glimpsed through the clearing stood on top of a 100-foot long series of single-storey façades and colonnades of varying heights, all surmounted by balustrades. Most of the windows were blind, and from somewhere inside the building came the regular *thump, thump* of a water pump. This, however, was only a service wing of the building. The main block was situated further down the drive, where Mabel already stood waving on the steps – a small figure made smaller still by the twelve thirty-foot tall columns that ran along a low terrace in front of the house. The four central columns supported a portico that extended over part of the driveway, and it was here that their father parked the car and the youngsters ran out into their mother's arms. Either side of them, the main section of the building stretched away for seventy-five feet, with twenty large windows arranged symmetrically on two storeys. If the new arrivals had stepped back, they would have been able to see a further nineteen windows hidden on the roof, skylights of tiny bedrooms once intended for a company of domestic staff, but never inhabited. The building seemed endless. Counting all the attics and cellars, it had more than one hundred rooms.

The children ran up the three shallow steps and through the twelve-foot high double doors into the lofty, square entrance hall. It was slightly gloomy inside, and the marble slabs felt chilly under their feet; but what caught the girls' attention were the glass display cabinets arranged around them. There were foxes and weasels, owls and jays, a magnificent if somewhat decrepit golden pheasant, and larger collective displays of stuffed ducks, songbirds, hawks, gulls and kittiwakes, as well as a particularly attractive arrangement of smaller seabirds, presided over by a handsome puffin.

A door to the right led to a second hall, the sole purpose of which now seemed to be to accommodate a tall organ housed in a case richly ornamented with Greek designs and with pipes rising to the ceiling. Lying incongruously beside it was the top of an old coach that had had its wheels and shafts removed. But it was to the organ bench that the twins scrambled, each wishing to be the first to send a volley of sound crashing through the house. Neither could play, but they had watched organists frequently enough at church services, so where were the keyboards, the stops, or the pedals? Alas, they soon realised, the only thing they could play with this organ – with its cavernous space where once the manual had been – was hide-and-seek.

The most remarkable features of their new home, however, were yet to come. A large door opened into the 'Saloon', designed as a showpiece of the house, but now showing ominous signs of wear and tear. The circular room, nearly twenty-four feet across, was lined with imitation red marble panels. Eight lofty pillars of the same dark red material, with Ionic scroll capitals like those on the columns along the outside terrace, held a gallery with an iron railing that ran around the top of the hall. Above was a domed ceiling; in its centre a round glass panel was painted with what was later claimed, probably spuriously, to be a copy of a picture by Michelangelo, and surrounding it, on smaller glass roundels set in the flaking ornamental plaster, were naked angels, signs of the zodiac, and symbols of the seasons. Much as the children may have admired the architectural features, they soon appreciated this part of the house more for its potential for games – pretend battles in which the gallery became castle battlements, roller skating around the hall, or playing tennis between its pillars. Conditions for playing were much improved when the cupola collapsed during a storm; the smashed marble floor was replaced with wood and plain glass substituted for the Classical scenes above.

On the left of the round hall was a door that hid the staircase to the gallery and the first floor rooms. On the right, a heavy door led into what Ursula and Barbara had expected to be the greatest treasure of all in their new home. Both were prodigious readers, so when the twins complained about moving away from their friends, or tired of the moralistic volumes at the strictly Nonconformist house in Bromley, their father spoke of the magnificent library they would have at their new home. "There are hundreds of books there," he told them. "They should keep you busy for years." If this account, often repeated by Ursula in later life, is true, his care in checking the details of the property before signing the lease must have been less than diligent.

The library was certainly a magnificent room, the largest in the house, extending across almost the full width of the building, and with three double-height windows opening onto the south terrace. Between the ornate ribbed pilasters stood high shelves apparently filled with titles in English, Latin and other languages, many with what appeared to be fine leather bindings. In fact, when the children tried to take them down for inspection, they were shocked to discover that neither the bindings nor the titles that they supposedly contained were what they seemed. Most of the apparent cabinets were little more than boards to which book-ends had been glued. Others pulled out to reveal six-foot long drawers. "We secretly hoped to find relics of some past tragedy," Ursula later wrote. But there was no such success; there were in fact no books in the library and no relics other than those that the children might invent for themselves.

At the back of the house lay other rooms, most of them empty and without plaster – homes now to mice and insects, and frequented by birds. There were many cellars, some of them without ceilings and open to the skies, others storing items linked with the maintenance of the four hundred-acre estate, all of them thickly strewn with cobwebs. The judge's mother and sister still occupied a few end rooms, reached by a separate entrance, and estate employees lived in tiny lodgings at the back of the northern service wing. Nevertheless, as Ursula and Barbara made their way to bed that night, carrying candles up the stairs to the gallery, past oil lamps that were the only other source of light, and along the vast first floor corridor that stretched one hundred and twenty feet into the darkness, the only sounds were their own footsteps and excited chatter. From the bedroom window they could look out upon a a great cedar below the house, or up towards a plantation of ancient yews. Hidden from view within the grounds were artificial lakes and islands that invited exploration. From outside came the hooting of owls, and perhaps the calls of nightingales, which guests would later complain kept them awake at night.

The house was cold and draughty. It had no electricity. Parts were dilapidated or unsafe. It was in the middle of what was now a largely neglected woodland, a mile and a half from the nearest proper road. The house was decorated with imitation marble, to a plan never completed, designed to accommodate servants who never came. It held a deteriorating collection of dead birds and animals, an organ without a keyboard, and a library without books. What a place they had come to. What a life they would lead. What stories they would tell.

Chapter 2

"The way was long, long, long, like the journey in a fairy tale."
– *Christmas-Tree Land,* Mary Louisa Molesworth[1]

The decrepit mansion might have been an improbable family home, but it suited Arthur Moray Williams well. He had just been promoted to Hampshire County Director of the Red Cross when he took on responsibility for the convalescent Home of Recovery. He could walk to his office through Stoneham Park, or drive from North Stoneham House to the charity's headquarters in Southampton in 15 minutes. He was not without a theatrical sense of the absurd, but even if very few of its rooms were furnished or habitable, the idea of living in the imposing pile rather suited the image that he wished to cultivate among the patrician hierarchy of the Red Cross.

For Moray, as he was known to his family, was a snob. Both his daughters later said so,[2] and if corroboration is required, it might be seen in the way that he used his name. Until abandoning his teaching career during the war he had been known simply as Mr Williams, but it had no doubt polished a small spot of vanity to christen each of his children with the middle name of Moray. Red Cross colleagues and records then generally refer to him as Mr A. Moray Williams. Strangers invariably called him "Mr Moray Williams," and by the time of his retirement, his name often acquired the distinction of a hyphen.[3] This had the odd effect of ruling out Moray as a familiar term to those who met him for the first time in later life, for he could not be Moray Moray Williams. As he preferred to remain somewhat aloof, this presented few difficulties.

Moray, pronounced "Murray", was born in 1878, the third of nine children. His father, the Rev. John Alfred Williams, vicar of Alderminster, Warwickshire, was a genial but conservative disciplinarian with a tendency to xenophobic outbursts. Asked at a celebration lunch to give the simple toast "Church and State," he could not restrain himself from coupling it incongruously with the cry, "the Anglo-Saxon race against the whole world." But it was cricket not politics that was his passion, and his metaphor for life. Players should do as they were told both on and off the field. He complained at the village club's annual dinner that other team members did not always accept his decisions as captain. Greater discipline was required, as he splendidly illustrated: "They did not say that the great charge of Balaclava was a good order," he said, "but think what credit it brought on the British army as regarded its cavalry. Cricket was the same."[4]

Within a few years of taking up his position in Alderminster, however, the vicar's authority started to diminish. He started to miss matches and meetings. His hands trembled. Aged only forty-two, the Rev. Williams made a terse farewell, sold the living, and never worked again. Moray avoided talking about his father, but Ursula discovered the truth from others. The spirit that drove him was not that of the Holy Trinity. "Grandmother Williams was very hard on him because he was so fond of drink and had to move on from parish to parish," Ursula told her brother Alan years later. "She didn't like it when he drank.... I never heard her mention him and neither, I think, did my father. They were a bit ashamed of him."[5]

Grandmother Williams, the former Evelyn MacLeane, Grandmother Williams, the former Evelyn MacLeane, came from a long line of settlers, soldiers and clerics who had made their marks in the West and East Indies, in India and the Middle East. She chose the names of her third son, Arthur Moray, after her clergyman father Arthur, a Classical scholar and headmaster, and her uncle Moray, a major general. It seemed as if those names were auguries of the boy's career, for after boarding at the military-oriented Felsted School and obtaining only a third-class degree in Classics at Selwyn College, Cambridge, Moray took up a post to teach Latin and Greek at Weymouth College. There he was appointed as lieutenant of its Engineer Corps and trained the boys – in their Ruritanian cross-belted uniforms and high-peak caps – in such skills as musketry, signalling and camp disciplines. The association was not to last. After the Corps' captain accused the headmaster of embezzling funds to send his son to Eton, the latter departed and the Corps was disbanded. In 1902 Moray too left the troubled establishment.[6] He was young, headstrong, and wondered where this strict, conservative upbringing with its emphasis on martial values was leading. He thought about his father, about the drink, and decided to join the teaching staff of Bedales in the lovely village of Steep, near Petersfield, Hampshire – one of the most informal, liberal, pure-minded and anti-militaristic schools in the country.

One of the first friends that Moray made at Bedales was Sidney Unwin, known to pupils and staff as "Bunny Unwin." The nickname had an affectionate bounce to it, and it stuck with the science teacher who also gave lessons in gardening, kept the school chickens and helped on its farm. It suited too the rather shy personality who loved the peaceable character of a school where pupils dug potatoes, and were let off lessons to go haymaking.[7] Sidney was also a boys' housemaster, so when, in 1904, a vacancy arose for a girls' assistant matron, he suggested that his younger sister Mabel might apply.

It was no surprise that Mabel should follow a path indicated by one of her brothers, even one as mild-mannered as Sidney, for her childhood had been shaped by the male competitiveness around her, at home and at the Congregational Church that dominated family life. Their parents, Edward and Elizabeth, ran the household in the London borough of Lee according to strictly Nonconformist principles. The

Bible was read aloud morning and evening and a grace before and after meals. Manifestations of wickedness, such as playing cards, going to the theatre, or anything remotely frivolous on a Sunday were banned, and as demonstration of the triumph of the soul over the flesh, not a drop of alcohol was permitted into the house. Mabel's youngest brother, the future publisher Sir Stanley Unwin, described the extent to which religious observance occupied their lives, especially on Sundays:

> We and all three maids solemnly trooped into the drawing-room, where we sang a hymn. After the Bible reading we all knelt down and my father prayed. His capacity for extempore prayer was unrivalled. There seemed to be no reason why he should ever stop, and there were times when I irreligiously wondered whether he ever would.[8]

A distant uncle of Mabel's, the Rev. William Jordan Unwin, had been an early advocate of the theories of the educator Johann Pestalozzi, later developed by Friedrich Fröbel, including the idea that infants should be taught at home. Accordingly, Mabel was sent to study at the Fröbel Institute in Germany and then enrolled as one of the first students at Sesame House near Regent's Park, an establishment founded "to fit girls and women more fully for the woman's life – a life whose natural character has been somewhat overweighted in these days by an excessive attention to intellectual accomplishment." A highlight of the year was a visit from a dairyman who brought his cow.[9]

Mabel was "an astonishingly sweet character," sympathetic, retiring, loving and timid. Ursula called her mother "the sweetest, most gentle peacemaker ever born."[10] Yet the humility of the young woman able to radiate such warmth seems also to have contained the anxieties of imperfections visible only to her. Under a quotation from Milton, "Nothing is here for tears," she wrote Biblical references against what appears to be a checklist of worries: "Depressed … losing confidence … discouraged about work … out of sorts." There may also have been other emotions at work. Mabel, pretty, well educated, sympathetic and single "received an embarrassing number of proposals of marriage," all of which she declined.[11] When the last of these came from the only other resident teacher at the school she had joined in North London, it seemed time to move on.

Bedales was different. Influenced by the moral aesthetics of John Ruskin and the Arts and Crafts Movement, its charismatic headmaster John Haden Badley insisted that his pupils must be able to "handle an axe as well as a bat." Co-operation not authoritarianism was the model, and Badley led by example. Each week the older boys cleaned out the latrines from which the headmaster shovelled the waste to the very top of barrows wheeled away by the younger pupils. Visiting inspectors praised the school's "enhanced vitality," while critics referred to "enthusiastic amateurs dealing with children of cranks."[12] But the particularity that set Bedales apart and for which it won both commendation and derision, was that it had just introduced residential co-education. When Mabel joined her brother Sidney on the staff in 1904, the school had about forty-five female pupils, one third of the total number of students.

One of the benefits of the change, the *Bedales Record* reported that year, was the inclusion of "real girls instead of sham ones" in school stage productions. Moray had already established himself as a star writer and performer in the entertainments, for which he soon gained popularity and the dubious compliment of the nickname "Smirk." Mabel took a minor part in a Greek play, then, in 1906, the attractive assistant matron was persuaded to take the leading role of Lydia Languish in Sheridan's *The Rivals*, with her lover Captain Absolute played by Moray. In fact the production called for Moray to clap Mabel to his bosom not once but thrice as, after opening before a "boisterous" school audience, the production was repeated with equal success in Steep and at Petersfield Corn Exchange as a "Penny Pop" – founded as an alternative attraction to public houses on Saturday nights. Despite the absence of alcohol, the failure of the gas supply, and footlights that filled the stage with smoke, the pair took their final bow before an enthusiastic house which "applauded the entertainment to the echo."[13]

On Saturday, 31 August 1907, the Nonconformist daughter and Anglican son were married neither by minister nor clergy, but by a registrar in his modest office at Park House, Bromley. From there the couple went to the grounds of The Mount, Shortlands – Mabel's parents' imposing new home – for a solemnisation ceremony and reception. In front of a semicircle of eighty guests, two Congregational ministers stood on handsome carpets surrounded by banks of flowering plants and potted ferns. In this "sylvan glade … two tall palms rustled a gentle benediction, as the breeze stirred their fronds over the bridal pair," the *Bromley Times* reported. The Rev. Williams stayed away.

For a brief time, the newly married couple lived at a large, secluded cottage that boasted a paddock, stable, and pigsty, but which lacked more basic amenities such as electricity, an inside lavatory or a mains water supply. Within a year they had moved to Cherrycroft, at the top of Bell Hill, Petersfield, a five-bedroom house with a view over a valley (now the route of the A3) to the Hanger hills. Below, the top gable of Dunhurst, the Bedales preparatory school, was just visible through the trees. It was there, on 19 April 1909, that their first child was born.

The boy, christened Ronald Moray, seemed healthy enough at first, but the following spring brought the usual influenza outbreak at Bedales. It swamped the sanatorium and for a fortnight turned the school into a hospital with more than seventy cases. Ronald caught an infection and, on 23 February 1910, died of bronchial pneumonia, aged ten months and four days. Mabel, who had previously noted in her diary that, "We must … educate primarily and chiefly for motherhood,"[14] thought the house had not been kept warm enough and blamed herself for the rest of her life.

The tragedy came as a final blow during their early years of marriage when it seemed that each happy event was countered by calamity. A month after their wedding, Moray's younger brother Philip had died of tuberculosis and typhoid fever. Moray's father was taken seriously ill at the end of 1908 and died before seeing his first grandchild born. Then Sidney, the brother whom Mabel had followed to Bedales and in whose company she had lived almost daily for five years, suffered a nervous breakdown.

One cannot causally link these events with what followed, but the loss of his brother-in-law, father and son within a short period may have given Moray a particular sensitivity to an appeal for the Red Cross to establish the Voluntary Aid Detachments that were later to become invaluable in the First World War. At the time of their launch, response was relatively slow, but in 1910 Moray enrolled as Assistant Commandant of the first men's unit formed in Hampshire.

On 19 April 1911 Mabel gave birth again: first to one daughter, then ten minutes later to a second. To the happy mother, it was as if a kindly fate had dictated that they should be delivered two years to the day since Ronald had been born. "We were given two babies for the one we had taken away," Mabel would say.[15] Like Ronald, Barbara and her younger sister Ursula were given Moray as a middle name, as if in recognition of the fact that they were identical. As babies their duplicate appearance and reactions added to their charms. Visitors and relations fussed over them. "They are the sweetest, dearest little couple, so sturdy and rosy and happy," said one. Myfanwy, daughter of the poet Edward Thomas, became a childhood friend. The only way that she could tell them apart was by a tiny mark Ursula had on her cheek.[16] Those who lacked the intimacy or effrontery to stare never could tell.

Ursula was three at the outbreak of the First World War. She later wrote about it as "one long thundercloud of dread to me, yellow and grey, that went on and on." Written some years later, however, the description may owe as much to fears about another coming conflict, as to actual recollection of events.[17] Contemporary photographs of the twins show nothing different from a normal, peacetime childhood, except for their father sometimes striding rather stiffly across the background of their lives wearing a civilian uniform. Moray had been reprieved from immediate conscription because he was too old, partly deaf, and because three days before the outbreak of hostilities he had been appointed as an Assistant County Director of the Red Cross.

Naturally the twins were photographed together: in a double-hooded perambulator, identically dressed with identical dolls, or in a babies' race on the Isle of Wight. They dead-heated. These were happy times. Other photographs show them playing with a menagerie of cuddly toys, or reading picture books on their bed or in the garden. Elsa Mueller, an artistic Danish nanny fond of wearing large bows, arrived in March 1914 and taught them to draw. There was a cook too, who warned the girls not to talk to the gypsies who camped on the common between the house and the hill. "They like to take away little children," she told them, and as a result they "scuttled past the caravans in silence and never waved a hand."[18]

There were also older girls to play with when Cherrycroft took in boarders who could not be accommodated at Dunhurst. One can imagine, therefore, a feeling of consternation when four years of undivided, curious and loving attention were undermined on 17 June 1915 by the arrival of a brother, Robert Alan Moray. "We were just a bit bored with him, partly because the nurse was very possessive, and partly because, as the precious boy child, he stole our popularity," Ursula wrote.[19]

The charmed circle within which each twin had a like partner to share every activity, every game of make-believe, left little room for another.[20] The problem for Alan as he grew up was that he desperately wanted to be let into the circle. A garden portrait taken when he was four seems to sum up the situation: Barbara and Ursula sit back comfortably on a bench, a new picture book spread equally across their laps. Alan has been asked to pose with them. A hand has been tucked under a sister's arm, but there is not quite room enough on the bench, and turning sideways he half sits, half stands on its edge for the time required to take the photograph. Clearly neither book nor bench were intended to be shared with him.

It was probably Mabel who ruled out Bedales for the girls' education, and not only on the grounds of cost. She knew what they might expect if they went as boarders or day pupils. The writer and Bloomsbury Group member Frances Partridge recalled with horror her experiences there as a young girl in 1915. Every morning her head girl "would stand at the door and call our names, whereupon we had to leap out of bed, strip naked except for a very small towel round our shoulders, race along the passage and jump into a cold bath." Then there was the naked bathing in the swimming pool, "the only exception being that something had to be donned when diving off the top board, since it was 12 feet high and its occupant visible for miles." Presiding over all of this, and passing comment on the girls' practice, was the impassive figure of the headmaster. The bathing was therefore "not popular with all the girls by any means, particularly the fat ones."[21]

Mabel provided their early education at home, reading sometimes in the garden to the twins who sat in suitably Fröbelian child-sized chairs, and teaching them to read when they were only three. From the age of about seven, they attended Lincroft School, at Heath Road, Petersfield, which was opened by sisters Sybil and Norah Nixon around 1907. It offered, according to a former pupil, kindly discipline, "a good grounding in the three Rs" and a firm foundation on Christian principles. The latter was evident in the scripture instruction that Ursula and Barbara sat through on Wednesday afternoons. They evidently failed to take to heart the framed text that greeted their entrance each day – "Whatsoever thy hand findeth to do, do it with all thy might" – for the lessons had to be repeated the following year. Ursula hated going, so much so that her parents decided she and Barbara should be educated at home permanently.[22] Neither of them ever went to school again, apart from a few months at a school in France a decade later. Ursula hated that too.

Elsa had returned to Denmark during the war and recommended her friend Ellen Stubb as a governess. Pictures of the gently smiling, well dressed, pretty young woman appeared in the family album, a privilege indicating that she must have been a popular choice. Ellen covered academic subjects while Mabel taught English and read constantly to the twins and later to Alan. "We greatly enjoyed her doing this, and always begged her to read another chapter," he recalled. "There was, however, one rather unfortunate feature of these readings. My dear mother lived the plots of the stories so intensely that when something tragic happened, like the death of Dickens' Little Nell or Hardy's Tess, tears would roll down her cheeks." The girls usually were more stoical and embarrassed, but "ached for her even while we despised such wasted emotion."[23]

The twins were six when they heard Collodi's story of *Pinocchio*, first published in England by their great-uncle T. Fisher Unwin. As well as Sherwood's improving stories of the Fairchild family, Ursula loved the books of Mary Louisa Molesworth, especially *Christmas-Tree Land* with its final reunion of the children, the chosen tree and their long-lost father. *The Secret Garden* by Frances Hodgson Burnett and *Two Little Savages* – the story of two boys camping among Indians by Baden-Powell's friend Ernest Thompson Seton – became favourites, and although the cannibals and sharks of R.M. Ballantyne's *The Coral Island* captivated the twins' imagination, it was Ballantyne's *The Kitten Pilgrims* that they really adored – its words and frightening pictures relating the perilous journey of two kittens sent out into the world by their mother to overcome evil beasts such as Giant Sloth and Rhinoceros Sulkyface. Mabel had known *The Kitten Pilgrims* as one of the "Sunday" books approved by her parents Edward and Elizabeth, and now her own girls demanded that she read it over and over again.

The twins found more serious works, many of them with Highland connections, when they visited their now widowed Scottish grandmother Evelyn at her house in Chesham Bois, Buckinghamshire. The excitement of staying there was, as Ursula recalled, "the rich banquet of children's books that had belonged to my father and my aunts and uncles, that was ours for the choosing, and with nobody to take the slightest notice of what we read."[24] Her appetite for books was prodigious. Not counting the annuals that she felt unworthy of recording, by the age of ten she had read or heard her mother read at least sixty-three books, including classics by Sir Walter Scott, George Macdonald, Mark Twain, Charles Dickens and H.G. Wells. Mabel believed in choosing books a little in advance of the age of her listeners, so the girls soon recognised when she hesitated on or skipped an unsuitable passage. The following morning they would run downstairs to check on what they had been denied, but usually found, to their disappointment, nothing naughty. They preferred, however, stories about children, and the books they liked best touched on common themes: kindness to animals, the grandeur and terror of mountains, the natural world, the courage of small adventurers and the security of a happy home. These were themes that Ursula would make her own.[25]

By the end of the First World War sixty-five names had been written in gold on the dark wood panel of the Roll of Honour commemorating former Bedales pupils and staff killed in action.[26] In Petersfield alone, one of twenty-eight Red Cross districts in Hampshire, more than five thousand patients had been treated in the auxiliary hospitals set up in once grand houses lent to the Red Cross by their owners. Moray had thrown himself into the work, providing x-ray facilities and ambulances, arranging help for Territorial medical officers, and overseeing the distribution to hospitals of sugar, tea, bacon, cheese, dried fruit, jam, meat, margarine, butter, fish and suet as each became scarce. On 17 December 1918 he and Mabel travelled to Buckingham Palace where he received the Order of the British Empire medal from King George V.[27]

Bedales had continued to pay Moray's salary even though from 1916 the war had occupied all of his working time. As the conflict drew to a close, he had to choose between the school and the service. His decision was made easier by what had been happening at the former. There had been indications for some time that the increasing experimentation and radicalisation encouraged by the headmaster was leading to a sense of disorganisation – not a quality of which Moray would have approved. A parliament of pupils and staff led to the temporary abolition of punishable offences, and the junior school had started a programme that would, by 1919, allow children to do as they pleased in a regime with "no time table ... no rewards, no punishments, and apparently no compulsion."[28]

There was no guarantee that the administrative position offered by the Red Cross would be permanent, but it was no surprise when Moray left Bedales in the summer of 1918. In doing so, he changed social environments as well as employment. He left behind one that was intellectual, Bohemian, avant-garde, artistic, socialist and Quaker, in which his replacement Miss Peskett "built herself a hut to live in on the school grounds," for one in which his county president would be a marchioness, her successor a countess, his secretary and treasurer a brigadier general, and his colleagues would further include five countesses, six ladies, four honourables and three colonels. He received an apparently one-off honorarium in 1919 of £391 13s. 4*d.*, worth around £60,000 in average earnings today, plus motor and other expenses.[29] Soon there would be a change of home too, which outwardly at least seemed to advertise his elevated social status.

In 1921, looking to create a permanent ex-servicemen's convalescent home, Hampshire Red Cross bought Stoneham Park House – set in twenty-two acres, north of Southampton – from the Willis Fleming family at a bargain price of £7,250.[30] Moray, who had just been promoted to County Director, agreed additionally to manage what would be the Hampshire Home of Recovery. It was while visiting the premises that he came across another, even larger mansion on the estate, which had, rather uncomfortably, housed injured Belgian officers. After the war, it again stood empty and barely habitable until 1920, when a colonial judge, Mervyn Tew, moved in temporarily with his pregnant wife before they and their baby went back to Nigeria. It was quickly agreed that Moray should take over the lease at North Stoneham House at a cost of £60 a year,[31] and in August 1922 the Williams family took up residence. A few months later the roof fell in.

Chapter 3

———

"Those silly children on their hobby horses. They think they're real."

Ursula and her sister had been sorry to leave Petersfield and so many friends like Myfanwy Thomas and John Greenwood[1], the barrister's son who would crawl through the hedge from next door. The twins had also transferred to the local Girl Guides as soon as they were eleven. They loved the uniforms with the dark blue wide-brimmed felt hats, the games and stories about woodcraft and home skills, and life in the open air.

In the summer before the move to Stoneham, their idolised Guide Captain took the girls to their first camp to put into practice those so-called frontier skills that had been drilled in the meeting hall. It proved memorable. Rain poured incessantly. The "frightful" pits used as outside lavatories became so slippery that both Ursula and Barbara fell in and both longed to go home. So naturally when Mabel and Moray visited the camp on its Open Day, sheltering under umbrellas, the twins told them how tremendously they were enjoying themselves, and went back to their tents to console each other in their misery. A weakness such as homesickness, Ursula seemed already to have concluded, was a condition to be confronted.[2]

Even more than they missed that first Guide company, the girls were sorry to bid farewell to the horses that they had learnt to ride at the riding school run by the retired Major Fenn and his wife a mile from their home. Pictures of horses were hung around their bedroom walls, small models ran along the mantel shelf, and the twins longed for the day they could have a pony of their own.

Even before their riding lessons, however, this lack had not prevented them from joining the local hunt, at least unofficially. Mabel had provided the means and Moray the socks. These were old bed socks stuffed with rags, with buttons or tiddlywinks for eyes, and long woollen manes. The twins had been rather proud of the leather reins that draped over the broomsticks or the branches from the woodpile that made up the bodies of their hobby horses. They built up a quite a stable of favourite mounts: Trixie and Brownie, Victor and Kelpie, Bracken and Briar, Madcap and Mischief. There was McTurtle too, apparently a creature of uncertain bloodstock, indeed species, created for Alan.

Barbara and Ursula, Bubble and Squeak as they liked to be called, hacked and chased on their trusty one-legged friends, and at the age of ten were ready to take the adventure to a new level by going along to a meeting of the foxhounds that regularly gathered outside the Cricketers Inn at Steep. The girls were splendidly turned out in scarlet jackets with silver buttons and black velvet caps made by Mabel and Ellen, with real whips, black gumboots and white breeches that only the unkind might have called pyjamas. They even had a hunting horn brought along by Mabel's younger sister Ella. To the twins' delight the Master and a fellow huntsman gave them both rides on their horses, but a younger onlooker was not so amused. Ursula told an interviewer fifty years later, "I can remember the scornful remarks of a well-turned-out little rider on her smartly groomed pony: 'Those silly children think they can go hunting on their hobby horses. They think they're real!'"[3] That naturally was the point and in her books *The Twins and Their Ponies* and *Hobbie*, which very precisely re-tell these incidents of the author's childhood, the exploits of their wooden heroes more than match any by animals of mortal flesh, and put to shame those riders who might be regarded as "show-offs, and snobbish and selfish."[4]

The taunt probably did not sting too much at the time. The twins were starting to outgrow the fantasy, so the hobby horses were exercised less often. When a friend asked Ursula many years later what happened to them, "she looked rather sheepish and said they were left in the attic and got all moth-eaten."[5] Their claims on the girls' affections had been usurped by their rivals at the stables of the Major Fenn, who had been so struck by his pupils' enthusiasm that he had started giving them an extra free lesson every week.

Now at their new home, much of the twins' effort was directed towards acquiring their own pony. There was plenty of space for animals. Fluffy stuffed versions had been replaced by a real dog, a cat, bantam hens, guinea pigs, and for a time ferrets, which bit the twins and terrified the guinea pigs. The equivalent equine presented a greater challenge. Money would be needed not only to buy the pony, but also for its oats and hay, for shoes, and tack.

The girls saved pocket money and added to it birthday and Christmas gifts from aunts and uncles. Soon a sizeable amount had built up, which their father had promised to double, but the rate at which they could save still seemed insufficient. The problem was solved by Mr Kitcher, head gamekeeper of the estate, who offered the family two white goats. Moray agreed that these could be looked after by the girls. Soon 'Pip' and 'Peter' produced a kid, and from that point the twins had a regular source of income from selling the milk to their mother. The cat liked it too.[6]

The output meant that they soon had enough money to buy a small, plain Welsh pony for £10 from the milkman. Yet with the new pleasure of riding the gentle, bob-tailed Puss, or having her pull the cart that was donated by a kindly neighbour, came new responsibilities that began at 7.30 each morning. After a quick mug of milk (cows', for the twins refused to drink their own wares), an apple, bread and cheese – eaten while reading a book at the kitchen table – they took it in turns to groom and ride the pony, or to milk the goat and clean the stable.[7]

Goats feature in one of Ursula's earliest surviving stories, *The Blue Wizard* (written in 1927), in her first two published books and in five of the first ten. Three later titles are based entirely on their misadventures, *Tiny* (1971 in the collection *Hurricanes*), the unpublished *Tim's Goat* and the full-length *Beware of this Animal* (1963). The last of these was based directly on the twins' goat Peter – a "devil" that creates havoc in gardens and allotments, butts those to whom he takes a dislike, and defies capture. The eponymous anti-hero is fed rhododendrons mistaken for laurel, and has to be treated with castor oil, an incident repeated in *Tim's Goat*, and *A Castle for John-Peter* (1941), suggesting that this really happened in the rhododendron- and laurel-filled woods of North Stoneham. With so many details in the latter title reflecting faithfully the manner in which the animals were kept, Peter looks a likely suspect also as the inspiration for another incident when a goat wanders into the kitchen and is taken upstairs to frolic around, but bounds downstairs and charges against a door, waking both the mother of the house and the maid.[8]

The goats were free to wander for much of the day through the wild and mostly unkempt park and woodland, grazing off the bushes and wild flowers. They were not alone. At night rabbits attacked almost everything Mabel planted in the garden that she had created at the back of the house, and stoats attacked the rabbits – their cries waking the children who ran from their beds in the hope of bringing rescue. The summer night air also brought the sounds of birds, five or six nightingales calling in unison with a song that "echoed off the moon," and the burring undertone of a nightjar.[9] Ursula and her sister learnt to mimic the sounds of owls and to lure them closer. They learnt every inch of the ground by heart and could tell where and when most of the nests were made.

The cuckoo, they discovered, always came in the first week of April at around the time that goat kids were born. It was the "high time of the year." The girls collected primroses and sent them in boxes to relations in London and Scotland; then there were bluebells to pick, and in autumn blackberries, nuts, and sweet chestnuts that they roasted on the fire.

As he had done at Cherrycroft, Moray built a tennis court, levelling part of the field below the main western façade of the house. Here on summer nights, glow-worms spotted the grass "like eyes," and the twins found additional entertainment by arranging them in a clock pattern – which to their delight the creatures had largely maintained the following evening. East of the house, below the walled garden that the children had passed on their first journey into the grounds, lay a large lake surrounded by trees, with a weir at one end and an island at the other. The island was inaccessible, but a larger lake just beyond the steps from the south terrace had an island that could be reached by a causeway. It became a favourite fantasy land where the children made houses and secret places among the twisted rhododendron roots.[10]

"Trees and flowers are all children of God," Mabel had written as a young woman in her treasury of thoughts and quotations. Indeed animals and nature were to be one of the main sources of inspiration to Barbara in her career as an artist, and were never far from the foreground of Ursula's writing. It was not a sentimental attachment; both observed and understood the gentle spirit of Puss and the wilfulness of Peter. They had tamed a robin but seen the ruthlessness of stoats, weasels and foxes. For Ursula, unlike her pragmatic and agnostic sister, such things were to inspire something more: a pantheistic faith confirmed by the miraculous and irrepressible life forces that surrounded her every day.

Ellen Stubb had returned to Denmark in the summer of 1922 and Moray advertised for a successor to come to North Stoneham. The first applicant, a Miss Maxwell, was sitting on the edge of a chair in the dining room when the twins were told to come downstairs to meet her. The girls were hostile, Miss Maxwell nervous, and within a few minutes she had departed by taxi. By contrast, the second applicant remained as the children's governess and began a friendship that was to last sixty-four years. Evelyn Rattray was the thirty-four-year-old daughter of Scottish naturalist Thomas Rattray, co-founder of Westonbirt arboretum in Gloucestershire, and had inherited her father's love of trees and wild life. Perhaps it was this that had persuaded her to take the job, as no interview seems to have taken place. "Anyone who has Miss Rattray in their house may count themselves a lucky family," a friend had written, and this appears to have sealed the contract.

Lessons followed a regular pattern of school terms, between which Miss Rattray – who for reasons now forgotten was known as "Tchat" – went home. In the evenings, while the girls knitted "unevenly matched" socks for friends, Mabel continued to read aloud adventure stories by Jules Verne and H. Rider Haggard, classics by George Eliot, Rudyard Kipling and the Bronte sisters, and Kenneth Grahame's *The Wind in the Willows*, which at the time became Ursula's particular favourite. Tchat extended the girls' reading with Austen, Dumas and Hugo. Such was her love for literature that even the essay subjects she set on these topics were "entrancing." Ursula remembered the drawing and painting sessions, continued from the time of Elsa and Ellen. Tchat also taught French, probably natural history and home economy, but if other subjects were taught, they seemingly made little impression. "We all loved her dearly," Ursula wrote of the time. "I remain so grateful to Tchat and my parents for their emphasis on books and reading aloud. I'm sure I would not have become a writer without their encouragement."[11]

Lessons took place at first in what was still rather grandly termed the library. The large panels glued with handsome fake leather spines of fake books that had reached to the ceiling had by now been removed. In their place were conventional, low shelves of genuine books, stacked irregularly and regularly used, with others spread across the large refectory table that effectively defined the classroom. The cases of stuffed birds and animals had been rescued from undignified neglect in storage and arranged on top of the bookcases, and the placement of a large, wooden, diamond-shaped heraldic crest over the entrance gave quite an appearance of baronial grandeur to the room.[12] It was not to last.

Disaster struck first in the domed hall. Once home to long-departed busts of George III and George IV, the children had found it perfect for ball games and roller skating. During their first winter in the house, the Williams family were awakened by what they thought was the echo of thunder as it crashed over the clearing between the trees. In fact the storm had split in half a large cedar behind the house, but a worse scene of devastation lay inside to be discovered when Moray came downstairs in the morning. The glass in the centre of the dome had shattered and its potentially lethal shards, three-quarters of an inch thick, had cut through the floor below. Estate workers boarded over the missing panes to keep out the rain and later replaced them with plain glass; wooden slats were laid to fill the gaps between the unbroken floor tiles. The children continued to play there, but not without their parents' anxiety that the roof might fall in again.

The family might have suspected a few days earlier from faults like worry lines in the ceiling plaster of the library that something was seriously wrong with the structural integrity of the building. The faults seemed no worse than in other parts of the house until one day, during a lesson, there were sounds like pistol shots and the cracks were suddenly transformed into a lattice work above their heads. Moray decided that the classroom, its large table, authentic books and varied taxidermy should be moved. The false bookends were restored, the library locked, and the pupils, teacher and furniture installed in a sombre chamber on the first floor under the portico. Unfortunately, the roof leaked in this room as well as the guest bedroom nearby, where rain dropped into receptacles in a musical scale of plops, keeping visitors awake at night. So this room too was abandoned for an even colder but at least brighter one further upstairs, with a lovely view over the lakes. For the next six years, this would be the sisters' schoolroom, and it was here that Ursula wrote her first published books.[13]

Ursula could not remember when she and her sister started inventing stories. It was some time around the age of six, or to put it more precisely, a few minutes past seven o'clock. Bedtime always came early – not until their teenage years were the girls allowed to stay up until supper – and unable to sleep they would tell each other stories. "Now you!" one cried, throwing the narrative to the other when she was stuck. Each carried on, avoiding violent changes, trying to keep the invention airborne until the next "Now you!" sent it flying back. First they invented three families, taking it in turns to make up their adventures, then animals, and inevitably horses. From the age of about ten Ursula's cast of characters included a little wooden one.[14]

From an early stage the twins started to write down by day the stories they had made up by night, adding their own illustrations. Ursula claimed to have written her first full-length book while staying away from home at the age of six, "about a rather horrid little boy." (Alan would have been two at the time.) She could remember little about it, except what his drawing looked like, and that she had given the whole thing to her hero of the moment, a young man who had given her a ride on his horse. "I expect he gave it to the horse," she concluded.[15]

At first, they used their father's old envelopes, split down the side; then exercise books for their stories, with pictures in paint or chalk; and for a few months produced a magazine, typed on a broken old machine and sold to relations for a few pence per copy. Like most magazines, it lasted only a few issues, but in its place came something more significant. The twins agreed to write and illustrate full-length books for each other for Christmas and birthdays as long as they lived. Remarkably, the promise was fulfilled for more than six years. They probably produced the first for their last Christmas at Cherrycroft, but it was of writing them at North Stoneham that Ursula left the most vivid account.

For twelve weeks from late September and again from mid January, they worked simultaneously with pens and paint boxes at opposite ends of the schoolroom table for two hours at a time. Each guarded her work from the other's eyes with a barricade of open dictionaries standing end to end, and there was uproar if either felt the rival had peeped. "Much as we loved my parents and governess," Ursula recalled, "the real and personal part of our lives was segregated even from them. Once lessons and meals were finished we were off together to our mainly imaginary and vastly superior world, which we defended fiercely from adult intrusion or participation."[16] They wrote, always about children or horses, in their father's discarded old board-covered ledgers, having torn out the early pages filled with his exquisitely neat Latin and Greek handwriting. Not a word must be seen before the special day, when the books, two hundred to three hundred pages long and with many watercolour pictures, would change hands after breakfast. There were always other books, bumper volumes and girls' annuals to be enjoyed between more approved reading, but nothing among their presents had so much importance for the twins as these treasured works. By the time they were fifteen there were around twenty-six volumes on the shelves of their bedroom. All were lost during the Second World War, much to Ursula's regret,[17] and sadly denying the opportunity to compare the work of the two sisters – each trying to surpass the other, as much for the joy of possession as for the satisfaction of creation. Alan, who wished so ardently to become a successful writer, later noted somewhat scantly that after opening "of course we were all expected to read and admire [the] little handwritten volumes."[18]

The family were not the only audience for their talents. Douglas Bunce, then aged nine, who lived with his family in a cottage by a stream deep in the woods of the estate, was one of about a dozen children and grown-ups invited to a special performance of *St George and the Dragon* that Ursula had written, and which was performed in a glade of giant yew trees about a hundred yards from the house. "It was just like a cave, a lovely setting," he said. "It was all yew needles that you sat on. I remember the dragon passing along, pulled by one of the princesses." A copy of the play, illustrated by Barbara, was found among Ursula's papers. It is not known who played the hero, but we do know that, waving a wooden sword made by the author's craftsman uncle Bernard, he proclaimed:

> Ho dragon! Monster, eater of the fair,
> Upon whose dainty bones thou lov'st to gorge!
> Know this, I'll fight thee to the death and more,
> I'll kill thee by my cross – I am St George![19]

This and nearly all compositions by Ursula to have survived from this period were written to be read aloud. From the end of 1926 the fifteen-year-old had been writing stories to read to her Brownies, who must also have met among the impressive yews. *A First Class Parcel* – with its clever comparison of the wrapping skills to be learnt by the pack of Brownies and the drop made by an owl of a closely-packaged skeleton of a mouse – would have gained her audience's immediate attention:

> The Pack was sitting under the largest yew tree in the wood, and it had just had tea, so everybody was rather crumby, and rather sticky, and not very inclined to move, and the bits of paper that had been wrapped round the tea were gradually fluttering out of the Brownie ring and trying to hide under the bracken where they wouldn't be noticed.[20]

The story was one of seven that appear to have been copied from earlier drafts, or written especially for the Guide camp on the Hampshire coast that the twins attended at Staniswood Farm, near Fawley at the end of July 1927 – the most recent having been completed less than a week before. It was the seventh time that they had been to camp, so Ursula and her sister were accustomed to being in great demand as storytellers. Even these early tales included themes that would recur in more mature work – the natural world in particular. Most, such as *The Blue Wizard*, are rather contrived, written to illustrate skills such as the use of knots or aspects of camp craft, but proved so popular that they had to be repeated. During the week Ursula told at least nine stories, and the younger the audience, it seems, the more she enjoyed telling them.

We know this from a diary that she kept at Fawley, her earliest still in existence, rewritten like later diaries in her then scrupulously neat handwriting from notes made at the time. Ursula recorded the habits of long-tailed and coal tits, the herons, redshanks and cormorants, and of Guiders too, like another Barbara who slept with a bottle of whisky, and another Miss Williams who, in a blanket bag away from everyone else, slept with Marjory, "sloppy things." The twins loved it: up at 4.30 a.m. before the others, paddling through a bog, confronting a bull, bathing in the sea, first to fetch and chop wood for the kitchen – which was "ripping fun." The Girl Guides, Ursula concluded, were "a great movement for females."

The twins stood out, and not only because they were identical, though that distinction continued to draw immediate attention. Before acquiring the nickname of Squeak to Barbara's Bubble, Ursula's pet name was "twin",[21] as presumably was her sister's. Collectively they now referred to themselves as "we" in the accusative as well as the nominative, and to each other as "the other of us." At home their identical appearance was a gift to be manipulated for their own amusement. Finding it tiresome to wash and change for visitors to North Stoneham, the girls would hide in the open space of the disembowelled organ. When the hiding place became known, they took it in turns for one to come downstairs, clean and tidy, to be introduced and shake hands, disappear and return to be presented again as the other. Mabel, embarrassed, carried on, and guests were no wiser.[22] At the Guides camp too the girls had fun by switching between patrols without anyone noticing; however, the stares from the curious adult Guiders when the twins were together was unwelcome, as was the habit of one leader who studied their faces intently to find differences. "She wouldn't like it if she was a twin – still we don't believe she really knows," Ursula wrote.

The frequency with which twins, particularly identical twins, appeared in Ursula's later fiction is perhaps the most obvious example of how she based many elements of her stories on features of her life – themes that were already evident by the time she was sixteen. As well as the horses, other animals and nature being the focus or the context for plucky heroes, there are many direct descriptions of North Stoneham, its house and the surrounding countryside. Her camping friends noticed another passion that distinguished the twins: food. Ursula noted virtually everything that she ate: sardines, potatoes, tomatoes, bananas, lentil soup, kippers, trifle, Ixion biscuits, and bread fried in lard with jam. She herself seemed to specialise in making the porridge and trifle, and noted how she and her sister were allowed to lick out a jam pot. "It was plum jam," she added with satisfaction. So the twins earned the additional nickname of "Ash bin", for their ability to dispose of leftovers. On their departure from camp they were given cards lovingly inscribed: "For the Royal Twins – we(e) in speech but NOT in size."[23] For the time at least, Ursula, who was in reality only slightly overweight, seemed happy enough with what she described as her "buxom" appearance in adolescence,[24] and in later life became celebrated for her home cooking. References to food occur in nearly all fifty-five of Ursula's full-length works, invariably associated with home and as a deliberate or unconscious allegory for a happy and secure family life.

It was possibly as a result of her success at Fawley that a friend sent copies of Ursula's stories to George Harrap. He sent a "very courteous and interested letter" in reply, commenting that the writing was full of promise, but not yet ripe for publication.[25] The immediate outcome of the submission might have been unsuccessful, but the choice of publisher proved a happy one. Harrap was to become an admirer, a friend if a rather reserved one, and from 1932 to 1955 the house of Harrap was to publish twenty-five of Ursula's books for children, including many of her most successful. Ursula, therefore, had the extraordinary good fortune to have not one, but two of the country's most important publishers interested in working on her behalf.

Stanley Unwin had taken over George Allen & Co in 1914 (forming George Allen & Unwin) and by 1927 was a wealthy man with an annual income of around £3,000.[26] He could be privately generous, but in publishing his parsimony was legendary. He had little interest in including juvenile titles in the company's lists, especially after finding at George Allen a large stock of plays for children which cost more to produce than they could command in sales revenue.[27] He was, however, very fond of his nieces, who had joined his family on holiday at their bungalow at Thorpeness, and keen to encourage their talents. Not long after Ursula's disappointment at rejection by Harrap, Stanley commissioned the twins to write and illustrate books for his own children. The handwriting in the surviving title suggests that Ursula wrote most of the words and that Barbara provided most of the pictures for *The Backwards Boy*; the story of a contrary child eventually cured of his predilection for doing everything the wrong way by being thrown through a mirror by his exasperated aunt. The book probably draws upon the girls' own observations: a pony cart, the mother who darns her dressing gown "under the collar where it doesn't show", the sage (Moray?) who uses long words, the teacher (Miss Nixon?) who kept pupils in late if they arrived after the bell. The central idea of doing things backwards might even have been taken from the rather farcical, but apparently popular secret code by which Agnes Baden-Powell had recommended that Girl Guides identify themselves. "D'neir felt til?" one asked, to which she should hear the answer: "Deraper peb."[28]

The best feature of the *The Backwards Boy* – one hundred and thirteen pages with three full-page colour illustrations and ten sketches – is its sense of collusive fun with the reader.

> All babies – or nearly all – are rather contrary, and prefer to do things just the opposite way to what their mothers think, and they are certain they know best … And, being babies while their mothers are not, they may quite possibly be right, for all we know.

Such whimsy would become one of the most appealing traits of Ursula's books;

however, she was not to have the chance to write another book for eighteen months. She and her sister had a remarkable knowledge of the literary classics and a reasonable ability to speak French. They knew more about the natural world than most people would learn in a lifetime, and had shown a natural aptitude as popular leaders and organisers in their first positions of responsibility with the Brownies and the Girl Guides. Other aspects of a more conventional upbringing, however, had been neglected, and in early 1928 it was decided that they should go to a college at Annecy in the Haute-Savoie, France to finish their education. "My father realised with some horror that we hardly knew the name of the prime minister of England," Ursula later explained.[29] How their knowledge of British history and politics would be enhanced by spending a few months in France is unclear. It is quite likely, however, that their parents, Mabel in particular, simply wanted their daughters to experience the challenge of living abroad, and the joy of doing so in the mountains. Mabel had been nineteen when her parents had taken the entire family to Lake Geneva for six weeks to celebrate their silver wedding anniversary.[30] Stanley had been nearly ten years old. He would later holiday regularly in Switzerland, and he and his sister Ella, a polio victim who was to spend much of her money on good works, agreed to cover the cost of the twins' stay in France in order to broaden their education. The product of their generosity was to become an inspiration.

Chapter 4

_____

"Meet the Muggets."

Ursula, Barbara and Mabel were met at Annecy railway station early on Wednesday, 4 April 1928 by Constance and Gaby Noyer, niece and granddaughter of a pastor, at whose home the girls were to spend the next six months. Their home, Les Muguets[1], a large house on the west bank of Lake Annecy, with a fine view toward the Parmelan mountain, also served as a classroom for Gaby's French dictation when the girls were not required to attend the town lycée. With up to seven other "Muggets" staying there, English girls of a similar age, there were many amusements including tennis, cycling, sailing, card games, knitting, and visiting favourite patisseries for gateaux and meat patties. The food was a delight, so Ursula was undismayed, and her colleagues amused, when the Noyers gave the twins illustrated texts for their seventeenth birthday, hers reading: "Donne-nous chaque jour notre pain quotidien."[2]

While others went to a gymnasium, Ursula and Barbara would sketch the lake, the mountains, or houses in the old district, and had painting lessons with a Mlle. de Banck, who "loves splodges" and "daubs on paint like jam." When she saw her pupils' work, she urged them both to become professional illustrators. At Les Muguets, Ursula had started to illustrate a copy of Charlotte Mew's poem *The Changeling* for a friend, Georgina Coles, and soon was in great demand to do similar work for others. Her ability to write was equally appreciated, particularly when employed in the popular game of poking fun at teachers and other girls whom the Muggets did not like. That talent had great opportunity to express itself at the lycée.

Accustomed to the special freedom of being taught at home by a governess she adored, Ursula had probably already decided that she would hate attending the college. While conceding on her first day that some of the staff and her fellow pupils were quite nice, she noted the "round and bulgy" art history teacher, whose class was incomprehensible, and the tall, pasty French mistress with pince-nez who compressed her lips "in a malicious manner when annoyed" and had the class of twenty recite poetry by rote. By the fourth day, her attention was entirely concentrated on writing a minute-by-minute diary for an hour recording sixty reasons she hated the place. A day's absence with a sore throat was "infinitely preferable to that hole of hell", and on her return a further lesson was entirely diverted into the composition of a long poem on imprisonment. It opens:

I am sick of the sight of the Lycée
My stomach recurs at the look
Of the blackboard all scribbled and greasy
And the blots that occur in my book …
The door, it is fastened and bolted,
The windows hermetically sealed,
And the room is all stuffy and scented
With the odour of girls fully-mealed. …
I wish I were up in a mountain,
I wish I were out on a plain
With nothing but freedom around me
And never a lesson again.

By the time that she returned home to England, Ursula spoke French almost perfectly, though she claimed to have learnt little else from the lycée. Instead, it was from the mountains, from time spent among orchids, crocuses, gentians, lizards, snakes and Camberwell beauty butterflies, watching hawks and listening to blackcaps and willow warblers that she brought back a lifelong inspiration. "It was all so beautiful … like living in a fairy tale."[3]

One of many expeditions with an Alpine club took the twins through thick snow and up steep, rocky slopes to the summit of the Chardon where at noon exactly the party sat down for a lunch of pâté de foie gras, oranges and chocolate. Behind them stood Mont Blanc, cut in half by a ridge of cloud. Among the group was "a rather nice looking little boy of about fourteen, very reserved," called Jean Pierre. Ursula, for perhaps the only time in her life, wished she could change sex, to enjoy the outdoor life more freely. She had always preferred the company of boys younger than herself, and his name must have stuck. Three years later it became the title of her first published work, about a boy and his goat who go climbing in the French Alps.

Other associations certainly remained long after the twins returned from their six months in France. Like a long-flowering tree of abundant fruits, Ursula had an inexhaustible ability to make friends and keep them over a long period. From Annecy, Georgina became godmother to her first child, and Gaby visited Ursula in England for nearly six decades. Back at North Stoneham, Tchat's employment had ended, yet, in 1985, sixty-three years later, Ursula was still paying her regular visits.

———————

While Barbara and Ursula had been enjoying the happiest time of their lives, their brother had been sent to a senior boarding school with a reputation for strict discipline and manly punishment. To Moray's great pleasure, his son was an intellectually gifted boy, good at languages, and seemed likely to progress toward an academic career. Nevertheless, at the time it cannot have seemed to Alan an equitable distribution of parental favour. Largely ignored by his sisters, he had grown up feeling lonely and insecure. Whereas North Stoneham had become a fantasy land for them, in which each had a permanent playmate, for him it was a place of isolation. Alan was not allowed to play with the 'common' children of the estate. Conversely, due to that acute awareness of social differentiation most discernable to the British middle classes, when the judge's son David Tew and his cousins came to visit their aunt, who still occupied the end flat of North Stoneham, they were forbidden to mingle with the Williams children.[4]

Mabel had largely determined the education of the girls, but Moray was going to decide what was right for his son. He needed, it seemed, toughening up. According to one story, the intellectually brilliant but recalcitrant boy was exiled to study in one of the abandoned rooms at the top of the house for refusing to obey his peremptory father. (The rooms were freezing, and crumbling. The children had found a bees' nest in one, with honey that tasted of the plaster.[5]) Alan was sent first to board at a preparatory school at Seaford, Sussex where the headmaster liked to discipline naked boys with the tawse. Once he caught Alan in the testicles as he swung the leather strap with abandon and was afraid the pupil would tell his father. He never did.[6] Moray decided the boy should then attend Malvern College. Its headmaster was also a Classical scholar from Cambridge, keen on tennis and on drama. In ethos, however, the college could not have been more different from Bedales. Information for new pupils stated that rounded collars were "obligatory for the first two years, all jacket buttons had to be fastened for a year, one hand in a trouser pocket was permitted after three terms and both after six." As a new boy, Alan would be required to sit in his study with one foot in the corridor in order to arrive in the shortest possible time when called to fag for older boys. When there he would be expected to hold bread slices in his bare hands in front of the fire because it was not allowed to use a toasting fork. Alan was searching for somewhere to belong in life. It was not Malvern, where he made almost no friends. "You have managed to escape from being overpowered by Father's so powerful influence," he told Ursula years later. "I could not escape from him and the Public Schools' mental tyranny."[7]

When they returned from Annecy, Ursula and Barbara were still uncertain about their futures. Both wanted to write, but both were also talented artists – Barbara had a particular aptitude for drawing plants and animals – and their most recent professional advice, from Mlle. de Banck, was that both should earn their livings with pen and brush rather than the pen alone. So neither knew what careers lay ahead when, in the autumn of 1929, they enrolled on the course in decorative painting at Winchester School of Art, travelling nine miles by bus every day to be taught by Andy Wilkinson, an "unattractive, rather tired, very disappointed, dispirited" man of forty-five.[8] One of the other students, who supplemented her modest means by posing for his life study classes, was Jean Gemmell. She became a close friend of Barbara and before long was invited to stay at North Stoneham. "This is the maddest place: enormous rooms and no electric light and parts of it are falling to pieces on top of you," she wrote on the back of a photograph taken at the time. Not far off eighty years later, her memories of visits were still vivid.

"You went into this tremendous looking house but the marble and the tubes of the organ were all painted," she said. "The water used to get so discoloured. I remember Alan, who was very blond, washing his hair and it would come out quite red. There was no electricity and when it was cold it was very cold. I remember at one stage trying to warm my bedroom with a candle in an earthenware pot. The room was along a narrow corridor, and you moved from one room to another as things in there got wet.

"Mr Moray Williams, very conventional and upper crust," would put on a jacket with a fresh shirt and tie for dinner and insist that everyone else changed, which was "a lot of trouble and rather a bore." His wife, however, was "very, very gentle. She was kind, and generous, and good. She had to put up with this job of putting up the lamps, cleaning the shades, trimming the wicks and filling them with paraffin every day." Jean tried, without success, to teach Mabel to drive so that she would be able to fetch visitors from the bus stop over a mile away.

Jean remembered North Stoneham Park becoming a popular venue for friends to meet one February when the upper lake froze hard and Moray pronounced it safe for skating. Ursula also recalled the event, with the alarming settling noises that sounded like cracks running across the ice, and another occasion when a goose got frozen to the ice with its breast feathers. The twins, who could not reach it, saved its life by throwing out pieces of bread for five days.[9]

Jean was seventeen or eighteen when she first came to North Stoneham, two years younger than her sister Maureen who was the same age as the twins. The Gemmell girls were tall, slim, and with the good looks to catch attention. Young men in the North Stoneham entourage courted them, and Moray must have been delighted to cast both of them in the Gilbert and Sullivan operettas he was producing at Romsey. Their popularity did not go unnoticed. "Ursula and Barbara were very clumsy, they were not elegant. She saw me with no clothes on – I had a marvellous figure and I know Ursula was envious of my sister and me who were better looking," Jean said.

Whatever the justice of this cool assessment, made by a woman of ninety-five more than seventy years after the event, Barbara clearly enjoyed greater confidence with the opposite sex than her sister. Ursula did not have a boyfriend. Barbara had encountered at least one too many. In the middle of the house was a deep, inner courtyard, level with the cellars and smelling of damp. Pestered by a young man whom she did not particularly like, she invited him to tea, and served it there, among the ferns, creepers and spiders. He did not return.[10]

There was no suggestion of anything more than a platonic relationship between Ursula and John Greenwood, three years her junior, when the former boy from next door came to stay in July 1931, although Barbara made herself scarce for most of the time. With Ursula, and occasionally Alan, John cooked, played cards, tennis, and stump cricket in the domed hall, and – that old device of juvenile flirtation – tried to teach Ursula billiards. He went with the Williams family to see Moray play Gonzalo in a production of *The Tempest* with the Rogate Players, and with Ursula and Alan for three consecutive days to watch a county cricket match. Ursula fitted in with what would interest her younger guest. That extended to his greatest passion, butterflies and moths, as the two set out with large nets on late "gloaming" expeditions, with Ursula being greatly congratulated on retrieving a Black Arches pupa from the trunk of a larch. Despite frequent rain, earache caused by the wind in his bedroom, and a "record nose bleed of 127 drops," at the end of the fortnight John went home happy.[11]

Given past experience, it cannot have come as a great surprise to Ursula's parents when, in 1930, before completing the first year of her course, she told them that she disliked attending art school every day and wanted to stay home to write. Mabel must have suspected something was wrong when her daughter burnt her hand with an iron and was forced to stay at home. The injury, as Ursula confessed many years later, had been deliberate.[12] Their reaction, reflecting a tolerance not to be accorded to their son, was generous. "While all our friends were doing jobs, and I *ought* to have gone off and earned my living, I was kept, and had a £20 dress allowance. It was small even in those days, but my parents weren't well off," she wrote.[13]

Before agreeing, Mabel and Moray had no doubt sought advice from Stanley, who could be relied upon for a realistic assessment of Ursula's prospects. In the winter of 1929 Mabel had joined her brother and his family on their annual holiday at Lenzerheide near Zurich. It had been a joyful reminder of their childhood trip to Switzerland, and her husband had been happy to stay at home and give her a break from the chores of looking after North Stoneham. Moray, British to the core,[14] disliked travelling abroad, probably a welcome reason for Stanley, who had little regard for his brother-in-law, not to ask him to come. A year later, Stanley invited his nieces. The prospect was immensely exciting. The twins had always loved their somewhat eccentric uncle – the one who had "jam on his dinner" as the young Ursula referred to him because of his liking for cranberry sauce. They were returning to the adored Alps, and the trip offered the great opportunity for an aspiring writer to spend three weeks in the company of one of the world's most respected publishers.

It was to be a glorious holiday. After a day of skiing, the twins would sit with their cousins David and Ruth to hear Stanley read Arthur Ransome's recently published *Swallows and Amazons* from one end of the table while their aunt Mary sat smiling at the other. Ursula had appropriately brought along *Heidi* by Johanna Spyri, and she may also have read to the company something of her own. Earlier in 1930, based on her memories of Annecy, she had written a story, all in verse and fewer than six hundred words long, about a mountain boy and his goat, and prepared four delightful full pages of coloured paper cut-outs and numerous black silhouettes. She had sent the manuscript first of all to *Punch*, whose editor said the piece was too long for his magazine. Stanley had then sent it on her behalf to a couple more publishers, now with Ursula's illustrations, but again without success.[15] Back in England after the holiday, he tried again; this time he sent *Jean-Pierre* to A&C Black in Soho Square.

Chapter 5

"Darling babies in their perambulators."

Ursula was not yet twenty when she received, via her uncle, the contract from A&C Black agreeing to publish *Jean-Pierre*. They probably liked the lilting rhythm – the boy skipping "away through the bracken all dewy and curly" – the repetition that would appeal to very young listeners, the art deco collages, mountain setting, and, at a time of deep recession, the fact that it was extremely short. An "engaging very small book," the *Times Literary Supplement (TLS)* called it. The author, whose language thereafter was always robust and direct, soon regretted the affected spellings, correcting "faeries" and other archaisms in her own copy after printing; however, it was in other regards an achievement of which she was justly proud. It was a precursor to the modern picture book and an indication of the themes to recur in her fiction for the next fifty-seven years: nature, faith, courage, food, shelter and homecoming. For good measure, the story concludes not with one, but with two homecomings: for Jean-Pierre, whose mother:

> Kissed him, tucked him up in bed,
> 'Angels keep thee safe,' she said.

And, after a bit of a butting from dad, for his little chamois goat, whose mother sought him in the hay, gave him all the milk she had, and licked his tears away with a goodnight plea:

> 'May the faeries guard my son,
> Sleep … O little wicked one.'[1]

Ursula signed the contract with A&C Black immediately, and returned it to her advisory uncle with a diffident enquiry as to whether she would have to give back part of her advance if sales did not reach a sufficient level. Stanley told her that although authors theoretically should so favour their benevolent publishers, they never did so. Diffidence, however, was not usually Ursula's style. She turned down Stanley's suggestion that *Jean-Pierre* might carry a dedication to all her friends at Annecy in favour, first, of "To Barbara and also to the rest of my family," and then simply "To my twin." Having written and illustrated the book, she then set about marketing it. Sometimes prompted by her father, she asked A&C Black for twenty-five publicity leaflets "as I know where to make good use of all of them" and advised her publisher to send review copies to *Punch*, and urgently to *The Guider* – for which she had written articles – in time for its December books' list. After the title had been on sale for a few months, and having heard little from her publisher, Ursula wrote a brief note informing A&C Black: "As I shall be in London on Thursday, I propose to call at about 4 p.m. and would be obliged if you will be kind enough to inform me as to the present position of the sales of my book."

Stanley had filled the window display of his offices near the British Museum with copies of *Jean-Pierre*, a rare occasion of one publisher promoting a title of another. Ursula asked if she were "presuming on [his] avuncular relationship" to seek his help in getting other works published. Her uncle unfailingly obliged, answering Ursula's letters on the day he received them, and sending manuscripts to publishers in Britain and America as her official but unpaid agent. "I can see," his grateful niece wrote at the end of the year, "there would have been many more books published if every would-be authoress was born with an equally gifted and generous relation." It is fair to add, however, that without Ursula's determination, and at least a degree of commercial awareness, it is unlikely that she would have established a writing career so early, whatever the benefits of avuncular assistance.

By the time that *Jean-Pierre* appeared in September 1931, Ursula had completed *The Princess, the Prisoner and the Pettabomination*, a story filled with humorous absurdities and private jokes. The palace has cellars (like North Stoneham) and conservatories (like The Mount), and there is a garage that the impoverished King had bought for the day he could afford an Austin Seven (just bought by Moray). *The Pettabomination* – under which title the book eventually appeared in 1933 – had been the name given by the Muggets to a hated household dog of uncertain breed. The story opens with what would become typical vivacity:

> The Princess's Papa lived in a very nice house in a suburb. It had a brass door-bell and a brass door-knocker and a brass door-plate with "The Royal Palace" written on it. On Saturday mornings the Royal charwoman polished them till they looked almost like gold.

The plot resembles the type of fairy story that Ursula's Brownies loved to hear. A wicked governess knits a spell and marries the king who imprisons a knight. The Pettabomination – a baby dragon found in a rubbish heap – helps release him and together they defeat a rival besieging the palace. The good knight marries the princess, and after the king's unfortunate marriage, the Pettabomination deals with the governess with unexpected finality:

> When the King had cut the wedding cake and was making a long speech, the Pettabomination suddenly got up and ate the Wicked Governess. You will not hear any more about her in this story, because there was nothing left of her to hear about.[2]

Ursula provided the line drawings, more than two hundred and fifty elongated Gothic grotesques that complement the story well, scattered around pages in a style that has been compared with that of Ernest H. Shepard for *Winnie-the-Pooh* seven years earlier. The central character, looking like a small, round, angry Pekinese, is, however, a curiously derived, unlovely creature. The book is long, with chapters of jarringly different lengths – some of only three or four paragraphs – and the author shows her inexperience in trying to interweave so many characters. Stanley probably sensed these weaknesses, as he offered the book first to publishers in New York in what he admitted was "a try-on" to excite interest at home. His persistence eventually paid off. Denis Archer published the title in the UK in April 1933. The *TLS* and *Manchester Guardian* praised its delights and unusual charm, although the former criticised the illustrations.

Anticipating the likely delay in finding a publisher for *The Pettabomination*, Ursula prepared what would now be called a marketing plan. In the autumn of 1929 she had been appointed as Brown Owl of the Brownie pack in the village of Bassett Green, close to North Stoneham, and for the next two years had continued to write stories for them and other packs, and to devise games and miniature plays for their Thursday evening meetings. The position also meant that she received copies of the Girl Guides Association catalogue. The issue for October 1931, she noted, listed two hundred books, mostly practical guides such as *Basket Making at Home* and *Peeps at the Union Jack and other Flags of the British Empire*, but few included the fresh stories and games that were "always heralded with joy by Guiders and Brown Owls." Ursula sent the catalogue to her uncle, pointing out that Harrap and Methuen published most of the approved titles. She enclosed her own illustrated material and said it might appeal to pack leaders, to Brownies wanting to read at home, and even to those outside the Guide movement. Stanley had until then been unable to sell *The Pettabomination*, and Ursula suggested that *For Brownies: stories and games for the pack and everybody else* would have more chance of success. "My only experience is that children seem to prefer books containing coloured pictures and short stories to others. I know my Brownies do," she wrote.

Her uncle agreed. His friend George Anderson, a director and co-founder of Harrap, planned to publish Ursula's *Hoot! Owl, Hoot!* – a story now lost – which also included illustrations and a simple music score by the author, but when next they met Anderson said they would publish *For Brownies* instead. The stories had been accepted at once. In a further agreement, the Girl Guides Association undertook to sell the book through its movement in return for a commission of 2.5%.[3]

The anthology contained eleven games and twelve stories. Among them was *The Blue Wizard*, previously recited at camps and during Ursula's time at Annecy; *Plumpy Cat*, with a pleasing amoral twist about a lazy animal who retrieves his lost mittens although "he didn't deserve it – but there you are"; and *The Story of the Twins*, who are "terribly alike," and learn to imitate owls and goats. A follow-up volume, *More for Brownies*, appeared two years later. The *TLS* was again complimentary about the "charming little imaginative stories reminding one of Hans Andersen."

After ten years in the guide movement, many of them as a patrol leader, lieutenant and Brown Owl of several packs and companies, Ursula had amassed a considerable number of her own stories and plays, all of which had been read and tested before live young audiences. As she and Barbara danced at a party to mark their twenty-first birthdays – watched from the balcony of the domed hall by children of the estate – it might have seemed that the path of her writing career was clearly marked. The short, lively fairy stories, with picturesque settings, purposeful twists and little need of deep characterisation were popular, and could be promoted by a still growing organisation with around 600,000 members.[4] But the style was a constraint for someone starting to address the business of writing with adult maturity. Her letters to Stanley had become more confident, whether about the terms of contracts, or in making acute assessments of the work of others anxious to exploit her special relationship with a leading publisher. One admirer who submitted a play had to be told that it was too old-fashioned. It was more difficult when friends pressed her to take their compositions to meetings in London. "It's you that I love," she told an offended Jean Gemmell, "not your poetry."

The next eighteen months were a time of uncertain directions for Ursula, creatively and in her personal life. Her writing was a vigorous shoot, struggling to burst from a tight husk. It was still unknown what shape it would assume. A&C Black, which after some deliberation had rejected *For Brownies*, took instead *The Autumn Sweepers*, a collection of four plays and two mimes that had been written for, and performed by Ursula's Guide and Brownie groups. She had sent the collection directly to the publisher without Stanley acting as intermediary. From the precise stage directions, it is clear that the author had learnt from experience – her own and her father's – how to command effective performances.

The title play drew its inspiration from mountain folklore; not of the Alps, but Scotland. Moray had inherited a love of the Highlands. In the summer of 1931 he had taken the family to join his sister Hester and her husband Graham, her first cousin, on holiday at Loch Garve in Ross.[5] Ursula read at least nine books about Scotland in 1931 alone, including the massive, ancient, and interminably dull Book of the Clan Maclean that she found in her grandmother's library. The Autumn Sweepers, dedicated to Ursula's Scottish governess Tchat, includes references to the buttering of cats' paws for luck, and the placing of a Samhain penny in the kirk box for good fortune on All Saints' Day, but carries its research lightly.

Further sophistication is evident with the carefully observed and anything but juvenile character of some of the dialogue.

Miss Elspeth (slyly): "I'd think shame of you, Margaret, that you should be peering after the minister at your age like a silly girl looking for a lover. And who else there is to be peering after the Lord Himself may tell us, since he has not seen fit to provide us with variety."[7]

News soon followed of performances of *The Autumn Sweepers* in England, Scotland and South Africa. Meanwhile, Ursula's career had taken yet another new turn with the publication in February 1933 of *Grandfather*, the most adult and one of the most intriguing works that she ever published. The six loosely-linked stories, written in verse without rhyme or metre, include two deaths, two murders, a suicide, a mad woman, the birth of a grandchild, and unmarried lovers. It is unlikely that Ursula ever sought the opinions of so many relations and friends for a book, or that they were so divided. She sent copies to authors she admired. Ernest Raymond was mildly encouraging: "It is in you … go on and on and on," he wrote. J.M. Barrie as usual failed to reply. Instead she received a formal acknowledgement "so cold and superior," from his secretary, which Ursula tore up.[8]

In 1932 Edward Unwin was ninety-two years old and clearly approaching the end of his life. Ursula saw how those who held him dear anxiously offered every service and forgave every physical failing. She began to describe her observations in a notebook, but soon found it easier to express her feelings by transforming what had begun as an "essay," into a fictional story set in the serenity of the Alps. In this imaginary account, the old man gazes with pleasure from his last resting place at the mountains and flowers beyond his window, whispering brown mice scuttle along the bedroom floor, and children and grandchildren season his soup or prepare the shroud that he will be happy to wear: "It is very pleasant to be old, and to be lying in this feather bed. If this is death I'm glad of it." It is a remarkable insight into old age by a writer aged twenty-one. This story, for which Barbara suggested the title *Afterglow*, became the first of six.

Ursula's favourite of the collection, and probably the best, was *Apples*, a strangely moving account of the mad wife laid in a room behind the kitchen "where the apples lie in long, cobbled rows." The wife kisses the apples, twists her yellow hair about the bed, and breaks the cups and saucers. "I fed her from my fingers like a bird," says her husband. All six stories share a faith independent of formal religious observances, and a wonder in nature. The description can be exquisite – the cows "sighing through their eyes," the snails wrinkled under their shells "like the petticoats of old women."

Despite its enormous charm, it would be hard to identify an audience to which *Grandfather* would have appealed in sufficient numbers to make it attractive to a commercially-minded publisher. Stanley was commercially-minded, but he was also an Unwin. It was usually a condition of any contract that he negotiated for his niece's books that they should be printed by Unwin Brothers,[9] now run by his brother Ted.

He also frequently helped Moray and Alan by offering them work as readers, and Barbara with art commissions. Most significantly, *Grandfather* was dedicated to his father. He published it in February 1933 – the only title by Ursula that appeared under the George Allen & Unwin imprint in his lifetime.

The work was not an unqualified success. Some metaphors lack consistency, and the writer can lapse into a prissy vocabulary that jars against the strict avoidance of sentimentality in its observation. Objects and animals that are not little are tiny or small. It was "a peculiar little work," according to *Current Literature*, which nevertheless concluded: "There is genius in these pages." Ursula was sensible enough to consider the critic illiterate and his judgement unconvincing. *The Morning Post* praised the sincerity that avoided the "terrible gulf between *simplesse* and *simplicité*." The *TLS* regretted those parts that descended from naive into the ridiculous, and "a too consciously continued ingenuousness," but praised the "lyrical and Alpine flavour which is distinctive and appealing."[10]

In Ursula's first five publications she had thus far produced a charming poem for very young children, fairy stories, games, simple songs, a short novel of about 14,000 words, plays, extensive sketches and colour illustrations, and reflections on life and mortality in fashionably free blank verse. Privately, she was writing poetry, plays and prose for adults and children, and the start of what looks to have been a romantic novel which opens with a scene on a London underground train. It would have been hard to predict at this time how her career would develop. Her output was prolific, but its diversity seemed to reflect a more personal uncertainty about the future. Two invitations were to have a significant impact on what lay ahead: one was to write a book; the other was to attend a dinner, and it was to change her life.

Ursula longed to be married and to have children. She would see young boys on buses or trains with their less than attentive mothers or distracted nannies, but she struggled to come to terms with all that entailed. It was, she supposed, a "sex oppression … beastly, horrible. … I want to be high minded and have beautiful ideals. If I could only marry and have children, boys, boys and boys, I know it would be different, or if I were attractive and never had the awful fear of not marrying. … I have a queer, entire faith in God, and I am always asking him to let me marry and have babies. I am so shy and self-conscious with men, except when they are younger than me. I want to adore my husband and mother him, and sometimes have him order me about and be a little afraid of him, and I suppose I am always thinking of sex really, even when I think it is other things," she wrote in her diary. She tried reading Freud, which didn't help, but watching nature did: "I saw two robins mating yesterday, beak to beak, with their little red breasts pressed together on the ground at my feet. They didn't notice me at all. I suddenly felt a pang of joy. I had been so worried about sex and being afraid, I was obsessed by it and fighting against it, but here was the real thing, unbeastly and beautiful."

Barbara was by now living in London. In early 1932 she had carefully wrapped an engraving on boxwood of bird skeletons and sent it to the Royal College of Art (RCA), hoping to gain admission that September. Not only were the entrance panel impressed, they gave her a scholarship and the British Museum bought the work – remarkable recognition for a twenty-one year-old.[11] She was soon winning other attention. Talented, popular, with the poise and social confidence among people of her own age that Ursula lacked, Barbara loved the intellectual and artistic life of the capital – and the parties and boyfriends that accompanied it.

When the twins' sociable uncle Ted and his wife Nell invited Barbara and some of her college colleagues to a dinner dance at the Strand Hotel on 20 February 1933, she happily accepted. Ursula also agreed to attend – though only after Nell sent the money for her fare – but, as she feared, found herself the odd girl out at the party. To her disappointment she got to dance only once, briefly, with Walter, a younger friend of Barbara who had spent the previous Christmas at North Stoneham.

Also at the dance was the twins' second cousin, Nora Unwin, who, by remarkable coincidence, had a near-identical sister, was studying engraving at the RCA, and would later publish children's books. Alongside Nora was her former boyfriend, Conrad John, known as Peter.[12] Ursula had probably first met him when the couple came to play tennis at Stoneham, and for a time it seemed as if the on-court partnership would lead to something more permanent. That prospect was changed by a box of chocolates. Peter had bought them as a present. Nora refused to hand them around, and in the wake of the row that followed had turned down his marriage proposal.[13] Ursula felt "desperately sorry" for Nora that the romance had not flourished. She did not seriously imagine that the tall, good-looking, former pilot would eventually turn his attention to her, and did not know him well enough to lean across her aunt Nell to speak to him at dinner. Peter was six years her senior, accustomed to the company of attractive women, and soon after his split with Nora started taking out one of Ursula's friends, Barbara Ward, leading to gossip that they might become engaged.

Ursula felt awkward, clumsy and shy. She watched in some bewilderment as her sister had a succession of romances in London. Ursula's affections had always been for younger boys like Walter, whom she had helped look after when he fell ill during a visit with his parents, or Robert, brother of a friend from Annecy who was "like a big puppy." There had never been anyone of her own age with whom she had shared a date, or anything more than a Platonic relationship.

When Ursula and Peter did talk later, she recounted a story she had read of a doomed expedition to the North Pole by balloon. He was intrigued. Young women did not normally talk to him so knowledgeably about things of such real and dramatic interest. He wanted to know more. Ursula promised to send him the book, but thought little more about it; it was over a fortnight before she did so. Peter quickly wrote back – "such a boyish letter" – which she had not expected to receive at all.

Ursula often went to London, visiting Barbara – whom she loved dearly, admired, and of whom she was slightly jealous – meeting with publishers, or staying with other relatives and friends. Sometimes she just enjoyed the freedom to wander alone through galleries, to admire the evening colours and reflections of the Thames, or to watch "darling babies in their perambulators." London, however, was uncertain territory. There were occasional sisterly arguments, though these were soon forgotten, and while Ursula was always excited by the prospect of discovery, of mixing with the most interesting of the capital's cultural set, there was often the disappointment, even the distress, of big city life. "In B's place it would depress me horribly," she wrote.

Ursula looked forward to nothing quite so much as the RCA Easter Ball in 1933. She had a new frock, a new partner – albeit a boring scoutmaster – and pictured herself dancing with witty, daring and clever young men. On the night, Barbara was on top form, surrounded by admirers, but Ursula felt only horror and embarrassment. The students "drag drunken bodies about the room aimlessly, stinking. It is so hot, and half-naked couples lie on chairs hugging each other like beasts. They are sick outside in the cloakroom." Walter, having arrived with Barbara, goes off with another girl. Couples form and re-form. Ursula goes outside hoping to escape, but is dragged back to join a chain galloping around the room. Clothes are being torn off and Ursula is afraid of falling, afraid of damaging her frock, of being thrown against the wall, of being heavy. Her dancing partner laughs at the frolics; she pretended to be amused.

The following morning Ursula went to see her grandfather, now close to death. Like his namesake in Ursula's book, he was lying in his comfortable bed, content in being looked after by the twins' aunt Ella and others. Ursula travelled home with Alan and Barbara. "I don't think anyone I know has such kind kinsfolk and such a home as we have," she wrote. "Alan and I are fast companions and everything is all right. We are back in the country and I shall begin again." The next day all was indeed all right. Ursula swept spiders from the bathroom and their webs from the corridors. She took her dogs through the woods starred with primroses and anemones. Summer was coming and the family was together again. Ursula and Alan would scramble through the bushes, snatching the flowers the other had collected just as they had in childhood, and Alan played Bacchus, making himself a wreath of laurel leaves.

Ursula's delay in sending Peter's parcel was understandable; she was working on *Kelpie the Gipsies' Pony*. This was to be the second momentous event in Ursula's life that year and a milestone in her career. By far her longest book to date, she completed it on 7 March; she sent *The Andrée Diaries* to Peter on the same day. *Kelpie the Gipsies' Pony* was to be her most successful title so far, selling more than 10,000 copies in the first two years, most of them in America. The tale of the pony allowed to run wild on a Scottish moor until befriended by a gypsy boy had also started with an invitation. In January A&C Black had suggested she write an animal story and shortly thereafter launched a competition for one of 40,000 to 50,000 words, suitable for children from eight years of age, which should be as true to life as possible. A good story about a horse or pony would be especially welcome, said a publicity leaflet.

Writing had now become a daily activity for Ursula – more a natural exhalation than a discipline. Her notebooks were filled with other ideas – poetry, fairy stories, a reverie on nature for *The Countryman*, 2300 words written in one day for a children's magazine – so progress was erratic. Ursula had plunged into writing *Kelpie* without great enthusiasm or an overall plan, but produced nearly six pages on the first day. Small episodes took shape; others were sketched to be incorporated later. Ideas came often in the bath. "Half the result vanishes with the waste water, but the essentials remain," she noted to herself. "The body being so utterly relaxed (the blood doesn't have to warm it any longer as the hot water performs that function) that the mind has time to work. I wish it were as simple to write down the ideas, but it's not easy sideways, in pencil and in bed, with a failing candle and many degrees of frost." Perhaps as a result of the writing being undertaken between other activities, the structure of the book is uneven, with some long, subsidiary passages delaying the main narrative. It seemed too that because the work would be judged as a competition entry, the author was trying too hard to impress. If like its predecessors it had been written to read aloud, she surely would not have written such overloaded sentences with up to nine subordinate clauses, or such an untypically clumsy phrase as that about a character who "ground knives as an appended means to livelihood."

Kelpie, a term for a ghostly horse of the lochs, had first been used by Ursula in *For Brownies*, and is one of several personal references to Scotland, gypsies, hunting, and somewhat incongruously to children attending a French school. Like the author, Tammas the gypsy boy knows much about animals and birds, and can mimic their cries. There is even a passing tribute to Ursula's riding teacher Major Fenn as Major Wren. Ursula was aware that some sections lacked incident, and that others might be shortened and rewritten more simply. But she let them stand and allowed the story to develop. As whole afternoons and evenings were dedicated to finishing the manuscript, the action increased in pace: boy, pony and dog rescue kittens from a flooded island; Tammas is left unconscious; and finally Kelpie's own fate is determined. All convey the excitement of having being written in concentrated spurts, and with the emotional punch of a writer who understood the realities of country life, and the natures of real animals, albeit talking ones. The author's ability to depict the character of Kelpie is extraordinary from beginning to end, from the approach of the nervous young pony blowing and "lipping" at the boy's hand and then starting back at the shock of being held, through to the speculation: "Who knows where ponies' thoughts fly when we suppose them sleeping?"[14] Ursula did, if anyone.

Ursula took a completed typescript to A&C Black in May, two months before the closing date for the competition. On the last day of July she learnt that *Kelpie* had been rejected. Harrap however accepted it without delay, and agreed that Ursula should do the line illustrations, which proved some of her best. Barbara would do the full-page engravings and colour plates. It was published in March 1934 and immediately became a Junior Book Club recommendation for the month. Walter Harrap wrote to the *Evening Standard* to endorse the title as "booksellers have taken up their usual apathetic attitude regarding it," and were waiting to see what reception it received in the press.[15] Publisher and author had to wait until the end of the year, when children's books were normally reviewed before Christmas, to find out the response. They were not disappointed. The *TLS* called it the best of eight books about children and horses. The *Manchester Guardian*, noting that the central character could talk, added "it is always in the most business-like way; the author makes no mistake, and never drops into unwelcome philosophy or sentiment on the part of the animal." Enthusiastic reviews followed in America, led by the *New York Times*. "The story is well written, but the brutal way in which Tammas's good-for-nothing relatives treat their horses may make painful reading for sensitive 9 and 10 year olds." In sales, and in recognition across the Atlantic, *Kelpie* was a breakthrough. More significantly, it taught Ursula valuable lessons about how to construct extended adventures, and the appeal of credible, plucky and sympathetic heroes, who through all vicissitudes of fortune find happy homes.

Chapter 6

"Someone to adore."

Ursula had written *Family Jane* in eight weeks during May and June 1933. With the embarrassing trip to London for the RCA ball still fresh in her mind, the work represented a return to all that was lovingly familiar. Eight months had passed since Barbara had gone to live in the capital. While the sisters remained very close emotionally, exchanging at least one letter every week, the twins who had spent such a large proportion of their lives in each other's company breathed a little more deeply in their own. Ursula no longer felt overshadowed by her more socially assertive sister, and with Alan away at boarding school she was left in sole charge of the North Stoneham heritage. She had in effect become the official custodian of their childhood memories.

The protagonist Jane, nicknamed Family Jane because of her wish to adopt so many of the babies she sees being wheeled in their prams, moves to the countryside with her governess – whose "thick shoes and country tweeds" seem "even nicer" than her city clothes. There Jane discovers an island, where – as at Stoneham – she and her friends play games of pretence: one to imagine a gang of crooks, another for a camp of Girl Guides, a third involving a goat, and a twin sister who magically and conveniently appears only on Sundays! Jane has lessons at home in geography, painting and literature with her friend Angela, and when the latter writes programmes for a concert, she does so "with the aid of Jane's paint-box … with an open book placed on end between her and the rest of the room, so that nobody should see or read what she was doing." Invited to recite a poem, Jane chooses Kipling – a favourite when Mabel read to her children – and at a campfire the governess tells a delightful story-within-a-story about glow worms, with a lively evocation of an Alpine mountain at night – and absolutely no relevance to the rest of the book. This digression aside, the narrative moves at a lively pace, with the childlike creation of a prison made from a few "stones, logs, branches and other impenetrable matter" to contain the imaginary crooks, and short, occasional but vivid descriptions of scenes as visible to the author from her window at Stoneham as to her fictional heroine.

> Everything had been so muddled and unsatisfactory lately. Over there it would be calm and peaceful again. The trees would drip quietly with autumn damp; the streams, clogged with leaves, would overflow and mingle with the marsh and bogs in winter comradeship. The old yew tree would be wet and black and smell strong and friendly.

Ursula had just sent *More for Brownies* to Harrap and must have intended her latest book as an extended adventure that would appeal to a similar readership. "When Hermione is big enough I feel sure she will want to become a Brownie," exclaims Jane, who finds that she too "liked being a Guide better than she had expected."[1] Despite these somewhat heavy-handed appeals, Harrap and other publishers were unconvinced. The original manuscript does not survive, so one cannot be altogether sure of its content, but from different précis versions that Ursula set down at the time it does seem that she was experiencing trouble in handling a story with more than a dozen main characters and many interconnected plot lines.

As well as writing, Ursula continued to work on her skills as an illustrator. She continued – or possibly resumed – art classes one day at week at Winchester. In her work for both A&C Black and Harrap, she had developed an individual style of silhouettes, coloured collages on black paper and ink sketches. As a result, in June 1933, Stanley asked if she would like to provide illustrations for one of Allen & Unwin's few juvenile titles, *Dan the Dog Detective* by George Wright. The fee, ten guineas and five more if it were published in America, was tempting. Ursula broke off from writing for another competition, this time for Methuen. Yet the sketches, and a completely revised set produced a few weeks later, failed to please the author. "He does not feel that the technique is up to standard," Stanley wrote, adding that "our own advisers agree in substance with his criticisms." Ursula was grateful for her uncle's efforts and conceded, "I am very conscious of my limitations and I never felt I would make a real success of it though I was keen to try."[2]

The Methuen competition, however, did lead to an art commission; not for her own book, but for *Vermilion* by Norah Shaw, a teacher who wrote short stories for *Children's Hour* on radio. The *Sunday Times* called the black and white sketches and cut-outs eye-catching,[3] and other critics were complimentary. Barbara's success in London had already indicated that she would be the greater artist in the family, but Ursula was a talented illustrator and may have hoped for similar work, especially as it paid relatively well. With editions appearing in Australia, South Africa and India, she received a fee of £31 10s, much more than she received as an advance for any of her books until the 1940s.[4] The illustrations were in fact the last that she would produce for another author's work. It is not known whether Ursula decided to concentrate solely on writing, or whether further art contracts simply did not materialise. Even if the former is true, her versatility and the diversity of her output to date still meant she would face a dilemma about her future direction as an author.

It would seem that at this stage the success of *Kelpie* provided the encouragement Ursula needed to focus on one style of narrative fiction. *Kelpie* had pointed the way toward more ambitious work with its big adventure, the trail and trials through the world of a brave and sympathetic main character with whom children could identify. It brought Ursula a sense of security, not just financial but psychological, in the sense that it allowed her to break away from a dependence on writing short stories for guides and brownies, and develop the confidence to use her imagination and experience to write works of greater scope.

As the distinctive character of Ursula's writing started to become clearer, the uncertainties of her personal life were also being resolved. As it turned out, it had been a happy chance that just before the dinner at which Ursula and Peter had accidentally met again, an aunt had sent Ursula *The Andrée Diaries*, an account of the ill-fated polar expedition in which Salomon Andrée and two fellow balloonists perished. Peter had been as fascinated by the story as Ursula. He wrote back, explaining points as a pilot about the conditions they would have encountered. When Ursula replied, asking to know more, Peter suggested that they might together visit Worthy Down, the RAF base just north of Winchester, where he had done his pilot training.

If it was a date, it was an unconventional one. Peter knew how to get really close to the runway to see the incoming Vickers bombers, but it had to be done at night. He led the way through rough country, helping Ursula across ditches and over barbed wire until they reached the very end of the airstrip. It was there, he told his awestruck companion with permissible exaggeration, that he had overshot the landing area, running onto tarmac where a sergeant's wife was pushing her baby in a pram. The wing of the aircraft clipped the pram's edge, sending it and its contents into a ditch. Mercifully neither mother nor baby were seriously hurt, although the RAF had to provide a new pram, he said. Peter then described, with practised delivery, his shame-faced visit to a hospital where "thorns were being picked out of the poor baby's bottom."[5]

The letters became more frequent though exactly what happened next is uncertain. The correspondence went on for nearly two years. Ursula described their relations as an acquaintanceship, but a stormy one.

Peter and Ursula seemed to have few interests in common. His father had been a professional artist, and Peter had been given the name Southey after his maternal great-grandfather, the Poet Laureate Robert Southey. But the artistic gene inherited by Peter's sister Jo, a concert pianist, had apparently skipped the male lineage. Their elder brother worked in a railway office and Peter's own recreations were masculine and practical – sport, flying and motor cars.

In an autobiographical profile Ursula wrote that Peter "had been in love with one of my cousins, who spurned him … I remember praying fervently that he would like me enough to marry me, and in the end he did!"[6] His affair with Nora was already over by the time Ursula and Peter began writing to each other, but, as the relationship developed, Ursula became uneasy, as her diary makes clear. Perhaps some flames still flickered for Nora for a time, or maybe there was some further rival after Barbara Ward for his affections. Of all the characters in *Grandfather* – the only one of Ursula's

hitherto published works describing in any depth the emotions of mature adults –
the one with whom she identified herself was the climber Michel, who murders his
unfaithful wife and her love child before killing himself. "I know it is pitiful to be so
jealous," she wrote in the diary kept hidden under her mattress, but Ursula did feel
"out of place" in casual flings. Marriage and children filled her imagination, and when
the possibility came along with someone for the first time in her life "to adore … and
sometimes … order me about," her passion became the greater with the fear that
she might lose him.

Money was tight at North Stoneham. Ursula worried when lack of funds made it
difficult to keep up appearances. She made excuses when friends invited her to go to
a skating rink, for example, and felt embarrassed at the lack of hospitality that could
be given to guests. On one occasion, having impetuously invited callers to come in
to enjoy a sloe gin, she suddenly remembered guiltily how much her father said it
cost. After carefully pouring the contents into other containers in the kitchen, she
reappeared with the empty bottle and an expression of regret. They had small glasses
of cider instead and went away amused but happy.

It is difficult to judge Moray's financial circumstances. There is no record of his
regular salary, and despite the considerable honorarium that he had received after
the war, circumstantial evidence suggests that any pay was modest. He enjoyed
extravagances befitting the expression of the social status that he wished to convey
– of which the North Stoneham was the main symbol. The family employed a
succession of married couples as servants, including an accident-prone cook and a
handyman with a weakness for the bottle. When a stranger telephoned to say that his
dog had chased the family's "drunken butler" up a tree, Moray was so pleased at
being credited with having a butler that all parties were forgiven as he went to rescue
the unfortunate man. On the other hand, staff were still relatively cheap to employ,
and Mabel, suffering by now from arthritis, was finding it increasingly difficult to
cope with the everyday tasks in an isolated house without modern services.

Eva, a kind-hearted girl devoted to "the master" and "the mistress," had been
with the family for six years. She always seemed ready to perform extra services for
"the miss Ursula," such as fetching hot water upstairs on the frequent occasions when
the furnace broke down. With the reliable Eva, so many spare – if spartan – rooms,
the lovely countryside, and a shortage of cash, it made sense to advertise for guests.
Among them was Luc Perrelet from Switzerland, who arrived in 1933 to learn
English. It was agreed that his family would host a return visit at their holiday chalet
in a village above Lake Geneva. As so often with events in Ursula's life before her
marriage, her fiction seems to provide missing details. *The Outlaws*, written in 1972,
tells the story of a French-speaking boy who comes to learn English with the

"Williams" family: a father who ignores him; a kindly mother; their two daughters; and the son whose return is awaited from boarding school. Mrs Williams has written to the boy's father about the house set among laurel woods, with tennis and riding available – both of which the real Luc wrote about in letters home. The visitor goes camping and fly-fishing, which happened to be one of Ursula's particular skills. At night the woods come alive with the calls of owls. But the house has its discomforts as "mosquitoes hummed away in discontent, repulsed by the oil of verbena" used to drench his pillow, and by day wasps swarmed around the kitchen.[7]

Luc was twenty-two at the time of his visit – the same age as Ursula – although naturally in a children's story his alter-ego Robert is much younger. Intriguingly, in *The Outlaws* it is the girls' younger brother who is due to go on the return holiday. He contracts measles, his return from school is delayed, and the story leaves open the question of whether he will go. The real-life brother still had a year to complete at Malvern at the time of Luc's visit. It seems appropriate that Alan should have had the chance of the trip to Switzerland that summer, or in the following year before going to university, especially as Barbara and Ursula had previously enjoyed the delights of six months in the French Alps, as well as Stanley's hospitality at Lenzerheide. Whether it was because Alan had measles, or for some other reason, it was in fact the twins who took the train to Southampton in August 1934 to spend a month in the lovely village of La Forclaz, above the town of Les Haudères. It was to prove as inspirational as their time at Annecy six years earlier.

The visit was a great success. The twins joined climbing expeditions up to 12,000 feet, traversing glaciers and crevasses, camping, finding nuts and wild bilberries to eat, encountering marmots, the occasional snake, and large herds of mountain goats. Much time was spent painting, drawing, or sketching wonderfully witty cartoons of life *chez* Perrelet. In Ursula's case she recorded incidents to use later in her writing. Luc's father, Paul, wrote: "The Moray-Williams [sic] twins are charming girls who know exactly how to win everyone's hearts … They are always in good spirits, and, because they come from a life that lacks everyday comforts, they are always ready to accept whatever situations arise. They can both draw, and Ursula is writing a book with very good illustrations."

Paul was a professional artist with a considerable domestic reputation for scenes of the Alps, and unsentimental portraits of the ordinary people who lived and worked there. He sat with Barbara over sketchpads and easels opposite the lake, then at home gave his young pupil a master class in oil painting. Ursula was persuaded to sit as their model and to take a miniature portrait back to England. Apart from being a splendid gift, the picture also represented, at a time when economic hardships made it difficult to get work in Geneva, the most beautiful business card.

It was Paul's good fortune, therefore, that the Williams family had recently come into a little money. Harriet, the last of Mabel's five aunts from the wealthy Spicer family of paper merchants, had no children of her own and left £48,000 to her nieces. Unfortunately for any prospect of a grand fortune, Mabel was one of twenty-four nieces.[8] Even so, her share would help pay for the expected weddings, and a few unaccustomed luxuries – a cruise to Norway for the whole family, and a series of grand portraits. To Ursula, there was something uncomfortably hubristic about the commissioning of formal, large-scale portraits of individual family members, particularly those of herself and Barbara – so different from the comical, self-deprecating figures that she had drawn in her souvenir of La Forclaz.[9] Moray, on the other hand, although professing little knowledge of art, was delighted at the prospect of being immortalised in oils. It would show him, like his grandfather the Rev Arthur. J. Macleane, a Classical scholar and headmaster of Bath College, as a man of intellect and means.

Paul arrived at North Stoneham in May 1935. He set up his studio at first in the domed hall, now empty and dilapidated, but had to move after thieves got in through one of the permanently insecure windows and made off with some of his equipment, chased by Ursula's dog. It was not the only difficulty. In his bedroom the casements shook at night making it hard to sleep, and by day the "glacial" air blowing through made it impossible to work. Painting had to be done by the light of oil lamps, and Mabel, nervous and slightly deformed from her arthritis, stirred constantly. Moray, however, "a strapping fellow the colour of a cooked lobster, with clear eyes, thick lips and a good child's smile," posed confidently, staring rather importantly into the middle distance. Ursula, in a delightful smaller portrait, full-face, head on hand, looks with happy contentment directly at the viewer, the light picking out her gilded, rippling hair.

For a Bohemian spirit like Paul, life at North Stoneham could be disappointingly predictable – with punctual attendance required at every meal, including the obligatory tea and cakes that interrupted work every day at 4.30 – but the house, in which the old furniture seemed to disappear as if eaten up by space, and the woodlands were endlessly fascinating:

> This afternoon everyone has gone, and it is as if I am in Sleeping Beauty's castle … or in the atmosphere of *A Midsummer Night's Dream*. The only noise is the singing of birds that are everywhere around this abandoned, ruined old mansion, encircled by the invasive vegetation. … The greasy water reflects the large trees and the varied greens of the lake create great beauty; the solitude is exquisite … A fish darts out of the water to catch a mosquito. … Cuckoos in the distance give their questioning cry, and in front of me, by the water-lilies, there are gurgling wild ducks preening their bright plumage.[10]

It was the time of the Silver Jubilee celebrations of King George V and Queen Mary, and the family had a special reason to see the aerobatic display over the south coast arranged as part of the festivities, as one of the pilots was Peter. Paul had met Peter for the first time a few nights earlier when Ursula had proudly introduced her fiancé, "l'aviateur." He rather liked the straight-forward manners of this true English man of action, who was more impressed by Paul's ability to chop wood to make a painting platform than by the purpose to which it was put. The ducks were not all that caught Paul's eye on his morning walks around the lakes. A charcoal sketch had been going well, and his spirits were high as took a stroll before lunch and came across Ursula and Peter entwined by the water and the flowers. He thought of the landscape he had been preparing, and a scene by Watteau, *The Embarkation for Cythere*, with two lovers embracing, their dogs, a boat and flowers. It was not an image that Peter would have appreciated. He didn't even like the portrait of Ursula, but the painter was not too upset by this verdict. After all, as Paul privately observed, Peter had no artistic taste whatsoever.

With early sales of *Kelpie* being encouraging, Harrap were keen for Ursula to follow its success and contribute titles to complement its *Milly-Molly-Mandy* series aimed at girls aged from five to nine. The result was three books completed before Ursula's marriage, and published in a little over twelve months from February 1935. *Anders & Marta*, *Adventures of Anne* and *Tales for the Sixes and Sevens* were all illustrated by the author, and drew upon familiar themes – as is evident from a preface to the first title, in which Berta, when asked what she might like more than anything else, answers "Twins." There are also references to twins, identical or nearly so, in the two later books, and all three include short stories that celebrate acts of kindness and the unspoilt beauty of nature and its creatures. Goats turn up almost as frequently as they did on Ursula's Alpine expeditions. *Anders & Marta* most likely took Annecy as its inspiration, with a dedication to Gaby's baby daughter, and the first adventure of Anne begins with a private acknowledgement of uncle Stanley's generosity at Lenzerheide:

> In the summer holidays Anne's uncle and aunt took her out to Switzerland to a lovely little village in the mountains, which might have been built, Anne thought, straight out of a fairy-tale.

The three books were largely written in the reverse order from that in which they were published. The five stories about Anne had already appeared in *The Guider*, and had almost certainly been told to Ursula's Brownie packs. They would have loved the local references to New Forest ponies, to gypsies like those that brought their fair to Petersfield, to the hall like the corrugated iron hut at St Nicolas's church, North Stoneham, that was so cramped for games, and the laurel woods in which they longed to hold a party. Perhaps something like the incident in which the Brownies ill-advisedly bring together a dozen cats, resulting in "a surging mass of grey and black fluff, tumbling and tossing, in a whirlpool of black tails" actually took place.[11] *Adventures of Anne* appeared in September 1935, and with her wedding planned for the end of that month, Ursula had other things on her mind as she prepared the typescript of *Tales for the Sixes and Sevens.* Not for the first or last time, she solved the problem by reworking stories written much earlier – one of them, *The Way of the Wind,* when she was only fifteen.[12] Like *Anne*, it contains lively and cleverly executed silhouettes. The first story Susan and the Witch has crisp dialogue, creates tension between episodes, and ends happily with an unexpected switch. For the rest, *Tales for the Sixes and Sevens* represents the final pickings from the Brownie bran tub. The public seemed to agree. Despite positive mentions from the *TLS* – "quaintly illustrated" – and the *Manchester Guardian* – "very pleasant reading … well-accredited inhabitants of the wonder-world," – the book sold fewer than 1200 copies over five years.[13]

As the later two *Milly-Molly-Mandy* titles largely contained earlier work, *Anders & Marta*, although published before them in February 1935, should be considered as the most recent example of Ursula's writing before her marriage. It shows in the greater range of imagination and the skill with which the ideas are handled. Nor does it seem accidental that, after the opening wish for twins, four of the thirteen stories are about babies or young children. Although all the stories are set somewhere in the Alps, the range of ideas is remarkable, from the opening tale, probably based on real life, of a grandfather who feigns sleep while his photograph is taken, to an allegory about the spirits of nature whose tears form a mist that deters a millionaire from building an intrusive hotel. The collection contains some of Ursula's best short stories. The direct, expressive vocabulary seems to creep up to take quite difficult issues by surprise. Clouds "dress themselves up" in washing as a storm carries away clothes; mountain people "weep for avalanches and for deaths, and for the last of autumn and for great cold and loneliness." Swallows summoned by an unusual whistle bring good fortune to the valley, but eventually swarm into Anders' house in a frightening black storm before peace is restored. In another story, poor Anders and Marta leave hay for Santa's horse, only to find that the fussy animal turns away. The happy ending is nevertheless provided, not by the hoped-for Christmas gifts, but by the children's own industry. for they are able to keep a wandering little yellow cow, attracted by the free food, and start selling its milk. The final story, *The Miracle of Mother Rosa Katrina,* ends appropriately enough with a variation on the most famous story of a baby's birth. Rosa Katrina, old and lonely, sees a child accidentally left asleep in a stable at Christmas. She thinks it a miracle, and creeps away "with a new thankfulness and joy in her heart, to thank God for sending her this miraculous vision."[14]

It seemed as if Ursula too was bursting with joy, and the confidence to express it. Probably also, as her wedding approached, she felt some nervousness about the physical nature of marital love and childbirth. No diaries or personal letters survive from this time, but as so often fiction and real events overlap to such an extent in her life, it is reasonable to extrapolate some elements of the latter from the former.

Out of the Shadows, published in *Hurricanes,* a 1971 collection of Ursula's short stories, relates the discovery of an old diary. Its fictional author writes that she is about to wear her grandmother's wedding veil to marry Edward, who had previously courted her sister Mary. Ursula cannot have forgotten that she had worn the veil of old Honiton lace in which her grandmother Elizabeth Spicer had married Edward Unwin,[15] nor that his brother had married Elizabeth's sister Maria. The similarities, and the fact that the story goes on to say that the woman later died in childbirth, suggest therefore that on the eve of her own wedding, Ursula shared the anxieties that she attributed to her supposed diarist:

> Why am I so frightened? I know he will be good to me for he is a good man. But I know so little. I know nothing about being married. Mamma does not like me to speak of it. I love little children but I do not know how children begin. I love babies, but I do not know how babies are born.[16]

On Saturday, 28 September 1935 at least fourteen Unwins, eleven Williamses, local friends and those from Annecy, Girl Guides colleagues, and acquaintances from the Red Cross filled to overflowing the three hundred seats of St Nicolas Church, North Stoneham – with latecomers settled on chairs around the nave. Ursula walked down the aisle wearing an oyster-tinted satin dress with a short train, and wearing Elizabeth Spicer's long veil that came down to her calves. In spite of Ursula's fantastic capacity for making friends, and the great number of Peter's RAF connections and Hawker aircraft colleagues, the couple cannot have known all of the guests, who included a vice admiral, two major generals, a lieutenant colonel, a countess and a generous smattering of knights, ladies and officers of lesser rank. The main local newspaper – noting the descent of Flt. Lt Conrad Southey John from a poet laureate, the bride's father as "the gentleman whose name has been outstanding for many years in Hampshire" with the Red Cross, and giving a lengthy summary of the history of the church itself – barely mentioned the bride's occupation as a writer, but still thought the event worth a report of nearly 3000 words.

The bells rang for an hour as the guests departed for a reception in a marquee on the lawn in front of North Stoneham House, decorated with palms and roses. "The grounds looked lovely in the sunlight, of which there was fortunately plenty," the *Hampshire Chronicle* reported. More than two hundred guests had accepted invitations. George Harrap was unable to come, but sent a handsomely-bound volume of love lyrics.[17] Moray had sent the list of acceptances in advance to local newspapers, and as a result the *Chronicle* included the name of Sir Mervyn Tew's sister-in-law Winifred Davies, who had in fact died a few days before the ceremony. Although she had continued to occupy the end flat at North Stoneham, she was not well disposed toward Moray, and had discouraged her nephews from playing with his children. Ursula's departing gesture at the end of the afternoon was, therefore, the more poignant. After posing for photographs with her bridesmaids, Barbara, her cousin Peggy, friend Barbara Ward and Peter's sister Jo, she went back to the church, carrying her bouquet of pale pink roses tied with white ribbon, and placed them on Miss Davies' grave.[18] It was a small kindness in the manner of those for which she would be known for much of her life.

Chapter 7

"Revolt! Revolt! Revolt!"

Like many descendants of immigrants, the boy born Conrad Southey Jahn, grandson of a naturalised jeweller, grew up to be more English than the English. His grandfather had died in his native Germany not long before the outbreak of the First World War, and because of his name and ancestry the boy had been bullied at school at Kingston upon Thames – and not just by the pupils. Returning to retrieve forgotten books, he was once confronted at the locked gates by the caretaker, who hit the lad on the head with heavy keys. They left a permanent bruise and sensitivity to being thought of as anything less than a true Englishman.[1] In January 1919 the family changed its surname to John. As the threat of a second war with Germany began to loom in the 1930s, Conrad became more comfortably known as Peter.

Paul Perrelet had loaned his chalet at La Forclaz to the bridge and groom for their honeymoon. They returned again the following June. Days spent in the Alps had been the most magical of Ursula's life since that first arrival at North Stoneham, and she longed for Peter to share her delight in the mountains as Barbara had done. Ursula poked gentle fun at her Anglophile husband, with his pipe and trim moustache, his limited ability and greater reluctance to speak French, and his fond expression that the English were "the Cream of the Earth." She teased him for being short-tempered with noisy French children and less than charitable about the manners, clothes, relations and smells of their Swiss maid. Bitten by ants, sunburnt, suffering from stomach ache, Peter would probably have been happier at home. But all around were landscapes of spectacular beauty, through which wild goats seemed constantly to follow them – their irresistible charm penetrating even Peter's crusty reserve. A hearty meal also helped, and "did much to bring the Boy Scout back to his nature. Soon he was reiterating his sins with every appearance of contrition and self reproach, through which the realisation of his present wellbeing beamed like a glow worm in a dingy corridor." They returned with three souvenirs – a strong-smelling cheese accepted with some annoyance by Peter as a present from the abused maid – and packed with his hiking boots – and two mementoes carefully chosen by Ursula herself: a pretty handmade frock "in case they ever had a daughter about that size," and a pair of rompers for a boy.[2]

The end of Ursula's honeymoon meant relinquishing two romantic worlds – the majestic Alps and the folly at North Stoneham – for a modern second-floor flat at Hampton reached by an external fire escape. It was convenient for Peter to travel to the Hawker aircraft plant at Kingston upon Thames four miles away, but "pretty suburban" compared with what she had known. "I would have lived in a coal mine with Peter," she said.[3] She was happy, but it helped that she had packed her imagination. Of the four full-length books that she wrote there during the next two years, three were about horses and one about Switzerland.

The first lines of *The Twins and Their Ponies*, a fourth consecutive title for Harrap's *Milly-Molly-Mandy* series, could not have stated more clearly its autobiographical character: "This is the story of Bubble and Squeak, who were twins." Almost every episode and most characters can be traced to events and personalities in Ursula's childhood at Petersfield: the hunting incident with the hobby horses and the snobbish girl; the Danish nurse; the twins – of whom Bubble is the bolder – that walk thirty minutes to school and pick cowslips in the woods to send to their aunts in London; and references to specific locations, including the Cricketers Inn at Steep where the hunt used to meet. The twins have a younger brother, who wants to join in with their games, but offers a sad spectacle as he drags his own battered hobby horse the McTurtle – so much more ragged than the rest – "upside down, its long dismal ears covered in leaves."[4]

Following its success in Great Britain, *Kelpie* had won the recommendation of the Junior Literary Guild of America and by 1936 had easily outsold all of Ursula's other books put together. So when Ursula offered another pony book in July, Harrap accepted it at once despite having taken *The Twins and Their Ponies* just two months earlier. Both titles were published simultaneously that November. *Sandy-on-the-Shore* contains references to Ursula's childhood, in particular to a nearby convalescent home, dressing up as St George, and an occasion alluded to in *Kelpie* and in the later *No Ponies for Miss Pobjoy* when Puss the pony was taken inside North Stoneham House and got stuck – possibly after being encouraged to climb the stairs. Rather than relying on such incidents, however, *Sandy* draws essentially on the sympathetic feeling for ponies that the writer acquired by looking after her own and sets the eponymous chestnut-coloured hero free in a fast moving and convincing seaside adventure. As in *Kelpie*, the language is descriptive – an inexperienced rider feels "tossed up like an orange" – but the writing more vigorous. A scene in which the pony is almost swallowed up in quicksand was described by the *TLS* as "painfully exciting." There are no villains, the naughty children see sense, and the vicissitudes of fortune are ended typically with the final words of the book: "Sandy-on-the-shore was at home!"[5]

In *Dumpling*, another horsy book written a year later, the style is even more direct: "Dumpling was a round, fat pony who was rather ashamed of himself for being so round and fat. He had an enormous appetite." Readers were not to know of the memories that the writer had brought to mind, though those who had known Ursula as a girl might guess something of the sort from the introduction of his future owner: "Annabel Brown was eight years old, and rather fat, like Dumpling. She often wished she were thin and had a plainer and more ordinary name." Together they are inevitably called, kindly but still to Annabel's distress, the two Dumplings. Home and kindness are constant themes in Ursula's work, but – often serving as their metaphor – there are even more references to food. Here the reader is offered a diet of carrots, sugar, bread (two portions), apples, straw, dumplings, stew, cauliflower in creamy sauce, pancakes, dripping toast, eggs, rolls, jam, cake, buns and gingerbread – and all in a book of only ninety pages.

In fact, Ursula had never looked better. Photographs suggest that she and Barbara had each lost a stone or two. Perhaps Ursula, in the ecstatic early years of marriage, felt herself flying too, like the prancing pony with real wings in the picture that Annabel receives at the end of the story. She could now recall her own teenage anxieties with untroubled affection in telling the story of another dumpling who has learnt to diet. Gypsies make their customary appearances and Dumpling himself finds his way into a girls' dormitory, as seems to be the habit of ponies from the Williams stable. What is new is the writer's greater confidence in her powers of invention. When a mysterious old man produces beans with special powers to help Dumpling, they turn out to be imbued not with magic, as might have been the case in earlier stories, but more probably with tonic for his withers.

Dumpling is a much better book than the brief attention it received in the national newspapers would suggest. Regional dailies called it "appealing", "delightful" and the *Bournemouth Times* gave the most considered assessment about a story "full of useful information about the care of ponies, administered with great subtlety. The young reader should learn a lot without knowing it. Annabel is a remarkably real little person and will become a good friend to all who read the story."[6]

Between *Sandy-on-the-Shore* and *Dumpling*, Ursula completed two other books for Harrap; the first of them was the only one she ever published under her married name, and of all her titles the one with the youngest age group in mind. At the Hampton flat, in anticipation perhaps of the family yet to come, were two woolly toys: a small koala and a leopard. In *The Adventures of Boss and Dingbatt* Ursula produced an endearing story of just a few hundred words from the simplest idea: Dingbatt (the leopard) falls from the window and Boss (the koala), despite being put in the dustbin by the woman in the downstairs flat, brings home his spotty friend minus half-an-inch of tail. Ursula wrote the text and drew illustrations, but the real delight of the volume is the surprisingly expressive and lifelike photographs that Peter took of the inanimate pair around the flat. Harrap bravely used his pictures as full-sized 8" by 6" illustrations and claimed it was the first ever book of its kind. It sold very few copies even though, according to the *Daily Telegraph*, the book gave "adorable recognition" to children's "quick facility for investing any kind of stuffed beastie with life."[7]

The setting of *Elaine of La Signe* was equally specific. Apart from substitution of

La Signe for La Forclaz, the names of locations in the Valais district of Switzerland where Ursula had spent happy holidays with Barbara and Peter are preserved. Almost all of the incidents recorded from those times in her diaries and sketchbooks find their way into the story, be they expeditions up mountains or to the dentist. The plot loosely follows the fortunes of Elaine, as she crosses torrents, survives a snowstorm and climbs an ice face, but the book is more a series of loving miniature portraits of a hard-working community. Fragrant flowers and folk costumes are set against a landscape of looming mountains and pine forests, while occasional showpieces like a traditional cow fight to decide the herd leader, and a dramatic chalet fire leap from the pages.

> There was one great blaze and roar when the roof fell in, and hot stones jumped over the path, bowling down the mountain side to come to rest in the potato beds below, where the next morning they were lying, still warm.[8]

Barbara had provided exquisite full-page colour illustrations and engravings for *Elaine of La Signe* and for *Sandy-on-the-Shore* to accompany the author's smaller sketches. She had also been working regularly as an illustrator for other Harrap titles. Only a year after graduating from the RCA in the summer of 1935, Barbara had been accepted as the youngest ever member of the Royal Society of Painter-Etchers and Engravers. Her hardwood engravings and woodcuts, typically of small, delicate subjects from nature – cobwebs, worms, snails, flowers or raindrops – were being exhibited in England and America.

Her horizon was widening, but when, in 1936, she received an award to travel, she headed in an unexpected direction. She was a frequent visitor to the flat in south-west London, but in July she came with extra luggage as she was heading to Iceland to seek inspiration from its Sagas. Six weeks later she was back, with a snapshot of a rather older man standing on a river bank, wrapped in a bath towel. "That is an Icelander," she told Ursula, "and I am going to marry him."

Unlike her sister, she was not going to submit to any paternal insistence on a society wedding, and the following February Barbara was married "quietly" at North Stoneham to the painter, sculptor, composer and writer Magnús Árnason, and moved permanently to Iceland. Her parents' greatest concerns were that Barbara should also find happiness and that the twins should not miss each other excessively. "What actually happened," Ursula later wrote, "was that we were both so much in love with our own partners that the break was hardly noticed."[9]

By the summer of 1937, at the age of just twenty-six, both sisters had achieved extraordinary success in their early careers. With fourteen published titles, Ursula was already a prolific author, though not yet a particularly well-known one. There were to be hard years ahead for Barbara, working with Magnús at their small studio on the outskirts of Reykjavik, but she had already won artistic recognition at home, and had decided upon her course – the way ahead was clear if not easy. It was not, in fact, about Barbara that Ursula might have worried, but about her brother.

Unfortunately for Alan, the success of his more creatively gifted sisters sharpened his own sense of uncertainty and inadequacy to fulfil the great but ill-defined goals that he felt were expected of him by his father, and by himself. While his sisters had found their chosen paths, he had wandered from that chosen for him. His parents had been happy to let their daughters travel and to see their artistic talents flourish without earning much money, but it was in the knowledge that marriage would take care of their material needs. His parents' greater expenditure had provided the best education for Alan, and in return Moray expected him to work hard and get a proper job. All seemed to be going reasonably to plan when, in 1934, Alan followed his father, his grandfather and his great-grandfather Macleane in winning a place at Cambridge; in Alan's case to study modern languages at King's College. Moray the sportsman would have approved too as his son joined the rowing and cricket clubs – as much for comradeship as for genuine enthusiasm for the activities – but not of the other new friends that he was soon making at the university. Communism had swept through Cambridge in the 1930s following the rise of Hitler to the German Chancellorship. Kim Philby had left the university in 1933 and Donald Maclean just before Alan's arrival, but two other members of what was to become known as the Cambridge Spy Ring, Anthony Blunt and Guy Burgess, were still leading members of the secret Apostles discussion group, which drew its members largely from Trinity and King's colleges. Alan was unsure of himself, resentful of what he regarded as his domineering father, and unable intellectually to submerge his anxieties in the submissive Christian faith of his mother. Communism seemed to offer the only hope of resisting the spread of fascism. With its ideology of scientific determinism that purported to provide answers to all questions about society, it provided a formidable attraction to the idealistic, the naive and the lonely. Alan secretly joined the Communist Party.[10]

In the summer of 1936, as Barbara travelled to Iceland, Alan headed east to Salzburg and on his return sent a 25,000-word anti-colonialist manuscript by registered post to Stanley Unwin, hoping to recruit his help in getting it into print. Curiously, he proposed using the pseudonym Roy Maclean (without the –e). Stanley wrote back kindly but firmly two days later to say the work was unpublishable, but urging Alan to look at it again in three years' time. It, and others like it, did not survive so long. In a further letter to his uncle on 8 November, Alan wrote: "I celebrated Guy Fawkes' Day by burning all my manuscripts."[11] He did not, however, abandon either his views, or his desire to become a writer. By coincidence, in the following spring, relief organisers chose a site on farmland at North Stoneham on which to set up the British camp for Basque refugee children from the Spanish Civil War. Several weeks later, many of them transferred to Cambridge.[12] Political passions were high.

In a magazine that Alan edited and almost certainly wrote, with the self-explanatory title, *Revolt! Revolt! Revolt!*, he railed against a world of injustice, against the government and the authorities in his own college. The deans and tutors were unimpressed, and just before the end of the summer term rusticated the unruly student – or in their words "agreed to permit R.A. Moray Williams to withdraw from the College" – in effect delaying the awarding of his degree for a year. Moray, worried in the past about his son's tendency to adopt radical views, had repeatedly advised him not to go to extremes. Now the horror of the college decision was that Alan would have to acquaint to his father not only the fact of his rustication, but its circumstances and almost certainly his declared allegiance to Communism. A few days after the special College Council disciplinary meeting, Ursula received a telephone call informing her that Alan had locked himself in his room with a revolver and was threatening to shoot himself. She travelled to Cambridge to persuade him to set the gun aside, brought him back briefly to the London flat, and persuaded him to waste no time in facing up to the inevitable confrontation with Moray. He left for Hampshire the following morning.[13]

Alan had been persuaded by, but cannot have found much comfort from his sister. He does not seem to have stayed with Ursula again before the Second World War, although ninety-eight other guests came and went during that period, according to her meticulously-maintained visitors' book. The next time he spent a night at her home, he was in army uniform just after the start of the conflict. Nor were relations with his father easily repaired. After returning to North Stoneham again at the end of 1937, he informed his old school, Malvern College, that henceforth he wished to be known not as Alan Moray Williams but as Alan Unwin.[14] It must have been an eventful Christmas.

By comparison with her brother, Ursula appeared to have achieved a happy equilibrium between her writing and home life, but she disliked living in an urban flat. She and her husband started looking for a new home outside central London, with more "room to think," with a garden, and above all with the space and tranquillity in which to raise the children she longed for. "'Home' in the dictionary has nothing about mothers in it: I am sure it ought to have," she had written in a diary, but after eighteen months of marriage no children had arrived. Consultants advised on an operation, and in the spring of 1937 Ursula entered Queen Charlotte's maternity hospital, Marylebone. The shining months that followed were to realise the dream in full: a new home, a first child, and a book that would become a classic of its time.

In August, Ursula and Peter moved to Desborough Cottage, on Milbourne Lane, Claygate, Surrey. Immediately behind it was Rosebriars, home of R.C. ("Bob") Sherriff, who had bought the house and its large grounds on the proceeds of *Journey's End*, his enormously successful play based on his experiences in the trenches during the First World War.[15] Desborough could not compare with that impressive mansion, but it was still a substantial and attractive property, semi-detached with pebbledash and a dominating gable. Like all of Ursula's homes, it was rented, on the principle that it was better to have a large property immediately than to buy a small one slowly. It also avoided the unattractive association of debt and the millstone that a mortgage seemed to represent. She could hardly wait to welcome guests, to show them over the house and the rear garden where Scots pines laid a carpet of needles over the footpath that skirted Rosebriars. Nearby she could point out Claremont, the stately home built by Sir John Vanbrugh, or walk through the pleasant woodland of Esher Common. Six visitors came to stay, one after the other, in the last two weeks of August alone.

When Mabel came for the first time in mid September, she brought a symbolic gift; daffodil and tulip bulbs that promised new life to come in the spring. They had to be planted immediately, for early the following morning she was to set off with her daughter and son-in-law, and with Peter's mother Maud, for a short holiday in the Lake District. They stayed near Keswick, close to Greta Hall, where Maud's grandfather Robert Southey had lived for forty years. In glorious weather all four climbed the crags and rowed on Derwentwater. But, after scaling Scafell Pike with Peter, Ursula felt unwell and stayed at their hotel while Mabel and Maud walked beside the lake alone.[16] Shortly after returning home, she discovered that she was pregnant.

Full of joyful expectation, Ursula began writing what was to become the most loved story of her career, an international success in children's literature and one of *Time* magazine's Books of the Year. The book was not an easy gestation, but when it was finished, George Harrap took the unusual step of writing personal letters to the thirty principal buyers of children's books in the country to recommend a title for which he predicted outstanding sales that autumn.[17] The entry of *Adventures of the Little Wooden Horse* into the world was preceded by only a few weeks by that of Andrew Paul Southey John, at 2.30 a.m. on 16 June 1938 at Queen Charlotte's hospital.

Chapter 8

"I'm a quiet little horse."

When Elaine Moss, a leading commentator on children's literature, interviewed Ursula in 1971 about *Adventures of the Little Wooden Horse*, she asked about the books Ursula had read when young, particularly fairy tales. "We read those to ourselves. I adored *Pinocchio*," came the reply. Moss sat up on hearing this, recognising the parallels between Ursula's hero on wheels – who bravely ventures into a hazardous world to save his beloved old creator Uncle Peder – and Geppetto's wooden doll, whose courage is ultimately rewarded despite his running away from home. "Had it ever occurred to her that her childhood passion for *Pinocchio* might have been partly responsible for the creation of the little wooden horse?" Clearly it hadn't, the interviewer concluded.[1]

This association stuck in Ursula's mind, however, so when Anne Wood, the children's TV producer and later creator of *Teletubbies*, asked her to contribute a magazine article, Ursula re-examined the link between the two books. It is worth quoting at length:

> It took Elaine Moss to point out to me the source that inspired The Little Wooden Horse … As a child of six or seven my mother read aloud to my twin sister and myself the original translation of Collodi's Pinocchio. She read it again and again … And every time I listened I was consumed by the same distress at Pinocchio's treatment of his father Gepetto … the old man who sold the coat off his back to give his ungrateful little son a schooling.
>
> Each time I heard the story I hoped that this time things would be different and Pinocchio would behave better, but he never did, and the happier ending came after so long a period of desertion and selfish behaviour that it almost seemed an anti-climax.
>
> The Little Wooden Horse was, I think, an unconscious vindication of Pinocchio's guilt. He was Pinocchio as I would have wished him to be, although in writing the book I never realised that I had related him to Collodi's immortal story. But now I see that Uncle Peder's carved wooden hero must have risen very positively from the ashes of my early distress, as, armed with a staunch and loving heart, he marched out into the world to dedicate himself to the cause of his well-loved master.[2]

In a monograph written at around the same time,[3] Ursula referred again to the possible link, although always with the qualifier that this must have been an association of which she was unaware. There is no doubt that *Pinocchio* had indeed been popular in the Williams' nursery, although curiously Ursula failed to include it in an inventory of books that she had read, or heard her mother read; she had set out the list for her own amusement in August 1931, marking all those she liked best with stars, and kept it up to date for several years. Yet, although the catalogue included more than six hundred titles, *Pinocchio* was not among them. She first referred to it as a favourite childhood story in a piece written for a magazine run by storyteller and librarian Eileen Colwell in December 1938, three months after the publication of *Adventures of the Little Wooden Horse*.[4] Perhaps the writing of the latter did bring *Pinocchio* to mind, though it may also have been the publication that year of a new edition – after a gap of twelve years – by J.M. Dent & Sons.

There is no other obvious example of a thematic connection between Ursula's writing and the work of another author. As an adult, she avoided reading juvenile fiction. "I read enormously but hardly ever children's books for fear of unconscious plagiarism," she said. In New Zealand she told a reporter that she refused to read other writers' work for children because "I'm afraid that if I did I might subconsciously use someone else's ideas." If, in any case the inspiration for the little wooden horse was one of which the writer was unaware, it seems questionable whether one should consider the Pinocchio proposition as having much weight.

Ursula said of her best-known character, "His actual creation in my mind was not so straight-forward as it might appear. The idea came to me in a flash."[5]

The first two chapters "flowed from my pen as fast as I could write them down," Ursula wrote.[6] The first we know about the old toymaker's finest creation is that the little horse is "brave," but despite his courage, size, and construction, the tears that roll down his newly painted face at the thought of being sold are large and real. And what is more, he can talk. Outside those stories very much in the style of fairy tales, Ursula's animal and toy characters had lacked the power of speech, except like Sandy to express their inner thoughts, or like Boss and Dingbatt to each other. The little wooden horse at first keeps his thoughts to himself, then questioned by Uncle Peder, "at last … made a great effort and sobbed out, 'Oh, master, I don't want to leave you. I'm a quiet little horse, I don't want to be sold.'" It's a clever construction that forms a bridge between the real and the imaginary world, and is immediately followed by a virtuosic leap into a higher realm of illogicality into which only children may enter. The little wooden horse, rigidly attached to his platform as every picture makes clear, nevertheless "kicked his legs in the air, so that the four green wheels spun round and round." In the course of the adventures that follow, it comes as little surprise that he can win a race despite losing all his wheels, or that he can remove his own head in order to put coins in the hole in his neck. The culmination of such glorious absurdity comes after an unfortunate decapitation when he sets out "to look for his wooden head by the banks of the stream." He might have been fearful, but fortunately "he had no painted eyes with which to see his shadow in the moonlight."

His adventures begin after Uncle Peder falls ill. The little wooden horse's determined efforts to fetch an old woman living nearby to look after him are misunderstood. She flings him out, so he sets out to sell himself in order to help his ailing and impoverished creator. After being given five shillings for Uncle Peder to make another wooden horse like himself, he goes to work for the cruel farmer Max who imprisons him without pay. He escapes, but in the process loses all his money. It was at this heart-breaking instant of high drama that the writing came to a sudden halt.

"Inspiration died. The whole story went dead, and I stopped writing," Ursula explained. "Although it is quite an exciting moment in the story and one to which children constantly refer, it still holds a blankness for me. It was only by reading and re-reading the first chapter that I knew the story was still there in waiting, the little wooden horse was a real person, and his adventures were somewhere ahead waiting for him … till bit by bit they began to materialise. After that the book took charge, I simply followed."[7]

The wild, picaresque episodes that ensue are only loosely connected, and could almost be stories in themselves, many only as long as those that the author used to tell her Brownies. In an epic, exciting tale of bravery and astonishing strength, he survives encounters with unruly children, pirates, sea horses, and with jealous pit ponies, brought out of the dark only on Sundays to scamper in the daylight. As great as his courage is his kindness, and greatest of all is his longing to return to security. There are many tears from the quiet little horse before he arrives at last at the door of the cottage he left long before. Uncle Peder is at that moment marrying the old woman (whose name we never learn) who now deeply regrets having treated the little wooden horse so cruelly. All live together happily. "I shall never leave home again," declares the unassuming hero.[8]

It is a typical ending to one of the author's most emotionally powerful stories, and she herself, now approaching the due date for the birth of her first child, was moved by it. "I was in tears when I wrote it but by that time the story had so taken charge of me that I wasn't really writing it any more," she told Moss.[9] Later she recalled: "When parents tell me that their children have shed tears at the little horse's difficulties and setbacks I can honestly say that I suffered in the writing of them. … The suspense of the final homecoming was almost more than I could bear to write about, and I have never been so reluctant to complete a story, nor so adamant that there could be no sequel."[10]

Interestingly, it was Pinocchio's treatment of his father who had made sacrifices "to give his ungrateful little son a schooling" that had apparently caused Ursula distress as a young girl. When she first heard the story, Alan was one or two years old.

When she started writing *Adventures of the Little Wooden Horse*, he had just been rusticated from Cambridge. He had rebelled against his father's views by joining the Communist Party and heedlessly published an intemperate attack on the authorities. As a result, it was uncertain whether he would be allowed to collect the degree toward which the family had invested heavily in school and college fees. Imagination – always creative but not always just – might suggest that Alan was a Pinocchio, and *Adventures of the Little Wooden Horse* was a wish for a happy ending.

Whatever the possible resonances with what was going on in Ursula's life at the time of writing *Adventures of the Little Wooden Horse*, Ursula did leave a clue about his origin in a letter to a fan who wrote to her when she was in her eighties, describing how much he loved the character. She wrote back, "My chief memories of him, dear fellow, is of telling my twin sister stories as we huddled under the bedclothes aged about ten onwards."[11] The Little Wooden Horse, it seems, was born in Petersfield.

The thirty-minute walk from Bell Hill that the twins did for a year or more to Lincroft school led past the railway station and along Lavant Street, where they had their portraits taken at the photographic studio run by the Pickering sisters. A greater point of interest, however, was the Post Office a few doors away run by Llewellyn E. Bradley, for it also served as the town's bookshop. Wartime austerity meant that most books were passed on from relations or friends, but occasionally Ursula or Barbara would save up to buy something new, and it was probably there that Ursula earned Mabel's indignation by spending her seventh birthday half-crown on a book that her mother had not read, simply in order to feel it was entirely hers. The shop, advertising itself as "Bookseller, Stationer, News Agent, Fancy Repository", and home to Bradley's Library, was crammed with tempting items, books, postcards, lamps, baskets and toys. A photograph of the store from the time shows something that, given the girls' interests, they cannot have failed to notice on their daily walks. Standing out from all the clutter, hanging in pride of place from the awning immediately beside the entrance, are four splendid, striped, little wooden horses.[12]

George Harrap immediately took the book to heart. It is not known whether he decided at the outset to commission an outside artist, or if Ursula's pregnancy deterred her from undertaking the additional work, but the illustrator whom he chose demonstrated his faith that the title would become a major success. Joyce Lankester Brisley, creator of the *Milly-Molly-Mandy* series of stories – published originally in the *Christian Science Monitor* and now forming the backbone of the Harrap library for children aged from five to eight – was given the job.

Harrap had been following the progress of Ursula and her new son with interest, and in July he wrote back with good news of his own. J.B. Lippincott Company, of Philadelphia – which was to publish *Elaine of La Signe* as *Elaine of the Mountains* – had also accepted *Adventures of the Little Wooden Horse* for publication in America. He also enclosed a note that he was sending with copies of the book to the most important trade buyers. "I am, of course, very chary of writing such personal letters. I very rarely do it, on principle," he said. As Ursula read what her publisher had written, she could not have wished for a higher endorsement.

> I cannot imagine the boy or girl of from 8 to 10 who will not be thrilled by the story of the Little Wooden Horse. The test of a good juvenile is whether it can please and amuse the grown-ups and I aver that I followed these adventures from end to end with the keenest enjoyment. In my judgment it is the best story that Ursula Moray Williams has written and I have backed my judgement by producing it thus attractively. I have been ably supported by Joyce Lankester Brisley, who shares my enthusiasm, and I feel sure that if you will open the book you will be compelled to finish the tale and to recommend it to your friends.[13]

It had not been a great year for children's literature. As *The Times* reported, "Shadows over Europe have almost touched fairyland. Certainly this Christmas there is rather less magic about than in former years." Nevertheless, critics acclaimed the story. The *Daily Telegraph* called it one of the "most joyful and colourful children's books of the season." Eleanor Graham wrote in the *Sunday Times*: "Everyone who reads it must be struck by its classic simplicity. I believe this story will find a permanent place among books for the six-to-nine-year-olds, and will be loved by generations of children", and in its review of the year the same newspaper called it "a fine story worthy to rank with Hans Andersen's Toy Soldier." The *TLS* praised the "most appealing story of a gallant and lovable steed with a good brain, a loyal heart and tremendous courage and sagacity." The *News Chronicle* and *Yorkshire Post* said the book had the charm of Andersen, and *Christian Science Monitor* declared, "So exciting were the many desperate situations in which the valiant little horse found himself, that one's heart beats in company with his."

By Christmas, *The Bookseller* was reporting the "outstanding success" that more than 2,000 copies of the book had been sold during the previous fortnight alone, nearly a record for any children's book at that time.[14] Letters started to arrive from fans. One was particularly pleasing as it came from a popular novelist whom Ursula admired, A.S.M. Hutchinson, author of *If Winter Comes*. He had read the book twice in a few weeks to his younger boy after Christmas.

> Legion is the number of juvenile books I have read to his brother … and to him. I can say wholeheartedly that this of yours is the prince of them all … Yours is delicious simple entertainment all through. You would have loved to see him hug himself with joy at each repetition of the phrase 'I'm a quiet little horse'.[15]

The success was repeated across the Atlantic at Lippincott. The firm's advertising manager wrote after production of its catalogue the following autumn: "I wish you could have been present at our sales conference and heard the enthusiasm which the salesmen had for the possibilities of selling quantities of your books."[16] The commercial ebullience was justified. *Time* magazine's Books of the Year for 1939 – which also included *The Grapes of Wrath* by Steinbeck, Joyce's *Finnegans Wake*, and Hitler's *Mein Kampf* – listed *Adventures of the Little Wooden Horse* as one of its books for children aged four to eight. Incidentally, Walt Disney's *Pinocchio* was another. In the years that followed, the little horse was translated into many European languages, and has remained in print almost continuously since publication. Puffin Books alone reprinted the title twenty-two times between 1963 and 1987.

Harrap might have made his reputation from publishing more weighty tomes – such as the biography of Lord Marlborough by his friend Winston Churchill – and his money from French grammars, but he seems to have taken a particular interest in Ursula's books from the time he received her first "unripe" manuscript in the 1920s. Apart from her uncle Stanley, Harrap was the publisher that she most loved to visit, enjoying his courtesy and famed conviviality, and hearing him talk with pride about other titles on his lists. He in turn had the satisfaction, after supporting his young author for six years for sometimes modest returns, of reading the first euphoric review by the influential Eleanor Graham. Less than two weeks later, on 29 October 1938, he died following an operation to remove gallstones. His family and colleagues knew how much the success meant to him. In the window of his company's offices in High Holborn his photograph was framed by copies of *Adventures of the Little Wooden Horse*.[17]

———————

Rather like her little wooden horse returning home at the end of his travels, Ursula could look around with a sense of exhilaration and of hard work rewarded. At the age of twenty-seven, she had achieved nearly all her childhood ambitions: motherhood, a beautiful home, and recognition as a writer. Peter's interests, however, lay beyond the kitchen and the nursery. His chief delight lay in driving off with Ursula, often at short notice, for long car expeditions or to compete in rallies. One of the first they entered was the Lands End Trial in April 1936. The trip entailed an overnight drive in their Austin Seven via the official starting point at Virginia Water in Surrey, during which Ursula kept her husband awake by playing the mouth organ. Her greatest effort however was reserved for the ascent up Lymouth Hill in Devon, where her determined bouncing on the rear seat helped the car conquer the steepest incline – before sliding into a ditch.[18]

At this time of her own personal success and fulfilment, it seems an act of loving generosity that at the end of 1938 she should write her next book about something that primarily interested her husband. It tells the story of Peter, son of an artist, who discovers an old car in a barn, restores it, rechristens it the Wanderlust, and wins the London-to-Brighton Old Crocks' run. Among the adventures along the way, the car gets stuck on a railway crossing, is buried in snow on Exmoor, enters the London-to-Exeter and Lands End trials, and is swept away in a flood, before Peter finally outwits the efforts of a crook to steal the car for a wealthy American collector. The manuscript originally bore the title "Horse Power for a Hero," but after asking her husband to check the technical details, Ursula decided to call it instead *Peter and the Wanderlust*. It was their private joke.[19]

Aimed at an older audience, predominantly of boys aged up to thirteen, *Peter and the Wanderlust*, stands apart from most of Ursula's writing. As a mystery adventure, with an exciting climax and a well-concealed twist, it shows how she might have excelled in this branch of juvenile fiction if her real interests had not been confined largely by the centripetal influence of the home. "All the characters, whether children or grown-ups, are natural and completely alive," wrote *The Observer*, and the *Yorkshire Post* called it the most exciting of the children's books in its annual review. Among its attractions were undoubtedly the precise, detailed drawings of the old car by Jack Matthew, who went on to specialise in illustrations for boys' adventure stories. The TLS singled them out for praise, but their technical charm was probably lost on others. The critic from *The Lady* commented demurely, "The main interest, for us, at any rate, lay in the description of the trips in the car, and very interesting they are."[20]

In the beautiful wood-panelled offices at High Holborn, George Harrap's successor, his original partner George Anderson, was hoping for another Christmas bestseller; something more in the style of the little wooden horse which had sold nearly 6000 copies in the 1938 festive season.[21]

Ursula must have been thinking about possible subjects when she returned to North Stoneham in November 1938 to go through her old books and manuscripts. [22] There was talk of the old house being pulled down, and Mabel had suggested that Ursula might take copies of some old favourite childhood books. It was just three years since Ursula had left the house, but as she wandered through the half abandoned rooms, stacked with used exercise books, broken furniture and discarded toys, memories returned of earlier days when the family had just moved in. There was the golden pheasant in its glass case, no longer so proudly attired, foreshortened, with his fallen tail resting beside him.[23] Ursula felt sorry for him, but here was no hero to succeed the little wooden horse – a stupid bird really, a sad stay-at-home with no real pluck. The puffin, on the other hand, still stood erect at the head of his case of seabirds, his brilliant bill clearly marking him out as the boldest and brightest.

Adventures of Puffin was completed in three months from January 1939. Icelandic girls recommended by Barbara had started to stay at Claygate *au pair*, so that Ursula could usually find a couple of undisturbed hours each afternoon. But although free briefly from motherly duties, her hopes for another child seem evident in what she wrote. The story begins with the finding of an egg, and ends – against all the odds – with its happy hatch. The language is exuberant, bursting with energy and life. The opening moments are filled with tension with the fear that the egg might easily fall "rackety-cracketty" over the edge of its cliff, and the story ends with an explosive breaker of vivid detail surpassing anything the author had written before:

> Trotting out on to the ledge again, he put a wing around the tiny Puffin's shoulders … Sitting side by side while all the rainbow colours faded out of the granite cliffs, while the moon rose, and mermaids dived in and out of silver ripples, combing their hair, while seals barked, and waves washed sighs into hollow places, Puffin told his little companion the story of his life; and when his adventures told, they sat quietly in the moonlight, he began the tale of all the wonderful things they were going to do.

Along the way, Puffin adopts a cotton dog washed ashore, whose name Little Wo (derived perhaps from Little Wooden Horse) makes one suspect it was based upon a cuddly toy given to baby Andrew. The simple Wo and the smarter but sometimes short-tempered Puffin outwit wicked mermaids – who in the book's most exciting episode pursue the pair on seahorses – and escape from the clutches of a peregrine falcon, a cuttlefish and foxhounds. There is, of course, no doubting the outcome from the moment that the venturesome hero gloriously sings:

O! there's nuffin', nuffin', NUFFIN',
Quite so happy as a puffin
When he's busy doing nuffin' in the blue!
It may strike you that a puffin
Does an awful lot of nuffin'
But there's nuffin' that a puffin cannot do.[24]

The contemporary reader may have noted the allusion to real events in elements of the plot, as Puffin and Little Wo travel on the Coronation Scot express train – inaugurated amid great celebration in 1937 – then on the ocean liner *Queen Mary*, launched the previous year. The events, probably suggested by Peter, are rare examples of Ursula allowing her make-believe world to be punctured by the sharp intrusion of real events, and mar what might otherwise have become one of her most successful books. Critics praised its humour and the endearing charm of its bluff hero, but stopped short of the praise accorded to *Adventures of the Little Wooden Horse*. The new book of adventures, the *Yorkshire Post* declared, "somehow lacks the Hans Andersen touch of the Wooden Horse's odyssey."[25]

In the summer of 1939, Alan joined the army after two years of working as a farm labourer and a little freelance journalism.[26] Barbara and Magnús brought their baby son Vifill for a short visit, not knowing when circumstances would allow his grandparents to see him again. They were among the last visitors to North Stoneham, whose owners had decided to demolish the property rather than allow it to be requisitioned again for the wounded. Mabel could look forward to leaving a house in which everyday life had become so difficult, but must have had mixed feelings when Moray accepted a suggestion from his president at the Red Cross, the redoubtable Lady Malmesbury, that the county offices should transfer from Southampton to her home at Hurn Court, near Christchurch, and that the director and his wife should take up residence there. Public events were already roughly forcing the course of everyday lives onto new paths when, on the first day of September, Ursula, stood by her gate, overheard two workmen talking as they cycled past. "The Germans – they're bombing Danzig," one told the other.[27] Two days later, the Allies declared war.

Chapter 9

———

"To sit by the fire and sing like the kettle."

It was lunchtime on Wednesday, 4 September 1940 when a security worker at the Hawker factory at Kingston upon Thames scanned the clear blue skies that had been a feature of that fine, warm summer. Men were filing out of the shed now used for assembling the Hurricane fighters. Others were enjoying cigarettes in the sunshine. After the klaxon sounded, Peter would have had little time to scan the skies while running to the nearest air-raid shelter. Had he been able to, he would have seen two German aircraft swooping down out of the sun. In fact, they headed further west to attack the Wellington bomber plant at Brooklands. Up to six 500 kg bombs were dropped, killing eighty-three workers and leaving another four hundred injured.[1] For Ursula, after months of relative calm, and a spring of almost charmed peace and happiness, the conflict was coming closer.

Peter had not doubted the likelihood of war. Back in October 1938, only days after Germany invaded Czechoslovakia, he had enrolled as one of Surrey's first Air Raid Precaution (ARP) wardens. He was issued with his helmet (size 7), boots (size 9), a respirator and other equipment. Within three months, he was attending courses on first aid, poison gas, and how to build Anderson shelters.[2] Ursula bought yards of black-out material and criss-crossed the windows with white tape to reduce the danger of an explosion sending a shower of deadly splinters into the house. The small diamond shapes of glass that remained visible actually gave the house a rather pleasing Tudor appearance. Outside, the lawn and perennials in the large rear garden gave way to as many vegetables as the land was capable of producing.

The threat seemed real enough and suddenly close at hand. On 26 October 1939 the Nazi propaganda programme 'Germany Calling' identified an intended target less than a dozen miles away. "Croydon must beware," drawled Lord Haw-Haw: "We know the aerodrome is camouflaged but we know just what kind of camouflage it is. We shall bomb it … to a finish and we would advise the people there to evacuate the area next weekend.[3] No such attack took place, but even if the warning was largely dismissed as another absurd claim by the Hamburg radio station, it seemed clear that the area around London was likely to be attacked.

At the end of the year, Ursula listened to the Christmas Day message of King George VI. Mabel, Moray and Alan had come to spend the holiday at Desborough Cottage. All had their own particular reasons for wondering how the war would affect them in the coming year. For Ursula's parents, there was the uncertainty of life as guests at Hurn Court, while Cadet Alan Moray Williams of 8 Platoon 168 Officer Cadet Training Unit, Aldershot, faced the rigours of a career in the army to which he seemed ill-suited. Ursula, now pregnant, was anxious for Peter's safety, and for that of her children. So they listened together to the King's speech, his gentle voice gliding over the stammer that at other times affected his speech. Mabel was so moved that she wrote down his closing words and never forgot them. She had preserved her inspirational diary from her days as a student at Sesame House, and, in 1952, near the end of her life, she copied the king's words as her last entry: "Go out into the darkness and put your hand into the hand of God. That shall be to you better than light and safer than a known way."

Ursula's second child, another boy, was born on April 6 1940 and christened Hugh Maclean Southey John. Difficulties connected with the birth required his mother to spend three weeks in hospital. A series of helpers was arranged during the last weeks of her pregnancy, starting with a girl who had been in one of Ursula's Brownie packs in Hampshire. At the end of April, another nanny took over for a few months, Joan Gregory, who "promises well, very energetic, does everything." As was the case with several of the young women who came to help look after her children, Joan was to become a lifelong friend.

By May, life had settled into a more regular if not always comfortable routine. "It's lovely to see dimples and bracelets coming and to think it's ME that fattened him," Ursula wrote. "Andrew's favourite game is to cuddle under the eiderdown under my other arm while I nurse and … make loud kissing noises. He is always eager to deliver dozens of very gentle kisses as I stroke his head." Peter, on the other hand, was proud but indifferent to such sentimental charms, and was "waiting for a more attractive state to set in." Evelyn Unwin, the second cousin to whom these thoughts were confided, had also just had a baby, and despite domestic preoccupations at Claygate, it is clear that Ursula had been busy on her behalf too. "I posted books to you to-day and hope to send your nightie to-morrow but couldn't do any sewing over the weekend."[4]

The peaceful interlude was soon to end. "At the outbreak [of war] we waited moment by moment for the inevitable bombing attack we felt was sure to come, but instead there were … months when no bombs fell," Ursula recollected. It was the thunder that came first. France had fallen, and while she and Peter worked in the garden at the end of May 1940, they picked up the distant sound of guns at Dunkirk. It was, said Prime Minister Winston Churchill, "a miracle of deliverance" for the 300,000 troops who were evacuated, but with it came the expectation that the war would now be fought over Britain, prior to a possible invasion. Pillboxes, gun emplacements, concrete blocks and barbed wire were erected across counties like Surrey. The Epsom Downs, ten minutes drive from Claygate, where Ursula and Peter had loved to walk, were cleared of undergrowth to give defenders clear lines of fire against any enemy gliders or paratroopers who might land.[5]

"The Battle of France is over. I expect that the Battle of Britain is about to begin." Churchill was right. Within a month of his 'Finest hour' speech on 18 June, the battle had opened with attacks on Channel convoys, and on 24 July a Junkers-88 bombed the Hawker HQ at Kingston. Peter was employed in the drawing office, probably in Canbury Park Road. In a long room, painted a shade of dirty cream, seventy draughtsmen worked on modifications to the Hurricane fighter, seated around the glass-fronted box from which Hawker's chief designer, the brilliant Sydney Camm, could watch their progress.[6]

On 24 July, those on nightshift had been sent to the shelters, but the attack killed one man left on fire-watch duty, and blew out the office windows. Loss of the design centre meant alternative accommodation had to be found. The site chosen was just down the road from Desborough Cottage. In great secrecy, Camm and his team moved to Claremont House, the entrance to which faced Milbourne Lane, and remained there for the rest of the war. Windows were bricked up, tank traps laid in the grounds, camouflage netting fixed over the building, and an ARP post established on the roof. The story of what went on inside that former stately home became one of the best-kept secrets of the war. It is not known whether Peter also transferred there, but whatever the case, Ursula would have been aware of the potential German bombing target at the end of the lane.[7]

By early August, the Luftwaffe was concentrating its attacks on airfields, and on Sunday 11th, more than 500 bombers launched their greatest assault of the war. Vapour trails could be seen all day in the clear skies over Surrey. Four days later at least sixty people died in Croydon after the first air attack on civilian London. Thus began weeks of constant alarms. In Claygate the air-raid sirens sounded on every day except one for a period of 106 days from Friday 23 August until Friday 6 December. Three times during November, the small community suffered direct hits: bombs badly damaged a school and shops, and landmines fell on the outskirts. The local vicar recorded more than fifty high explosive devices having been dropped in the village by the end of the war. Many of his parishioners blamed the elegant but unusually high steeple of his church, which they thought the enemy used as a navigational aid.[8]

Of all the victims of the conflict, none was dearer to the John family than Dick Reynell, and of all the deaths of which they learnt, none came in more tragic circumstances than his. Like Peter, Reynell had joined Hawker after serving in the RAF, and remained on the reserve list as a flight lieutenant. Both had young families – Reynell's son being exactly a year younger than Andrew – and the friendship that the two men formed soon extended to their families. But Reynell was not at the Kingston site in the week of the 4th September raid, nor in the two weeks before that. The handsome and dashing chief test pilot had been working relentlessly, pushing each of Camm's modifications on the Hurricane to the limit, and by the middle of

August he was close to exhaustion. As far as most of his colleagues were aware, he was taking a three-week break. In fact, Reynell had gone to the commander of Fighter Command, Air Marshall Hugh Dowding, to volunteer for the duration of his holiday.

It was an act of great bravery. In the week before he climbed into the cockpit of a Hurricane of 43 Squadron, the RAF had lost at least seventy pilots, twenty-seven of them in a single day. But Reynell was one of the best fliers in the country, and he so nearly made it through. On 2 September he forced down a Messerschmitt 109 at Hythe where its pilot was captured, but on his last mission before returning to Hawker, was surprised by enemy aircraft. With his Hurricane on fire, he baled out. His widow was told he had been killed in action, but learnt that he might have survived had his parachute not failed to open.[9]

Even at a time of commonplace tragedies, Dick Reynell's death evoked particular sadness among work colleagues and friends, in both of which categories the John family could be counted. Heroism is a difficult companion, demanding of its admirers how they might act in similar circumstances. Ursula would later refer to Peter's employment at Hawker as an "engineer" and it is fair to say that his duties for the company were directly linked to the war effort. Engineers, draughtsmen, firemen, scientists, administrators may contribute more by continuing in their civilian occupations than by enlisting for the front line, although the fact may not always be appreciated by those whose loved ones are in mortal danger. There seems little doubt that Peter could have volunteered for active service, if he had chosen to do so. He might not have had experience of flying Hurricanes at Hawker, but he remained on the RAF reserve list. On his marriage certificate in September 1935 Peter gave his occupation as "aircraft manufacturer," but earlier that year he had flown in the aerobatic display watched by Ursula and the visiting Paul Perrelet. The following year his RAF records list him as a test pilot with Hawker, and his availability on mobilisation is marked "no restrictions."[10]

It would be wrong to overstate the hostility toward families of men who stayed at home, but as the war brought more disasters overseas, the loss of thousands of lives at sea, and the fall of Hong Kong and Singapore, there were those who could not forgive the good fortune of women like Ursula whose husbands returned to them every night. One of them was her childhood friend Jean Gemmell. "Ursula was tremendously, passionately and physically in love with Peter," she said. "So she would not let him join up although he had been a pilot. I really resented that. My husband was in the Royal Navy and I did not see him for two years."

Peter's dilemma was made all the more difficult by his German family background which had led to his being bullied at school. Andrew recalled:

The bullying made a really big impact on my father. His life was complex as a result. He would not have been called up because of his age, and in not volunteering, he could assuage his conscience in knowing that his work at Hawker was linked to the war effort, but I am sure he would have been very keen to join up. He very rarely talked about that period of his life. My mother was very concerned that Peter should not join up. And I think in the end he must have capitulated. She was so in love with him that she didn't want to risk losing him and she wanted a father for her children to see her children grow up and to be with her for all that meant. Not everybody had the opportunity to make such a choice. I know father always felt guilty about that.

Ursula's youngest son James confirmed this impression: "Father confided in me that he would have liked to have flown in the Second World War. I think mother was relieved but it was not discussed by them in front of me. I always assumed that building aircraft was as important as flying them but father never really bought that line."

So a frugal, disciplined but at least domestic family life continued into 1941. There was the "abominable" margarine, jelly packets cut up into squares by the local grocer that were bought as sweets for Andrew, packets of egg and milk powder, and the little bottles of onion flavouring to replace the real thing. Ursula brought home ideas from the Women's Institute for the "most nourishing and appetising dishes made from rations." She probably drew the line, however, at the mashed potato sandwiches that the Ministry of Food promoted in a campaign to get the public to eat more root vegetables. Clothing restrictions were occasionally lightened by the arrival of baby clothes from Moray's sister Cicely in India; coal rationing was not so easily supplemented. The routine left its mark. "Never will I waste any food, not even a bit of butter on the side of a plate," Ursula wrote after the war, "and for a very long time I made do with old garments to cut out new."[11]

Andrew and his baby brother Hugh were becoming accustomed to sleeping in improvised bunks under the stairs for safety. From there they could still hear the distant crumps and bangs when the London Blitz reached its greatest intensity. Claygate escaped most of the damage, but Ursula was in the East End on the day after one of the heaviest raids, and saw "the harrowing sights of houses reduced to skeletons with furniture hanging out of broken balconies, the timbers black, and streets on end devastated and destroyed."

Awful though the scenes were, Ursula responded with the same resolute humour shown by many East Enders. In the unpublished *Bombed out* she describes the plight of a family in the one undamaged house in a street that has taken in the residents of every other. This extract gives its flavour:

I can't discover where my car has gone
As 'Journey's End' has got my trousers on,

70

So if I go to work I'll have to hike,
'Dunromin' has gone shopping on my bike.
And all the kitchen rings with 'CornerCot'
Relating which was bombs and which was not.

Of her own situation, she wrote *Sobs from the Suburbs*, a wry satire, of which a central verse reads:

And if, O lord, my pleas should go astray,
And bombs, machine guns, sirens come our way,
Should Mr James, our warden, let the foe
Past our defences, then spare Mon Repos.
Let Byways crumble, let The Laurels lump it
And Elveden burn, we've got the stirrup pump, it's
Theirs, but surely only cads would cherish
Such selfishness as leaving us to perish.[12]

It seemed the closer the incident, the greater the need to see humour in the situation. Ursula, who had inherited her father's talent for mimicry, lovingly repeated a farmer's description of a bomb killing one of his cows. "Ay," he admitted sadly, "they punctured she." Then, while Ursula's parents were staying for a few days, incendiaries fell at the back of the house. They left a large hole in the garage wall. "Who did that?" Moray asked Andrew, seeking to make a joke of it. But the lad was nearly three, and saw a chance to show off. "I did," he declared. Even Peter laughed. He failed, however, to see the funny side of an incident that cost him the use of his beloved motorcycle. He had gone out on foot for an ARP night shift, leaving it at home in the shed. The blackout demanded elimination of unnecessary noise, but suddenly the horn on the bike short-circuited and started to blare. Ursula rushed out, and was confronted by the cacophonous but otherwise dumbly insolent machine, which defied all her efforts to silence it. She pressed buttons, pulled at cables, but all in vain. In desperation she hit the horn and its adjacent wires a few times with an axe. The noise stopped, much to her relief, but her prompt action did little to avert Peter's wrath when he returned early the next morning.

While black humour was in keeping with the usual wartime response to material misfortunes, one cannot doubt the anxiety that Ursula felt, especially after the incendiary device had fallen barely thirty yards from the house. On 18 June 1941, aged just thirty, she made her will, witnessed by her nanny Rita Wade, and by Mabel who had travelled down for the day. Peter, Moray, and her cousin Philip Unwin, Nora's elder brother, were made executors, with the manuscript of *Adventures of Little Wooden Horse* being left to Andrew. Most of her other manuscripts were bequeathed to her aunt, Moray's youngest sister Kathleen, who had shown keen interest in her work; but the will stipulated, remarkably, that the manuscript of *Kelpie the Gipsies' Pony* and five others to be chosen by Kathleen, should go to an American fan, Helen Ann Raiber, whom Ursula had never met. Miss Raiber had fallen in love with Ursula's books, and letters of admiration, forwarded through publishers, had been followed by parcels of tinned food and clothing from Delaware to supplement the John family's wartime rations. Here was an act of reciprocal kindness, the most generous that Ursula could make in difficult times. It seems evident, however, that the will was made because Ursula was afraid of being killed, not simply as a means of thanking her transatlantic benefactor. For the document remained in force for more than twenty years after the troubled Helen had committed suicide, and was only revised in 1983, a few years after Kathleen's death.

By Christmas 1939 *Adventures of Puffin* had sold almost 2000 copies in less than two months, almost matching the early success of *Adventures of Little Wooden Horse*. George Harrap's successor George Anderson was keen to get another Ursula Moray Williams bestseller. Since the signing of the *Puffin* contract that April, wartime restrictions and a shortage of paper had severely reduced the number of new titles. Publishers were eventually reduced to an allocation of 40% of the paper they had used before the war. Ursula was therefore fortunate in having achieved a peak of popularity just before the war, and in the support of Walter Harrap, who like his father championed the cause of juvenile publishing. As treasurer of the Publishers' Association, he argued that young people still had to be taught, and that books of entertainment were essential "to steady the morale of the public." With fewer titles on sale, long print runs were more profitable for publishers, and for those popular writers fortunate enough to continue to get their books into print, sell-outs were virtually assured.[13]

Less fortuitously, the opportunity for Ursula's sales to prosper came at a time when domestic pressures made it most difficult for her writing to do so. She therefore returned to a manuscript that had been set aside for several years. When, in April 1933, Ursula first came up with the idea for *Family Jane*, about children's fantasies that come true, she had briefly called it *Pretenders' Island*. Now she reverted to that original title as she worked to revise and update the unpublished manuscript. In the new version, set during the war, Jane moves to the countryside for safety. As one of the first rather well-to-do evacuees arriving by car and boarding under the care of a governess, she is followed by other children arriving en masse by train from the London – an unruly bunch that fall naturally into the role of a gang of crooks. Shamed by their reckless behaviour, they eventually settle into more laudable roles as would-be air-raid wardens. For good measure, and in keeping with the wartime spirit, the gardens lovingly tended in the imagination of Jane's governess are turned into allotments. The patriotic spirit did the trick. A contract was duly signed in March 1940. Ursula received another advance of £40, and Harrap turned again to Joyce Lankester Brisley for the illustrations.[14]

By the time of Hugh's birth, Ursula already had in mind what would become her most extended series: the Alpine trilogy that was to begin with *The Three Toymakers*. A difficult nursing period meant that the story had to be put aside and she may then have felt disinclined to tackle a large project, whose over-arching plot was of a greater span than anything she had previously envisaged. So with the outline of the trilogy allowed to lie on the shelf, Ursula looked elsewhere for ideas. They came again from North Stoneham. Of all the books it inspired, none provides a more detailed representation of the house and the land around it than *A Castle for John-Peter* – an obviously loving dedication to her husband but one that is perhaps rather more telling and artful to those closest to Ursula and Peter. The mysterious bastion in Hampshire is explored in every detail, until at last the hero from London who comes to possess it feels like a town boy no longer, "but belonged to the country for ever and ever" and is, of course, "the happiest boy in the world."

The scene that awaits the hero on his arrival exactly matches that which Ursula remembered:

The house was the biggest John-Peter had ever seen, and the oldest and most tumbledown. It had great pillars in front of it, holding up the roof, and dozens and dozens of windows looking out over the lawns, where the grass grew as long as in a hayfield.

There was a lake behind the house with an island covered with rhododendrons and behind the lake were more fields and trees and parkland, that went on and on and on.

There was a cedar-tree in front of the house, where a boy could climb and lose himself for hours among the thick branches, with the flat green cones. There were rabbit holes and yew trees and bracken, and the house stood in the middle of it all.

[Inside he] came to a stairway that led up and up and round and round almost to the roof … he came out at last on to another corridor, on either side of which were dusty little rooms, lit by skylights. Some of the floors were quite rotten, so that John-Peter's foot went through the boards when he stepped inside. All the rooms were empty and felt very lonely and cold.

Almost every incident, every detail of life has a parallel with North Stoneham: the pet goat that gets into the kitchen, the pony ridden by two sisters living elsewhere in the park, the maids who come to help with the housekeeping, the skating on the frozen lake. But in one regard – of which the author cannot have been oblivious – the balance of the cast was fundamentally changed.

Alan was away serving his country. Of all the Williams, Unwin and Jahn families, he was the only member other than Mabel's brother Cyril who had entered the armed forces in either world war. Cyril had never recovered fully from the injuries he suffered in the trenches of France. Ursula may well have felt a debt of honour toward the brother who had been so excluded from the twins' adventures in real life and in fiction. In a reversal of the roles depicted in *The Twins and Their Ponies*, the young boy was the central character; he is the principal inheritor of the castle whereas the girls are the established possessors of the surrounding estate. Contemptuous at first of the "silly little boy," they finally and happily cede possession of their lair to the intruder, encouraged by enjoyment of a large tea.[15]

On 20 September 1941, as *A Castle for John-Peter* appeared, *The Newsagent* announced the list of books to be published by Harrap in time for Christmas. Among them was a new title by Ursula, *Gobbolino the Witch's Cat*. The contract, signed that July, had agreed that the author would also provide thirty-six small and three full-page woodcut illustrations. For some reason, *Gobbolino* failed to make his appearance until the following February. The additional task of preparing the illustrations might have prevented Ursula from completing the book in time, or more probably Harrap decided to hold back publication. During the Blitz, the publisher's handsome wood-panelled offices in High Holborn were hit by an incendiary bomb, and many books were destroyed, including 3000 copies of *Kelpie* and *More for Brownies*. Meanwhile retailers were reporting high demand for *A Castle for John-Peter*, but slow sales of *Pretenders' Island*. With an extra 7000 copies printed earlier that year of Ursula's other titles, Harrap might have preferred to delay publication of *Gobbolino*, a move that may have suited Ursula well.[16]

The witch's cat was to become a classic, which makes its fate after publication rather puzzling. The initial print run was the standard 3000 copies, and by the end of the year, without the benefit of any special discounts, only four were left. Yet *Gobbolino* disappeared from bookstores for more than twenty years while Harrap continued to reprint books like *Adventures of the Little Wooden Horse*, *Kelpie the Gipsies' Pony*, *Anders & Marta*, *A Castle for John-Peter*, *Dumpling* and *The Twins and Their Ponies* in large numbers. Unusually, both the manuscript and Ursula's illustrations for the 1942 edition of *Gobbolino* are missing from the extensive archives of her work. No correspondence survives to explain what happened, but a clue lies in a letter from Kaye Webb, editor of Puffin Books, who wrote to Ursula in 1963 to suggest that she might include some of her original illustrations in order to keep down the cost of the abridged version to be published the following year.[17] In fact, the Puffin edition appeared with completely new artwork, and although the later and now more familiar spiky and sprightly Gobbolino might be considered an improvement on his plump and fluffy predecessor, his creation strongly suggests some further disaster at Harrap. The inescapable conclusion is that the original drawings, and probably the manuscript too, had been destroyed in the Blitz. This would certainly have made the expense of re-commissioning pictures and new typesetting difficult to justify, especially in wartime. Otherwise, it is hard to understand the publisher's failure to reprint such an instantly captivating and gripping story that seemed certain to repeat the success of *Adventures of the Little Wooden Horse*. Indeed, over the next forty-five years, *Gobbolino the Witch's Cat* was to sell a massive 635,000 copies in a succession of Puffin reprints.[19]

From the moment that Gobbolino and his sister Sootica tumble out of the witch's cavern, his steps are directed by an author on top form. While Sootica wants to be a witch's cat,[20] "to know all the Book of Magic off by heart, and learn to ride a broomstick and turn mice into frogs and frogs into guinea-pigs," Gobbolino wants only to be a kitchen cat, to "sit by the fire with my paws tucked under my chest and sing like the kettle on the hob." Dropped by his mother among toads in the darkest corner of the cavern because his one white paw shows he is not a true witch's cat, repeatedly abandoned in the wide world because he cannot entirely abandon his bewitching tricks, Gobbolino repeats good-heartedly "What a lucky cat I am" for every small comfort on his journey.

Many chapters form single stories, ideal for bedtime, as Gobbolino makes himself invisible, faces drowning, or helps a Punch and Judy showman after his Toby dog dies. At an orphanage, Gobbolino slips chocolate sauce into the cook's gruel. During a vividly-described storm, he outwits a sea-witch trying to sink a ship. But for all his good turns and a spirited refusal to bow to injustice, he seems to be constantly rewarded with rejection. What child did not sigh for him, as he is blamed for crimes he did not commit, is thrown into a cauldron for refusing to cast a nasty spell, or is thrown out into the cold because of who he is? And what child did not long for that certain happy ending, and to go to sleep contentedly, as Gobbolino finds the home where he will stay "for ever and ever," where "nobody would turn him out again. The children would become boys and girls and men and women. The baby would grow up and rock its own baby to sleep in the wooden cradle."[21]

Gobbolino was destined to make his first public appearance at exactly the same time that Ursula too was to find a new home, and with a similar sense of security and deliverance. For the ink was hardly dry on her signature to the will written in June 1941, when there was talk of moving away from Surrey to the comparative safety of Gloucestershire. Hawker had bought the Gloster Aircraft Company, and in 1938 started producing Hurricane fighters at its factory at Hucclecote on the outskirts of Gloucester.[22] Three years later the company asked Peter to consider going there as contracts manager. His discussions at home did not last long. Ursula's relief can be imagined. *Mon Repos* had indeed been spared. Her adored husband and children would be protected, rather like the evacuees of *Pretenders' Island*. As an added blessing, the move could also bring a return to country living. It was agreed that Peter would go ahead, find a suitable home, and that the rest of the family would follow. The clouds were lifting. Peter's ARP superintendent, already short of wardens, noted the unexplained absence of Flt. Lt. John at the end of August. A week later he heard that Peter had resigned and jotted in his notebook, perhaps somewhat testily: "Gone to Gloucester. Some job I expect."[23]

Chapter 10

"Tic-tic-tic and there was a Christmas tree."

The move to Gloucester brought the opportunity to live in the Cotswolds, those rolling hills of golden limestone, fat sheep and thatched cottages that for many epitomise unspoilt rural England. Peter soon found lodgings at Crickley Lodge, between Gloucester and Stroud, part of which had been turned into a guesthouse. Ursula came for weekends, in the course of which she helped to look for a permanent home during the day. In the evenings she enjoyed the pleasure of riding again, and helping to round up and feed the owners' horses. Their hosts' thirteen-year-old daughter loved having a writer to stay, and would later be a writer herself, but it was already evident from her phenomenal horsemanship how Pat Smythe was likely to achieve fame.[1] The parents of the future show-jumping champion were friends of the Holland-Martins, descendants of the founders of Martin's Bank, who bred horses and rented out properties on their 5,000-acre Overbury Estate which covered much of Bredon Hill in south Worcestershire. As a consequence, in February 1942 Ursula, Peter, Andrew and Hugh moved to Clifts, a Victorian red-brick house on the Evesham to Tewkesbury road at Teddington Hands, with large, cold rooms that had neither electricity nor telephone.

A couple of months later they were joined by Ursula's neighbour from Claygate, Joan Cotton, her two small girls Jill and Susan, and their nanny. Joan's husband, Jack, was serving with the RAF, and it was agreed that the family could stay for the duration of the war if necessary. Peggy Tandy, who had moved from Sunderland and married a tractor driver from nearby Beckford, came as a helper. For a girl from a fairly well-to-do family, the wages of an agricultural worker came as something of a shock, and now with a baby of her own to look after, she needed the money. It was a trial arrangement. Over forty years later, she was still calling, by which time not a lot of dusting was done. Ursula appreciated her visitor also for her workaday Northern humour, and sometimes would pay her simply to listen to the latest of her manuscripts over a cup of coffee, or suggest they went together for one in Cheltenham. When royalties came in, wages were supplemented by gifts. When, some years later, Peggy lost the money she had paid to a collapsed travel company for an air ticket to visit her daughter in America, Ursula gave her £200 as an advance and a Christmas bonus. "The notes have been lying under my bedroom rug for five days," Ursula said. Given the unexacting nature of the helper's duties, they had been safe from accidental discovery.[2]

The heaviest air attack on Gloster Aircraft Company had taken place at Easter 1942, killing at least nine people, including a bus driver and passengers in the company's car park.[3] Raids were, however, comparatively rare, and Clifts itself was a comfortable distance away from likely danger – surrounded by fields of wheat and barley. The family could live reasonably well. The garden produced a phenomenal amount of vegetables and plums, supplemented by what was bought from the orchards of the Vale of Evesham, or gathered from hedgerows. Chicken and geese provided eggs and sometimes a dinner, and for the children there was the occasional treat. A temporary American supply base was set up on the road to Stow-on-the-Wold. As convoys of military trucks, tanks and equipment rolled by, the friendly troops would toss bars of chocolate or sweets to the youngsters waving at their front gate. When they were gone, the lanes were as quiet again, but not empty. Discarded packing cases, lined with tar paper, were perfect for turning into firewood, or into the go-kart in which Peter towed Andrew and Hugh behind his bicycle.

As a key worker in the aircraft industry, Peter received a petrol ration for the Standard Eight that he maintained with an enthusiast's devotion. Ursula's conveyance was an even more delightful pony and trap. No amount of care could, however, ensure a trouble-free start for the two-wheeler. The pony, Nancy, had apparently been overloaded earlier in life and would baulk and go backwards unless allowed to start immediately when put between the shafts. As a result, the visiting aunt Ella, her companion and the cart once landed in a ditch. The only remedy, like kick-starting a car downhill, was for Ursula to load the children in the trap, to connect the shafts, and to jump aboard through the rear door after the vehicle started moving, to the dismay of onlookers.[4]

Jill Cotton loved the pony cart rides and bath times even more. Aged four, she would be put into the sudsy water with Andrew, who was a few months younger, and by the flickering light of oil lamps Ursula would tell them stories that she had just made up. "Oh please, just tell us another story," Jill would say, and sat there fascinated while the water got cold. "My memory is that [Ursula] was always smiling," she recalled. Children from Beckford were not left out of the fun. A tradition of parties began with birthdays and Christmases, to which all local youngsters were invited. Many of the children like Doreen Newbury were from poor homes in which treats were rare: "We sat on small chairs in the kitchen for tea parties, with jelly, and cakes and sandwiches. She was very much into crafts, and made lots of things for everyone to take." The children walked the two miles home, sometimes in the dark, carrying presents or balloons along deserted roads, safely and happily. Gifts were not confined to youngsters. On the day that Barbara Phipps' mother was due home after a stay in hospital, Ursula arrived with a huge bouquet of flowers. "When you had a conversation with her, there were no airs and graces," Barbara recalled. "She was an exceptionally nice woman, very generous, kind. My mum had several bouts of illness and she was always there. She was a lovely, lovely woman, a real lady."[5]

Within a week of the move to Clifts, both Rita Wade and the Cottons' nanny were called up for war duties. Not long thereafter, Peggy suggested that her 15-year-old sister Rita Gettings might look after the John boys, and she in turn recommended a friend to take care of the Cotton girls. Like Peggy, Rita became a lifelong friend. "It was the best thing that ever happened to her," according to her son Simon. Rita would take the children out for at least two hours each afternoon, giving Ursula time to write. There were other, less conventional childminders. Sometimes the boys were left to play in the garden and might wander under the fence into neighbouring fields. This was not a problem when Italian prisoners of war, who displayed an obvious love of children, were helping with haymaking or harvesting, as Ursula explained: "We put a label on Andrew's shirt "Please send us home at 12 o'clock" and a labourer … drops them over the garden wall. If not they scout the field for them with binoculars to spot their red and white check shirts and bright blue dungarees."[6] For the boys, it was a foretaste of the adventurous lives they would be encouraged to pursue as part of growing up. For Ursula, the immediate consequence of having time to herself was the production of another two of her most successful books; the first of them a Christmas classic. She wrote the story in peace, alone, then allowed in an audience as she set about illustrations for *The Good Little Christmas Tree*.

In the stone-flagged kitchen, Jill watched spellbound with Andrew as Ursula cut shapes from the coloured, gummed sheets spread across the large table and stuck them down onto black backgrounds. "She just went tic-tic-tic and there was a little boy, tic-tic-tic and there was a Christmas tree. She never drew the shapes first – just cut them out freehand, and even at that age, when I was only four, I thought this was so clever," Jill recalled.[7] Older heads were also impressed. It was, concluded one scholar of children's books of the period, "the best picture book produced during the Second World War in England."[8]

The book, dedicated to Andrew, Hugh, Jill and Susan "in our nursery at Clifts" became, in 1943, an instant and a long-lasting hit. Successive print runs, each of 10,000 copies, sold out. The BBC broadcast the story, adapted by Olive Dehn, as a play in *Children's Hour* on the Sunday before the thankful, happy Christmas of 1945, and repeated it at least four times thereafter. The allegory of sacrifice and redemption served its time perfectly. Yet, thirty years later, Eileen Colwell still chose the book as one of the best for reading to younger children. It was "a perfect story to tell at Christmas for it has all the essentials, family affection, compassion, the joy of giving and the anticipation of receiving" and was "typical of its author in its imagination and warmth of feeling," she wrote. As late as 1992, the *Sunday Telegraph*, with an appreciation of more modern tastes, called it "a truly heart-warming story that children up to the age of cynicism will enjoy," and recommended it to readers "if you're trying to steer your family away from rampant materialism."[9] Its international success was such that in 1983 a junior employee at Harrap mistakenly told an art student in New South Wales that she could go ahead with an Australianised version of the story to be called "The Beaut Little Christmas Tree." The original author and her agent learnt of this only six years later when contacted by an Australian publisher asking how she would like their acknowledgement worded. Permission was refused.[10]

With four children in the house aged up to five when the title was published, it was not surprising that it should be one of the shortest and most boldly illustrated books that Ursula ever produced, or that it was suitable for a very young audience. There had been a plantation of Christmas trees in the woods at North Stoneham, and there are faint echoes of Mrs Molesworth's *Christmas-Tree Land*, which Ursula loved as a child. But the style, the audacity of the Christmas tree able to pull up his roots and wander through the woods, and the repeated imagery of the candles flickering, the icicles sparkling, the toadstools gleaming, the diamonds glittering, and the cookies dangling from his branches "bobbing about like so many little brown mice," is inimitable. Like the Little Wooden Horse – made surely from similarly durable timber – the Good Little Christmas Tree wanders through a sometimes kindly, sometimes hostile world, careless of his own wellbeing, as he sacrifices all he has for the sake of the poor family to whom he hopes to bring happiness. Progressively deprived of needles and his best branches by goblins, wolves, and greedy children, the brave tree is reduced to a pathetic skeleton. Then Father Christmas intervenes. The tree is magnificently restored, and all march home in procession through the snow – including a pedlar of toys, from whom the tree has bought of all things a galloping wooden horse.

All was not as harmonious in the nursery. There were quarrels between the children of the two families, and relations were uneasy between the Cotton girls and the strict Peter, who insisted on his own children calling him "Sir." Jill was frightened of him. She was talking with her aunt, when he shouted out for them to be quiet, and the tearful girl ran to disappear under a table. This cannot have helped relations between the women of the house. There was plenty of space to accommodate two families, but crucially only one kitchen with its ancient stove. As future daughters-in-law and other relatives were to discover to their cost, this was Ursula's domain, and it became increasingly difficult for Joan to accommodate herself to the situation. At the end of December 1942 the two families parted rather thankfully, and good relations were restored.[11]

Before the move from Desborough Cottage, Stanley's daughter Ruth Brodrick had asked Ursula to become godmother to her baby son Michael. He was to be the first of eleven godchildren. Ursula maintained a regular correspondence with most of them when they were teenagers, but the boy received his first communication at the age of a few days, in the form of an embroidery sampler. It still hangs above the bed of the High Court judge, with the comforting thought: "God bless Michael. Dragons fear him, Stars light him, Little mice trust him, Water befriend him, and Mother tuck him up at night."[12]

Susan had become Ursula's first goddaughter shortly after, and although sharing the house with the Cotton family had not proved an unqualified success, the presence of the two girls was a constant reminder of the daughter that Ursula did not have. At about this time, Ursula wrote and twice redrafted a short verse in her workbook:

The creaking of the empty cot
The ghostling stir where child is not
Brings sweet remembrance in its train
And aches the womb to bear again.

In August 1943 Andrew and Hugh were sent to stay with relatives while Ursula was expecting her third child. For the first time, the baby would be delivered at home, and arrived in a hurry at 11 p.m. on the 27th, before a doctor could be summoned. The nurse coped, helped by Mabel and Peter, who "was very interested." Of course, Ursula wrote to an aunt a month later, "we had hoped for a girl but we are terribly proud of the Three Musketeers and Robin is the happiest baby I have ever known." By then the youngster had been for his first ride in the pony cart, travelling in a Moses basket for a picnic with his Athos and Porthos, together with Ursula, Mabel, Rita, and the nurse pedalling behind. Peggy was also expecting a baby and had already told Ursula that she would call him Robin if it was a boy. Faced with choosing a name for her own son, so confidently expected to be a daughter, Ursula asked her friend if she might steal the name. So when a few months later Peggy gave birth to another boy, she called him Roger. Robin and Roger became inseparable.[13]

The following year, Ursula finally got down to writing *The Three Toymakers*, the first part of what was to become the Alpine trilogy. The story picks up the names of Anders and Marta, although the characters do not correspond with their like-named predecessors. The later, older Anders' parents are alive, for example, whereas the earlier, younger Anders' parents are both dead. It seems odd that Ursula should have used the names again: Anders for the brother of the toymaker Rudi, and Marta for the mischievous mechanical doll made by his rival Malkin. The explanation is probably that since writing *Anders & Marta* the author had had a son called Andrew, and wanted to base the younger central character on him, and simply chose to re-use the name Marta despite the possible confusion.[14] Nor could she resist other family references: the benign old toymaker to whom Rudi is apprenticed is again called Peter; and Rudi, like Stanley, is one of six brothers and even has a disabled sister Elsa, like polio victim Ella.

The language is quirky and sensitive. Rudi first appears as "a very patched coat, a pair of long bare legs, and some boots that would hardly have pinched a giant's toes. There was a pair of trousers too, but so skimpy and so darned were they that they seemed to huddle away for very shame beneath the shabby coat-tails." Rudi grows up; now a toymaker too, he goes from tree to tree to find the right wood from which to make a musical box:

> … tapping and listening … to the strum of the wind on their fine boughs, to the vibrations running down to the roots. … When at last he had chosen a tree, he cut it down so carefully, with axe and saw and rope, that the trunk was not bruised and shattered but sank slowly towards the earth with all its sensitive chords unharmed.

Then, following a nail-biting chase through the woods with wolves in pursuit, there is a tremendous scene describing the fantastic toys entered to win the King's prize of one thousand gold pieces.

According to contemporary references in the trade press – probably based on publicity handouts from Harrap – *The Three Toymakers* is set in the Black Forest. Ursula had spent August 1932 there with Alan, but none of the incidents from that walking holiday appear here. What really sets the book apart from her previous, episodic works is the greater scale of a single, gripping plot, plus a new depth of characterisation. Marta herself is a great invention – not only is she a doll that can walk and talk, but she is wilful and manipulative – yet Malkin, her supposedly malevolent creator has tried to eliminate her personality defects, whereas Anders, in trying to protect his family from Malkin's tricks, acts far from honourably by kidnapping his doll. That the author was aiming to write a more extended adventure is clear at the outset. To advance the action, the narrative jumps forward six years after the first chapter, and the book ends with Anders telling his friend Janni that Malkin and his doll were never seen again, "so far as I know."[15]

The series that was completed by *Malkin's Mountain* and *The Toymaker's Daughter* was recognised among Ursula's finest achievements, be it rather belatedly. *The Three Toymakers* was dramatised by Olive Dehn for the BBC in 1948 and directed on stage two years later by Tyrone Guthrie.[16] But, to the author's chagrin, the initial appearance of the book passed almost without notice. Harrap delivered a contract in October 1944 to publish the book, but restrictions on paper supplies delayed its publication beyond the end of the Second World War. In response to her complaints, George Anderson wrote to Ursula in October 1945 explaining the further postponement: "It is quite evident that you do not realise half the difficulties that publishers have to contend with, especially over books with coloured illustrations. You have had rather more than your fair share of the paper we have had available during the last two or three years." The government had allowed Harrap sufficient paper to reprint 5000 copies of its *Standard French* dictionary, but even so these would not be available until the following April or May due to the difficulty of getting them printed and bound. In addition, the Army Education Department had ordered several hundred thousand books and these had to be given priority. As a result, copies of *The Three Toymakers* went on sale too late be included in national newspapers' pre-Christmas reviews – often the only attention that they gave to juvenile fiction during the year – and although bearing the date 1945 may not have gone on sale until January 1946. "I realise that you are working hard to make a name and we are assisting you all in our power," Anderson had added, but the damage was done and Ursula began to question more critically the relationship with the publisher responsible for eighteen successive titles.[17]

Ursula gave birth to her fourth child on 22 April 1945. In contrast to the previous occasion, Peter kept well out of the way and was lying underneath his car when the moment came.[18] The consequence was unchanged. The pretty handmade frock from Switzerland remained unclaimed as James joined the brotherhood. By the time that he was four months old, his mother had finished *The House of Happiness* with a dozen double-page paper cut-outs in the style of, but even more elaborate than, *The Good Little Christmas Tree*. The Harrap chairman bewailed the cost of printing in seven colours prompting him to seek a consequent reduction in the royalties paid to the author.[19] Production was again slow, with the book not appearing until the autumn of 1946, by which time Dehn was already preparing a free adaptation for *Children's Hour*, broadcast in November with Billie Whitelaw in the role of the brother. Like *The Good Little Christmas Tree* and later *The Three Toymakers*, *The House of Happiness* closely matched the criteria by which programme organiser Derek McCulloch, 'Uncle Mac', had built up Children Hour's audience to four million young listeners. "Our established policy is that nothing but the best is good enough for children," he wrote. "Our wish is to stimulate their imagination, direct their reading, encourage their various interests, widen their outlook, and inculcate the Christian principles of love of God and their neighbour."[20] *The House of Happiness* opens with words that suggest a familiar image:

> Once upon a time there were a little brother and sister who lived in a tumbledown house in a wood full of birds and flowers. There were spiders in the chimney and mice in the wainscot; at night the wind blew "Whee-ew!" through the cracks in the door and the rain dripped "pat-pat-pat!" through the holes in the roof.

Brother and sister agree to pull down their tumbledown home and to build a happy one in its place – North Stoneham House had been demolished at the start of the war. The plot then turns neatly on its head the author's own preoccupation with motherhood by having the children build and furnish their new house, then find first a suitable mother, whose "breast was made for the heads of small children and …

lap for fairy tales," and later a father whose "shoulders were broad to ride on" and head "full of stories." The groans of the empty house are gradually stilled to gentle sighs, but there remains the creaking of an empty cradle, a ghostling stir it may be assumed, until the children come home to discover a baby asleep within its blankets, after which "the little house was happy for ever and ever and ever."

Clifts too, although not so little, seemed perfectly happy, home to a devoted family. Blessed with four sons, Ursula was at the peak of her career writing books that inhabited a magical world of childhood innocence, courage and faith. She was admired in the community, and supported by a nanny and daily helper who had become close friends. American transports trundled past, but more infrequently. Overhead the skies once crossed by German aircraft heading for the industrial towns of the Midlands and Merseyside, were streaked by the vapour trails of American bombers in battle formations awaiting radio clearance to set off for Germany. The boys were growing up in the countryside, as safe in the affection of an adoring mother as Clifts was secure from the distant rumble of war. The turmoil of the world stopped at the stout farmhouse door. Nevertheless, a storm had threatened for a couple of years, and when it broke it created the greatest upset that Ursula had known, causing for a time a serious breach with Barbara and calling into question her relations with the rest of her family.

The wedding of Moray and Mabel. Their mothers sit beside them and Edward Unwin is between his wife and daughter. Moray's father pointedly stayed away. Bernard and Stanley Unwin are seated on the ground to the left, Ella on the far right.

Below: Mabel's Spicer aunts at the reception, with her mother, their sister Elizabeth (third from right). The scene probably inspired *A Picnic with the Aunts* (1972) in which their extraordinary hats are the first signs of the aunts swimming back to shore.

Model mothers – with twin dolls. Ursula "the sluttish one" is probably on the right, with her hair ribbon crooked.

Left: Elsa Mueller, the children's first nanny, who taught them to draw pin men.

Below: Reading time in the garden at Cherrycroft.

The twins make room, just, for brother Alan to share their reading.

Bubble and Squeak prepare to join the local hunt, on hobby horses made from their father's bed socks. "Those silly children think they're real," taunted one snooty young rider.

The twins as Girl Guides.

North Stoneham House: Ursula first arrived from the far end, disembarking from her father's car under the portico.

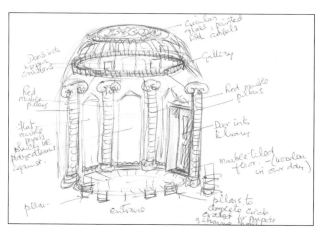

Left: Ursula's sketch of the pillared round hall, used for cricket and roller-skating, with the gallery that became a make-believe ship's deck from which pine cones were thrown at friends trying to board.

Alan, playing alone in the library. The false bookends had been put into storage and replaced by real bookshelves and the glass cases of stuffed birds and animals. The room was abandoned after the dome of the round hall next door collapsed.

Ursula's wedding day, 28 September 1935. She wore her grandmother's veil, and later that afternoon laid her bouquet on the grave of a neighbour who had recently died.

Left: The portrait of Ursula that Paul Perrelet painted at North Stoneham.

Right: "The Cream of the Earth?" Peter, the very picture of an Englishman, arrives at the chalet in La Forclaz for his honeymoon. He thereafter preferred holidays taken at home.

Above: Moray, right, at Hurn Court, Red Cross headquarters, with his demanding president Countess Malmesbury taking a keen oversight. It was her home, and she could be difficult to work with.

Left: Ursula and Andrew at Desborough Cottage. The sign on the fence shows that Peter is an air raid warden.

Right: The four-seater cart made by Peter from discarded US packing cases left on local roads.

Andrew, James, Robin and Hugh with their mother at Court Farm.

From left to right: Rita Griffin, Alan, Josephine, Barbara and Peggy Tandy.

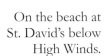

On the beach at St. David's below High Winds.

The story-teller.

The further adventures, aged 91. Son Andrew is the pilot.

Chapter 11

"That house on the hill."

An explanation of the extraordinary journey that Barbara made from Iceland to Clifts in December 1944 must be based partly on speculation. When Ursula travelled by trawler in the opposite direction in the summer of 1947, taking her two eldest boys, she wrote about the trip extensively, and enjoyed a certain degree of celebrity for the pluckiness of the enterprise. Yet neither sister talked about the earlier voyage that Barbara had made alone – in winter and in wartime. Nor is there a single reference to the visit in any surviving correspondence, although its consequences were to affect both women for many years.

The meeting was brought to light during research for this book. Tall and frail, but still with the discernible features that made her striking, the ninety-five-year-old Jean Burgess (née Gemmell) was easily tired by conversation, but she spoke vividly and with animation about the visit.

> Barbara was living very poorly, she was very hard up in Iceland, but she came back during the war to see her mother. You can imagine how difficult that was – it was hard enough in peacetime, but during the war! She went to see Ursula. She didn't have one of Barbara's paintings on show and she was critical of her. This upset Barbara very much.

It seemed an unlikely revelation. Communications between the sisters during the war "were confined to letters," Ursula told Alan,[1] but discovery of Ursula's visitors' book confirmed that Barbara had indeed stayed at Clifts for just two nights from Thursday, 7 December 1944. Questions remained. Although the Battle of the Atlantic had largely been won, it remained a hazardous voyage, and only a month earlier, on 9 November, the steamer *Godafoss* had been sunk by a U-boat on its way from Scotland to Reykjavik with the loss of forty-two lives, including a family of five.[2]

Barbara's journey was made a few days before her son's sixth birthday. "It must have been something important for her to go, and I don't remember the details, but I do remember that my parents discussed the risk," Vifill said. His father could speak from personal experience as he had been on board a ship torpedoed by a German submarine in the First World War. All those aboard safely evacuated the sinking freighter in lifeboats, but suffered the distressing sight of horses that had escaped from the hold being left to drown. Magnús nevertheless reassured his wife that she could go because he "had had a good dream and therefore they 'knew' that she would travel safely." Barbara joined an American military convoy carrying 1000 soldiers and supplies to Great Britain. It was a frightening experience, with the frequent sound of sirens and explosions beneath the waves as the accompanying battleships fired depth charges at suspected German U-boats. Barbara was scared, but yet more terrified for the fate of any young sailors in the submarines below.[3]

Why had Barbara found it necessary to come at so dangerous a time, and in the depth of winter? Even the journey to Teddington was difficult. There had been heavy snow showers, and on the very night of her arrival a Wellington bomber had iced up and crashed shortly after take-off from a nearby airfield.[4] In such circumstances and after a separation lasting nearly five and a half years, was it likely that a serious upset could be caused between the two sisters by the absence of Barbara's pictures on the walls? When Barbara confessed her distress to her friend, did this explanation mask more sensitive reasons that she preferred to keep to herself? Subsequent events and correspondence strongly suggest that Barbara had come to sort out a family problem: she wanted Ursula to take in their parents, and this she had been unwilling to do.

Mabel must have been secretly relieved to move out of North Stoneham and to leave behind all the practical problems and inconveniences that she had had to tolerate for seventeen years. There was the coal-fired stove that never worked properly and produced what Alan had fondly called "Mother's miscakes." There were the bitter winter evenings spent at supper in the dining room, always at Moray's insistence wearing an evening dress, while her husband sat in tweeds with his back to the fire.[5] There was the malfunctioning boiler, and the unreliability of hot water.

For Moray, the move to Hurn Court fulfilled all his social ambitions of living like the country lord that he longed to be. The Kaiser had signed the visitors' book. Handel, Lord Nelson, Henry Fielding and Lillie Langtry had all stayed in what he now regarded as his new home. They may even have been accommodated in the same bedroom, with its fifteen-foot high ceiling and a view over the front drive. For his office, Moray had part of the enormous library, overlooked by Sir Thomas Lawrence's portrait of the 1st Lord Malmesbury and illuminated by a magnificent chandelier now preserved in one of the London livery halls.[6] For Mabel, anywhere with an electricity supply would have been a blessed relief. For both, however, the blessing was mixed, and the other element in the mixture was Dorothy, Lady Malmesbury.

There had been tensions from Moray's early days in the Red Cross – not unusual perhaps in an organisation in which relatively untrained and often unpaid volunteers often assumed responsibility over professional officers and staff. Perhaps Moray had genuinely been ill when he failed to attend the official opening and dedication service for the Home of Recovery, although it seems odd that he missed an occasion led by the Countess of Portsmouth and conducted by the Bishop of Southampton only a few hundred yards from his home. There was no doubt, however, about his frustrations in the 1930s as wrangles and resignations followed his failure to win support from colleagues at Red Cross committee meetings. "After working so hard everything went wrong through people's personal prejudices," Ursula wrote in her diary. "It is so depressing for him and now everything will be as bad as before."[7] Throughout Moray's time as county director, the Countess of Malmesbury was his President; a post that in some cases was a largely honorary position carrying no formal responsibilities. That was not Dorothy's way. She was, according to her grandson James, now Lord Malmesbury, "a formidable woman, very hands-on. It was a good question who was the chief executive and who was the president." Another grandson, John, Lord Cottesloe, described her as "a very strong character who would have personally directed the affairs of the Hampshire Red Cross in a very forceful and hands-on way. She was a very powerful, rather frightening lady and liked her own way." Of course, domestic arrangements at Hurn Court were going to be difficult. The Williamses were treated as members of the family, Lord Cottesloe recalled, "but things got a bit mixed up as there was a sort of separate mess for the Red Cross girls."[8]

For whatever reason, Moray unexpectedly resigned as county director in 1942 at the age of 64. His departure was followed by that of the treasurer and two assistant directors. The closest reference to what had caused Moray at least to stand down came in a letter from Ursula to her brother nearly fifty years after the event. "Father went through a lot in his time poor dear and I doubt whether any of us really sympathised deeply. We more likely disliked Lady Malmesbury." The immediate consequence for her parents was dramatic – for they found themselves homeless, with little money, and few friends. Barbara had long objected to her father's social prejudices. Now she sympathised deeply with Mabel regarding their consequences:

> Isolation ... is rather what father suffered from. ... Mother, if she had been allowed to, would have known lots of people of all classes at Stoneham and never felt lonely. She was only encouraged to associate with one class and Daddy had the feudal system so engrained that he cut himself off from too many people and was always on the fringe of the class he preferred to frequent.[9]

Over the next three years Moray and Mabel had six addresses – sometimes living separately – including a hotel and lodgings in Salisbury, a London club, and three addresses in Winchester, one of which were rooms at the regional offices of the British Council where Moray had taken on a relatively junior position. Between leaving Hurn Court in 1942 and the spring of 1944, Mabel spent long periods at

Clifts, but by the time of Barbara's visit had not been there for nearly six months. Moray had rarely come for more than a few days, and during all of 1944 had spent a total of five nights under Ursula's roof. He had never managed money well, to his wife's distress, and the additional expenses now being incurred were contributing to a growing overdraft. He felt unfulfilled and had developed, according to Ursula, "an inordinate and regrettable love for the bottle."[10] His daughters must have been reminded of what had happened to their grandfather. Then there was the question of what to do about Alan.

Discharged from the army as medically unfit, he was living like a tramp, sometimes in a caravan, sometimes in a tumbledown cottage on a farm in Oxfordshire. According to his own account, Alan had not expected to remain in the army for more than six months, nor for war to be declared. After failing the examination for the diplomatic service in 1939, he had joined the Royal Army Medical Corps to gain experience until the end of the year, after which time his father had agreed to buy his discharge for £50. With the outbreak of hostilities, he applied to join the Officer Cadet Training Corps, and in December found himself at Aldershot. Inspired by the example of First World War poets, he wrote to colleagues asking them to contribute essays on the theme "What am I fighting for?" Rather prematurely he added that Chatto & Windus had agreed to publish the anthology and that he hoped Siegfried Sassoon would write a preface. Alan's own piece written in March 1940, "Wanted – a faith" – a title which could refer as much to the author as to the world he addresses – reads in part like the self-obsession of a man close to mental exhaustion, dwelling at length on his own "dreaminess and unpracticalness [*sic*] and out-of-touchness." Life, he concluded, "is not worth having." Of more concern to the authorities would have been his views about the war itself. The piece supported the war against the ruthless cruelty of Nazism and argued far-sightedly for a federal Europe, but supported German expansionism, stated that Poland and Czechoslovakia were not worth fighting for, and ended with a call for controlled human selective breeding. In May, after serving as a translator with the naval task force to Norway that destroyed German warships in the Narvik fjord, he returned to find that the War Office had banned his publication.[11] The decision precipitated a nervous breakdown and release from the services on the grounds of ill health.

Alan had joined the army to find a profession, attracted by the prospect of a six-month tonic for the mind and body. He left with his confidence shattered by discipline and regulation. He professed a faith that he hoped would revitalise the world, a pagan worship of the visible signs of God's presence: the sun, the moon, the stars, woods and flowers, and "the beauty of men and women and all living things." He clung to what he saw as its closest manifestation in the Soviet Union. By day he worked as a farm labourer. By night he worked at Russian grammars and textbooks, listening to gramophone records of the language, in a half-derelict cottage that he was allowed to occupy.[12] Remarkably, for one self-taught and in such a short time, Alan took the opportunity of Russia's entry into the war in 1941 to serialise an introduction to the language in the *Sunday Pictorial*, reprinted as *Russian Made Easy*, with much military vocabulary – air raid, spy, victor and declension of Танк – of a tank, to a tank etc.

Constantly short of money, Alan repeatedly sent ideas to Stanley for Russian works that he might translate, and examples of his own poetry. His uncle was supportive, sent occasional cheques for small commissions and gifts of books, but declined to publish any of the offerings. He gently advised him not to rely on writing for a living and to get a regular job.[13] Alan's anxiety to fit into a congenial intellectual community and his conflicting suspicion of authority meant that this did not come easily. He sent a letter hoping to obtain a post at Oxford University, the only consequence of which was a poem:

I wrote to a Don
And he did not reply.
He just did not answer –
I do not know why. …
And I was a stranger
And friendless and weak,
And lived in a garret
On two pounds a week.[14]

Despite his troubles, and the fact that he was living little more than an hour's drive from Clifts, contact between Alan and Ursula seems virtually to have ceased from the time of his discharge from the army until the end of the war. After coming to stay frequently during his few months in uniform, he did so only once during the next five years. By then, his nephew Hugh was nearly three years old, and it is quite likely that he did not see Robin for the first time until he was even older. Alan had always felt intimidated by Peter's brusque manner,[15] and he no doubt felt embarrassed to parade his troubles before his sister. She had after all rescued him once before from the consequences of another idealistic, but naive and injudicious publishing venture.

It is not known if some particular event in the lives of Moray, Mabel or Alan had prompted Barbara to board the steamer from Iceland. What seems indisputable is that she did so with their unhappy and unresolved circumstances on her mind. What the sisters agreed, possibly after some recrimination either during that short meeting or in later correspondence now lost, was that Ursula would take care of their parents, while Barbara would provide for Alan.

For more than thirty years, Alan received regular payments from Iceland, despite his sister's own early financial difficulties. When Moray died, he received Barbara's share of his legacy as well as his own. Despite the division of responsibility, Ursula also felt obliged to help. "Barbara always said she'd look after you and yours and Vifill and his. While I have the four boys to look after, now and hereafter, it seemed, and is, I think a fair arrangement," she wrote. Nevertheless, along with repeated statements of obligations to her more immediate family, gifts continued to arrive from Ursula – £100 after his bicycle was stolen, £1,500 left to her by a distant relative, and odd sums when royalties had been good.[16]

For Ursula the main consequence of the agreement, however, was that before long her parents came to live with her. Moray wanted to enjoy independence, and Clifts was far from ideal, as the experience with the Cotton family had illustrated. For some time Ursula had admired a lovely Cotswold limestone farmhouse, Court Farm, half a mile from Beckford on the lower slopes of Bredon Hill. Like Clifts, it was owned by the Holland-Martins, and when Ursula and Peter heard that the current tenants were due to leave, they asked to take over the lease. It was their two oldest boys who brought the good news. The landlords had been thinking over the proposition, and when they rode by, stopped to talk with Andrew and Hugh who were climbing on the gate. The elder immediately asked if they could go to live at "that house on the hill," and three minutes later, the time it took to run the length of the drive, both boys burst into the kitchen shouting, "They said yes! They said yes!"

On Friday 14 September, twelve days after the end of the war, Andrew, Hugh and Robin were helped aboard a furniture van to make the short journey to their new home, while James followed in his basket in the horse-drawn trap alongside his mother. A fortnight later, Moray and Mabel moved into two largely self-contained rooms on the ground floor and stayed for nine years. Ursula was to live there for fifty-three. For ten people, there was not an excess of space, with all having to share one bathroom upstairs. Bunks were fitted into the huge converted barn loft for the four boys, with an old rocking horse given by the family doctor. As at Clifts, original illustrations from *The Good Little Christmas Tree* were hung around the walls. Supplemented later by those from *The House of Happiness*, they gave the room the atmosphere of an art gallery into which only children were be admitted. From the large garden, dotted with elms, there were views of the Cotswolds to the east and the Malverns to the west. But of all the many delights, one above all thrilled the children when they first walked in. They stood at the entrance to each room, and for the first time in their lives had the pleasure of pressing switches, click-click, click-click, to see the lights come on.[17]

Chapter 12

———

"Home cooking, Morris 1000 cars and old bicycles."

Eight months after the move to Court Farm, Barbara visited her family in happier circumstances. She could see how well her parents had settled into their new home, but the fact that she brought seven-year-old Vifill this time, and that they stayed for five weeks, indicates that differences had been settled and she was happy with the arrangement. They would have come by air, but Magnús had had another dream, this time a bad one in which their aircraft crashed. As a result Barbara cancelled their tickets and booked sea passages instead. The aircraft did not crash, but in fairness to her husband it should be added that neither did the steamer sink. The visit went well. Mabel adored the grandson whom she had not seen since he was a baby, and as a bonus the boy had unwittingly helped solve something of an identity crisis for his grandfather. Those like Mabel who had known him since his less pretentious youth called him Moray, but this was confusing to those who referred to the family as the Moray Williamses. Given his patrician nature, the need for new acquaintances to address the old man with the undignified informality of a first name seldom arose, but for such rare occasions Vifill provided the solution. He called him "Afi," a seeming incongruous corruption of his ill-favoured first name Arthur, but in fact Icelandic for grandfather. The name stuck.

The countryside around Bredon Hill – an isolated northern spur of the Cotswolds celebrated in the poem by A.E. Housman, but far enough from its principal chain to escape the attention of tourists – captivated Vifill, as it had his aunt and cousins. From its summit, nearly a thousand feet high, could be seen the uncertain course of the River Avon, and the single-minded Severn beyond. Close to the foot of the lane passing Court Farm, in the centre of the village was Beckford Hall and its 48-acre estate, owned since 1936 by the Salesian community, and used to train young men for the priesthood and provide country breaks for boys from the London suburbs who had never seen sheep or cattle. Bill Bergen came in 1970 as a novitiate, but even then the area had changed little. "The whole area was as if one stepped back into the 1930s," he said. "It was dominated by captains and colonels in tweeds. The villages smelled of home cooking, Morris 1000 cars and old bicycles. It was lush with the smell of the fields. Everything seemed so perfect and well-kept, an atmosphere of idyllic picture postcard Englishness with a resonance like nothing else I had seen before. I heard Vaughan Williams or Gustav Holst. It reminds me now of country schools and a simpler but sophisticated lifestyle like black-and-white English films."

After the issue with Harrap's delay in publishing *The Three Toymakers* Ursula turned again to her uncle for advice about the terms of her contract. This was in June 1946, during Barbara's visit and probably after discussing the situation with her too. Stanley, critical perhaps of modest royalties offered by other publishing houses while noted for parsimony in running his own, did not think them "particularly generous to an author who now has such an established reputation," but advised that it would be difficult to obtain better at a time when every publisher had more books on offer than paper on which to print them. Ursula nevertheless passed on his suggested rates as her own proposals, prompting a rather indignant reply from Anderson. "Your letter … comes as a considerable surprise. We have never paid such royalties as these for children's books and I am not prepared to do so now." He agreed nevertheless to a small increase and wrote again in a more emollient tone a couple of weeks later. One of the difficulties in marketing her titles, he commented, was that no two were quite alike, and he suggested that she might create a character who could run through at least half a dozen books that could be produced in a uniform format on an annual basis "to keep the bookseller and children interested." Ursula had always responded to such suggestions by saying that she preferred to have a complete change from one work to another, but in this case she was happy to oblige. She had already written a sequel to *The Three Toymakers* to be called *Malkin's Mountain*, and was thinking about the plot for a third volume in the series.[2]

Several years have passed since the end of *The Three Toymakers*, when Anders expressed the view that "as far as he knew" Malkin and his doll were never heard of again. The central plot of *Malkin's Mountain* is nonsense of a type that the author had abandoned since writing for Brownies. Throughout her long career, Ursula wrote her most successful books when she was happiest, whereas at times of greater stress her powers of imagination seemed constrained, kept in at nights by the necessity of thinking about other obligations. With housemaid Rita Gettings having moved in, Ursula now had to cook every day for at least nine people, plus more often than not a visitor or two. As a result, perhaps, the usual lively narrative depends upon a central idea that, for all its symbolism, she would surely have rejected given more time to let her thoughts wander. It concerns a scheme by the evil Malkin, under whose spell a mountain is moving from the kingdom in which Rudi and old Peter Toymaker live, into his own, bearing with it the pines from which the best toys and furniture are made. As a result the mountain is dying. At its underground centre is its heart, a clock, which can be restored to normal working only with a magic key made from gold. Rudi triumphs after an exciting battle and thus the mountain returns home.

Some of the minor details of autobiographical reference are arguably of greater interest than the awkwardly contrived story itself. From the opening, with its rocking cradle, readers discover that Rudi and Margaret now have four children, including twins Paul and Peterkin, who, as seems inevitable, are later confirmed to be identical.

As the twins set out to save their father, and Anders provides the comforting information "that twins are protected against magic powers if they walk hand in hand," one can imagine Ursula and her sister hurrying past the gypsy caravans at Petersfield, or through the woods at Stoneham. Deep below the mountain is a passage leading to "a magnificent pillared hall topped by a dome," where a voice from the music box seems to express the author's sentiments when it sings that courage will vanquish all and faith solace the waiting mother.

Ursula had nevertheless achieved what her publisher had wanted: the continuation of a story with the same participants in the same setting. In doing so she had started to develop a new depth of personality to one of her main characters. Marta the doll, although continuing to help realise Malkin's plan, also seems secretly to be conspiring against him, and acts with apparent, if self-interested, kindness toward Rudi and his twins. At the end, bedraggled and shrunk to the size of a small, frail child, she is led away by her wizened, outcast and unloved master. The sad pair move Rudi's heart to pity, and for all the mischief they have caused, the reader longs for their redemption in what would have to be another story.[3] Anderson must have been pleased.

He could not however enjoy the satisfaction of seeing the book capitalise on the success of *The Three Toymakers* as quickly as he had hoped. Its appearance was unlikely before July or August 1947, he wrote, and by the spring of that year, post-war austerity had already pushed likely publication into the following year. Anderson explained that a coal shortage had reduced many print works to half-time working. "We are infinitely worse off today than we were a year ago. … [In] this four month period … we shall probably only get 50% instead of 90% of our quota. Really, our troubles are almost endless." Reprints of four of her other titles were also delayed, and *Malkin's Mountain* was eventually published in April 1948, twenty-one months after its acceptance. Ursula had every reason to be sympathetic. She had only to talk about the situation to her uncle Ted, who was printing the book at Unwin Brothers. A manager there had in fact simultaneously written to her lamenting that "the world of book production is now in such complete confusion – far worse than during the war." At the same time she could not ignore the fact that having all her most recent titles published by Harrap had meant that very few copies were currently on sale, and that as a result, at a time when she now had increasing responsibilities at home, her royalties for 1947 fell to about half of what she had earned for the previous three years, and to their lowest since 1941.[4]

While she was waiting for *Malkin's Mountain* to be published, Ursula had been planning what would have been a third picture book with scissor-cuts in the style of *The Good Little Christmas Tree*. *The House of Happiness* had appeared in an extraordinarily wide format, with double-page illustrations nineteen inches across plus margins, and Anderson had asked that the next should be designed as an upright.[5] Ursula started work on what was probably to be called *Ten Children*, with twelve colour plates, the first of them to be a depiction of home, and the last of a return to home. She got as far as drafting an opening about the seven sons and three daughters, but chose to write first the episodes about the girls: a ballet dancer who marries a prince, one who marries a farmer, and a third who becomes a missionary to cannibals who love her so much "that for her sake they gave up eating human meat and ate instead the apple dumplings her mother used to make." A list in Ursula's sketchbook – architect, road-maker, farmer, circus trainer, cowboy, explorer, sailor, cook – suggests a choice of the boys' future occupations, but not a word was written about them, and the work got no further than the first five hundred words. The reason may have been connected with frustrations over the delayed publication of other titles, but more probably the book was simply abandoned because of the more prosaic pressures of running the house. The fragment that survives tells that while the father is at work in the forest, the mother has plenty to do.

> There was so much scrubbing, ironing, so much mending and cutting out, so much washing and brushing and putting to bed.[6]

Despite such domestic chores, *Ten Children* might still have been completed but for the disruption caused by weeks of sub-zero temperatures in the severe winter from January 1947, when blizzards blocked roads and floods were widespread, causing shortages of food and fuel, and frequent power cuts. Access to Court Farm was difficult for two months. Pipes froze and throughout the coldest February on record, the household had to rely on a single tap in the kitchen for its water. Fine snow blew under the eaves into the roof space. The only way for it to be removed was for Peter to climb into the loft with a spade and throw down the snow onto the landing, from where Ursula shovelled it through the open window into the courtyard.[7] They were not circumstances that allowed much time for writing stories or that were conducive to making delicate scissor-cuts.

Barbara had meanwhile invited Ursula to visit Iceland in the summer and to bring the older boys. The air fare was expensive, and the steamer was often full, so she suggested half-seriously that the family come by trawler from Fleetwood. Peter decided to stay behind with Rita and Ursula's parents and to look after Robin and James. Nothing could be arranged in advance, but on 23 July the office of J. Marr & Son at the port rang Peter to say that a trawler was due to dock, and that any potential passengers should simply turn up in the hope that its captain would agree to take them. The following day Ursula settled Andrew and Hugh onto the train for Fleetwood, which her rudimentary knowledge of geography suggested was a suburb of Liverpool. On the next day all three were at the quayside when the captain, a fat little man in a grey suit and a small homburg hat, grudgingly offered to take them, largely as a favour to his friend in the fisheries office. He looked rather incredulously at his unlikely passengers.

"You must understand that my men have been fishing for three weeks. They can hardly be asked to give up their cabins to a mother and two children," he said. "Of course not," said Ursula brightly, as her heart sank. The boys did not wish to be deprived of their adventure, and had no such misgivings. "We don't mind where we sleep, just *anywhere*," piped up the elder. It seemed to do the trick. Perhaps this odd trio would not be such a burden after all. For the first time the captain laughed.

That evening Andrew and Hugh, looking like junior members of the crew in their Fair Isle sweaters, climbed aboard the *Kari*,[8] stepping over gutted fish and the wet cowhides used to cover hatches. Coal clattered into the hold, while great containers carried the catch in the opposite direction. As the trawler headed for the open sea, Ursula wondered what she was doing taking her boys in such a small boat for three days and nights across the North Atlantic. The smells were of dead fish, coal dust, engine oil, and of a stuffy cabin of twelve bunks that Ursula and the boys shared with six other passengers. When the weather turned rough there was also the acrid stench of all being sick over the side. There were compensations, at least for the boys, of going onto the bridge, of getting dirty in the boiler room, and of being lulled to sleep by one of the crew who played the mandolin. In thanks to Britain for her help in the war, and in admiration of its not least plucky inhabitants, the captain refused any payment.

The visit coincided with the longest and most serious eruption for a century of Hekla, the volcano about 100 miles east of Reykjavik. Ursula, Barbara and their boys set off in jeeps across black deserts and old peaks of jagged lava to stay at a wooden hut just five miles from the crater. Multicoloured smoke and steam belched from Hekla's fissures. By day, tentacles of cooling lava twisted toward the valley floor raising clouds of steam as they crossed flows of snow melt, and at night scars on the lower slopes glowed pink then scarlet as the light faded. Then, with the Northern lights behind it, the mountain would raise its own pyrotechnics, throwing fire flashes into the billows of smoke and ash thousands of feet above the summit, which seemed to spark electrical storms through the cumulus cloud. At night Ursula read Icelandic Sagas to the boys, and they felt the excitement of real adventure when earth tremors started to collapse the stone walls of a barn in which they had been playing.

The boys and their mothers took delight also in the wildlife. They noted whimbrel, phalarope, godwit and golden plover; picked the blueberries and strawberries that grew in the clefts of lava; and caught Arctic char, like large brown trout, in the fast-flowing streams. Barbara traded one of her paintings to hire horses. With Magnús looking after the children, the sisters made long excursions into the mountains, where farmers were trying to rescue the hay before the black ash destroyed it, and roped their mounts together with others to cross a swirling current. Much time was spent on rounding up the small, semi-wild chestnut-coloured

Icelandic horses that regularly slipped their bridles and headed for the mountains.

It was one such incident that Ursula used as the starting point of her story *Golden Horse with a Silver Tail*, published ten years later. It is an engaging description, written in simple, direct language, of the entire expedition which lasted nearly seven weeks. It might have been longer had Peter not sent a message asking if his wife was coming home. Almost every incident in the book was taken from the holiday, and almost every interesting event on the holiday found a place in the book, except, understandably for the time that Ursula stripped off at an isolated volcanic pool and enjoyed a bath with endless hot water, and "no-one likely to come and rattle on the door." That the story is told by a boy of nine – exactly Andrew's age at the time – adds to its charm, even if it rather limits the narrator's ability to convey any dramatic tension. "It was a most exciting sight," he says lamely as workers drive sheep across water. Nevertheless the deliberate coincidence of ages contributes to the amusement of tracing the transposition of characters in the book with those who spent that adventurous summer in Iceland in 1947. Ursula even made the narrator a twin, and cannot resist a little joke at the expense of Barbara born ten minutes before her. The story tells how Jean, a writer, comes with the boys to stay in Iceland with her sister Catherine, a painter. Jean is twenty-five, as Ursula would no doubt have liked to be. The reader is not told Catherine's age, except that she is "quite a lot older."[9]

Before the trip to Iceland, Ursula had been working on a new book. *Ten Children* had been set aside during the severe winter, and for some reason, possibly the likelihood of a long production wait for a picture book to printed in full colour, she abandoned the title to start on a new story that marked a further departure from her early writing. Tastes in children's fiction were changing in the more egalitarian post-war age, and subsequent works[10] indicate that Ursula was trying to achieve greater independence from the guides, horses, twins and crumbling mansion that had symbolised her curious childhood. Written in a lively present-tense staccato, *The Story of Laughing Dandino*, tells how the travelling showman returns home to a village where no-one smiles, where the priest is unhappy because he is not the pope, where the church door angels are miserable because they are not carved on a cathedral. One of the village children organises a nativity play, which the adults are reluctant to attend, so Dandino accepts a challenge that they will come if first he can make them laugh. Victory is achieved when the last to resist, the grumpy burgomaster, trips over a carving of his bulbous nose, and is fooled into thinking it is his own. Seeing his error when he looks in the mirror, the mayor laughs and all laugh with him, none louder than Dandino. Vannyenka will now be his home for ever.

Like Robert Thompson who carved a signature mouse on every piece of furniture that he made, Ursula could not help but leave her personal stamp of authorship on her work. Like the children of Vannyenka she had put on her own plays, Dandino's puppets long to settle down and have their own "wooden babies," and at the outset her widely-travelled hero's popularity is proven by the fact that he is known in "Reykjavik … and Annecy … and Little Beckford-under-the-Hill." The story nevertheless lacked the reassuring and customary support of being set in an environment familiar to Ursula, and she took the unusual step of seeking an outsider's opinion of the unpublished draft. Eleanor Holland-Martin had brought up five boys, including those now running Overbury Estate, and had often expressed interest in Ursula's work. After Ursula had returned from Iceland, Eleanor wrote back saying she felt "as if I had been deprived of a share in something very lovely to which the whole book was aiming" and urged Ursula to strengthen the final scenes. As a result, Ursula seems to have made some minor amendments, but one thing she declined to change. Eleanor had politely suggested that the story might end with Dandino packing up to make another journey to "the gateways of the world," leaving Vannyenka behind. Ursula picked up the phrase, but left the emphasis on the village being his home, wherever he travelled.[11] The destination of travel was always home, as surely as the end of a bedtime story was always being tucked up in bed.

Stanley shared Ursula's reservations about selling *Dandino* to Harrap. "Harraps are not generous with authors of juveniles, and with age dear old Anderson has tended to become more, rather than less, obstinate," he wrote to her in January 1948. "While the original George G. Harrap was alive something better might have been done." Reluctantly, however, he advised against switching publishers because of continuing difficulties in the market, and for fear of the book appearing too late for Christmas, but asked to see her next typescript as soon as possible in order to consider the matter again. Ursula had in fact already agreed to send illustrations of *Dandino* for consideration by Harrap by the end of that month. When they arrived, the publisher may have been taken aback to find there were around three hundred and fifty of the small black and white sketches, and at first turned down the book as being too expensive to produce. After an exchange of letters, however, it was agreed that the pictures would appear around the margin of small panels of text, and publication went ahead on schedule in early November 1948.[12] It was to be the last book that Ursula would have published for more than two years. This time the delay was caused by the first of a series of personal misfortunes.

Beckford tennis club had courts beside the village hall at the bottom of the lane leading to Court Farm. Ursula joined as soon as it opened and was playing with friends late one bright October afternoon in 1949. No one knows for certain who hit the ball that accidentally struck her in the right eye. Arthur Watkins and his partner had knocked the balls down the court at the end of their service game, and he was bending down at the net, when he looked up to see Ursula's partner checking to see if she was hurt. All gathered around. "Oh, don't fuss," she said, as she prepared to resume the match. "I'm all right." She was not. It was some time later that she sought help, but when she did, the eye could not be saved. She told Arthur and the others not to feel bad about what had happened,[13] and after she was released from hospital, she carried on much as she had before. She never played tennis again, but continued to drive, and those meeting her for the first time usually failed to discern the fact that she could not see through her right eye. Nevertheless it took her many weeks to recover from the physical and mental shock of the injury. Friends, relatives and professional colleagues sent messages of sympathy, among which the most bizarre came from George Anderson. At the end of a letter on publishing matters, he added, "I am extremely sorry to hear that you have lost an eye at tennis. This is quite unusual. With kindest regards." His son wrote a few days later explaining that his father was unwell. Unfortunately he addressed his letter to "Mrs Johns."[14]

Chapter 13

———————

"Long and weary dying."

On the day after Ursula left hospital, not knowing to what extent the loss of her eye would affect her daily life, or her stamina as a writer and illustrator, she wrote to a near neighbour who had suffered an infinitely greater tragedy. Michael Taylor turned five in the summer of 1949 and in the autumn started at the small primary school in Beckford. At the end of classes on Wednesday 5 October a teacher had taken pupils to the bus stop across the main road as usual. The boy saw his father working in the garden opposite; he let a vehicle pass before running across the road to see him, but did not see the lorry coming in the opposite direction. During the years that Ursula lived in Beckford, the village had no more than its average share of tragedies and hardships, but what was extraordinary was the extent to which, through many small kindnesses, she became known for comforting those affected by misfortune, great or small. She learnt of the fatal accident when she returned home on the Sunday, and wrote to Michael's mother the following day: "I think every mother in the village feels a part of your grief as if it were her own … I am afraid you are going to find life terribly hard for a long while, when other people seem to be going carelessly about their own ways, but do remember that we shall really be thinking of you perhaps long after you think we have forgotten."[1]

As a governor of the school, Ursula may have felt a duty to write the letter. Other frequent acts of kindness could be regarded only as spontaneous generosity. When a new family moved into Clifts, Ursula arrived "like a character from Beatrix Potter," or indeed like one of the mothers dispensing comfort food in her own stories, bearing a homemade steak and kidney pie. At Christmas she made chocolate eclairs and gave them to friends around the village, and every spring for more than thirty years she made dozens of posies of violets or primroses taken from her garden or the woods, for children to collect at Mothering Sunday services to give to their mums and grandmas. Nor were they the only recipients. When Ursula travelled to London to meet publishers, she usually took a few of the posies, planted in old margarine pots, to give to the toilet attendants at Paddington railway station.

Another incident stuck in the memory of Barbara Phipps for sixty years. During the severe winter of 1947 she struggled through snow up the lane to deliver the mail to Court Farm. "You poor creature, your fingers are so terribly cold," Ursula remarked as she handed over her letters. When the postwoman called the next morning, as well as the usual cup of tea or coffee, she was given a pair of green and white mittens that Ursula had knitted for her in a day from the wool that Barbara had brought from Iceland.[2]

The five years following the tennis accident were difficult for Ursula. At home, Mabel suffered a serious fall in December 1949. Professionally, relations with Harrap were not made easier by their mistakes, including attribution in publicity material of *The Twins and Their Ponies* to another author.[3] The post often brought letters from Stanley, enquiring about his sister's health, and offering advice about his niece's career. The one that arrived shortly before Christmas 1949 proved to be the most significant. Ursula had sent him a new manuscript, probably what was then called *Mrs. Binkleby and the Whooping Cough*, and he had sent it on to a professional reader. His reaction to the story is unknown, but like Stanley he advised against changing publishers "in view of the present slump in juveniles." His suggestion of greatest consequence, however, was that his niece should for the first time engage a literary agent, and he recommended Juliet O'Hea of Curtis Brown in Covent Garden. O'Hea happened to be a fan of Ursula's works, and had bought her books to give to young relatives and godchildren for a number of years. Stanley had mentioned Ursula's name, so it was no surprise when Ursula heard from O'Hea a few days later.[4] Neither could hardly have expected, however, that they would work together until O'Hea's retirement twenty-six years later, nor that they would become such close friends for even longer.

O'Hea's first major task was to place the new work, helpfully renamed *The Binklebys at Home*, with a hint of another title to come, as it did two years later in *The Binklebys on the Farm*. The title also brought to mind the archetypal down-to-earth British family that came smiling through all its troubles, and which Jack Warner and Kathleen Harrison had made immensely popular in films like *Here come the Huggetts*. In her early life Ursula had had relatively little familiarity with the ordinary, domestic lives led by the majority of her compatriots. She had seen only glimpses of deprivation in the early 1930s – like a march of unemployed, "a very big communistic-socialistic affair," that interrupted a visit to London, or the old man who supposedly lived for a week on the five shillings and sixpence that he earned by posing for her life class at Winchester.[5] Her contemporary, Geoffrey Trease, a prolific writer of children's novels, told how teachers in the late 1940s used to ask him, "Why are there no modern stories with working-class settings? Nannies and ponies mean nothing to the children we teach."[6] Now, in post-war Britain, with its Socialist government, Ursula had become much involved in the everyday life of Beckford, a village with a high degree of poverty in the cottages alongside its manor houses. Correspondingly she had written for the first time about a family from the world of Laburnum Avenues and Marigold Streets, with a plumber for a dad, who would regard a visit to the local gasworks as a rare treat. To make the point, the Harrap publicity department described the story as "essentially a humorous book for modern youngsters, written about the things and people they might encounter in the world of today."

One of its early fans was the young Jacqueline Wilson, the future Children's Laureate. It was a book she "adored and re-read many times, frequently laughing out loud," and not perhaps without relevance for her writing career. For it was just four years after its publication that Wilson, then aged nine, attempted her own first novel, twenty-two pages long, about an impoverished family with seven children, and called it *Meet the Maggots*.[7]

Ursula bequeathed her now abandoned idea of ten children to Mrs Binkleby, whimsically named Margarine; but her offspring had very different prospects from those fairytale figures destined for foreign adventures and careers as ballet dancers. Britain's National Health Service had been launched in 1948, and in the background of the new story is the battle of cheery and imperturbable Mrs B. – who has already personally suffered from measles, scarlet fever, tonsillitis, chicken pox, diphtheria, mumps and appendicitis – to cope as the entire family go down with whooping cough. Despite the washing on Mondays, ironing on Tuesdays, baking eclairs on Wednesdays, shopping on Thursdays, mending on Fridays, cleaning on Saturdays, and church on Sundays, Mrs B. still finds time to organise adventures; she borrows a postman's bicycle to chase a barrel organ, and takes the children – including twins Biff and Bang – to the country in a cart drawn by a recalcitrant pony. The family also smuggle themselves aboard a test flight of the Brabazon, here renamed the Skyscraper, the huge but unsuccessful airliner as big as a modern 747, that actually first flew from Bristol in September 1949, and which Ursula saw make a later test flight over Bredon Hill.[8]

The spirit of the book is complemented by superb illustrations by the author, even though she seems to have undertaken them reluctantly. Mabel needed more care after her fall, so Ursula, still adjusting to the strain on her eyesight, had asked a friend to supply the drawings that went off to the publisher. Walter Harrap was unimpressed. They were "not up to the standard that we feel should be enjoyed by an author of Miss Williams' standing," he declared and suggested commissioning another artist. He recognised that it would be "very inconvenient for [Ursula] to undertake the work herself, but if circumstances have altered in such a way that she can now tackle the task, then no-one would be happier than we should."[9] Stimulated by such a challenge, perhaps, the artwork delivered over the next four months, convincing, lively, varied images of children, adults and animals crammed with character, was some of the best she ever produced.

Harrap had bought options on further books in the Binkleby and Toymaker series, but Ursula's next title was so different from anything she had written before that it seemed to O'Hea the perfect opportunity to find another publisher, and, in April 1950, she arranged a lunch with Norah Smallwood at Chatto & Windus. Smallwood came back a month later with the offer of an advance and royalties rising to 15% – potentially more generous terms than any that Harrap had ever offered.[10] The typescript that had attracted her, *Jockin the Jester*, might be regarded as Ursula's first novel. The 70,000-word story set around the time of the Black Death in the fourteenth century, tells how the son of a poor peasant, despite his gawky manner and serious temperament, earns his cap and bells, and in an exciting climax rescues his master Sir Richard de Lacey's children when peasants burn down their castle.

Sitting at the scrubbed refectory table in her own kitchen, Ursula described in detail the refectory of the de Lacey manor, the conditions of labourers leading up to the peasants' revolt, and the situation of the real de Lacey family thanks to background reading provided by Cheltenham Library. It was the first time she had really needed to undertake research for one of her books. The vocabulary is enriched with medieval terminology – pattens, ewer, seneschal, hoydenish – but the dialogue is mercifully free from period pastiche, and the narrative from sentimentality. Jockin tells the maleficent dwarf who plotted his ruin, "Had your parents loved you as mine loved me, you might have been a better son to them,"[11] but unlike his obeisant father Jockin is offended by remarks of social denigration, and the story avoids the fairytale ending in which the jester gets to marry the earl's mischievous daughter Barbara. The choice of name for the rebellious girl who slips out of the castle to mingle with the common people, in defiance of her father's wishes, was of course no accident; especially as it was Ursula's sister who supplied the rich engravings for the story, and to whom it was dedicated.

Smallwood sought the opinions of trusted authorities on juvenile fiction, and they shared her enthusiasm. One, a librarian, told her, "The book is so alive; the picture she paints of the period, so vivid. It should be a joy to history teachers. She has that ability, which I think essential to writers of historical novels, of making her characters modern, or rather, timeless. I am sure a child's interest in the past is heightened by the realisation that the children then were fundamentally the same as now, and in *Jockin* they are real children." The book also caught the attention of Noel Streatfeild, author of the hugely popular *Ballet Shoes*, who wrote to O'Hea praising its "immense charm" and promising to look out for Ursula's name whenever she was editing collections of children's stories. The *TLS* called it a "solid achievement" that admirably portrayed "the stupidity, unceasing labour, poverty and animal-like qualities of the country people (and) the chasm that exists between them and the manor-house," and compared the book to Chaucer in its suggestion of the "completely different estimate of distance in that world of execrable roads and walking speeds."[12]

During 1950, Ursula found time to recast *The Pettabomination*, *The Good Little Christmas Tree* and *The House of Happiness* as plays. It was a labour of love, more to accommodate schools wanting to perform them than as a profitable exercise for the £20 fee she was to receive from publisher Samuel French. An original play, *All Aboard!*, a fairy story involving Father Neptune, seems to have been abandoned at an early stage, and Samuel French rejected another, *The Flower Show*. Most intriguingly, a letter from O'Hea refers to *The Winkle Society*, sent to Oxford University Press, where children's editor John Bell thought it accomplished, but detected "something a little distasteful" in the story.[13] No trace of it survives.

A bigger setback was the rejection of *High Haven*, a novel almost as long as *Jockin the Jester*, but set in the present day, and seemingly with little action. The book was based on High Winds, an asbestos-clad hut built 400 feet up Carn Llidi on St David's Head in Pembrokeshire as basic living quarters for non-commissioned officers at a wartime radar station. There was no mains electricity, no running water, and sanitation comprised a chemical toilet that had to be emptied through a manhole at the edge of the cliff. Visitors remembered finding the beds soaking wet, and shivering in the gales after which it was named. Nevertheless, the views were magnificent. A narrow track led half a mile through gorse and heather to a sheltered sandy beach, and the little port of Solva offered mackerel fishing and beer in the Ship Inn afterwards. Ursula and Peter had stayed at the hut when friends held the lease, and agreed to take it over when their hosts took another holiday house nearby. "Frightfully cold," Ursula wrote, when she and Peter made their first private visit in December 1950, but they loved its peace and spartan simplicity, so much so that they, their children and friends were to spend holidays there for twenty years. Perhaps for Ursula it brought to mind memories of childhood, or of the honeymoon chalet in Switzerland. Certainly, at a rent of £25 a year, it provided a cheap destination for a large family, and a refuge where she could write with little disturbance.

Ursula drafted the idea for *High Haven* in November 1950, at precisely the time that she was looking forward to taking over the property. The sense of tranquillity and escape seems to have influenced the plot. When she received the manuscript eight months later, the normally encouraging O'Hea concluded that there would be complaints about its lack of excitement. "Readers are going to demand more books like *Jockin the Jester* from Miss Moray-Williams [sic]," Chatto & Windus had somewhat presumptuously declared on *Jockin the Jester*'s cover. *High Haven* was not at all what Smallwood had in mind. When Ursula met her in London, she agreed to revise it.[14] By then, however, she was working on a Binkleby sequel. By the time that was finished, in July 1952, the increasing demands of looking after her parents and other duties at home had knocked out of her the enthusiasm for the major reconstruction required. Especially as Rita had left to work in a factory. *High Haven* was abandoned.

When Mr Binkleby won ten thousand pounds[15] in a football pool he told Mrs Binkleby he was going to give up living in Marigold Street and go to live in the country.

– The Binklebys on the Farm

Thus the author is on more familiar territory, even if the Binklebys are not. Yet they persevere through trials of learning to milk a cow, ploughing a neighbour's field by mistake, and building a rickety rick, to an unexpected triumph at the agricultural show. The scenes carry a conviction that the cor blimey housing estate never quite achieved, as Ursula was able to draw upon her own recent experiences. From a detailed description of floods around the farm, such as those of 1947, she invents a glorious episode in which Mrs B. goes to rescue a broody hen, then sits on its hutch as it is swept away. It is easy to imagine too the behaviour of wartime evacuee children, or those from London visiting the Salesian brothers, and the wild delight of the young Binklebys as they poke fingers into butter, blow ripples across milk and try to ride the pigs. It needed the author's inventive power, however, to add their innocent infusion of cake colouring into the milk churns to produce a choice of pints in yellow, green or violet.

Ursula said that the Binklebys were the only "funny ha-ha" books that she ever wrote,[16] but despite the farcical humour, events on the farm are marked with the rough grit of the real countryside. Nowhere is Ursula's unsentimental sentiment better expressed than in the pages where Mrs B. is captivated by the sight of fox cubs playing with a dead hen, until it is pulled to pieces. "Wicked thing … but she did it for her young," she declares. Modern readers may detect a hint of condescension toward the urban Binklebys, but not here as they settle into village ways, serving cakes and teas to neighbours. As she waves goodbye to the vicar and thinks of her children, Mrs B. concludes "There's nothing like a country life."[17]

Like Mrs Binkleby herself, Ursula was constantly busy, and after delivery of the typescript to Walter Harrap in the summer of 1952, she entered one of her most prolific periods as a writer and illustrator. While the appointment of Curtis Brown had reduced the amount of time that she needed to spend on routine correspondence, the overall effect of their services was to spread interest in her work among publishers at home and abroad and thus to increase pressure on her to produce books to satisfy their differing demands. Whereas for many years the relationship with Harrap had produced a steady output of new titles at regular intervals, Chatto & Windus, Samuel French, Brockhampton and others were now also looking to schedule books by Ursula Moray Williams on their lists. Another factor, albeit one unlikely to be acknowledged, may have been her desire to escape into her creative world, away from the harsher one in which she had to look after two increasingly infirm parents.

Mabel's small frame was further reduced by arthritis. She resembled a sickly bird, a bowed figure in a brown woollen suit, her arms painfully thin, her hands tightened into claws. Since her fall she had been confined largely to her room, and by now to her bed. Her hearing had deteriorated and she suffered increasingly from headaches, particularly at night. Relations between Ursula and her father were cool but respectful. He was restless at home, complaining often, and rather to his daughter's irritation, of insomnia at night, then during the day spent long hours on the hill. By good fortune, just below Beckford Wood, was the site of a Romano-British settlement. Beside it stood an abandoned slate-blue hut on wheels, where shepherds used to sleep during lambing. Moray had led archaeological digs for students at Bedales, and here he set up a new base. Children came to watch the slightly portly figure in a battered hat and tweed plus fours working meticulously for hours with his dustpan and brush; turning up coins, bangles and brooches, pieces of pottery decorated with lions and deer, and digging trenches that eventually uncovered the remains of the furnace in which they had been fired. Sometimes the children brought him coins, fragments or jewellery they had found elsewhere, for which, if they were lucky, "the eccentric, jolly old stick" would give them sixpence.[18]

Moray's health was also deteriorating, and when he suffered his first slight stroke, Ursula blamed it on the sherry and whisky that he kept in his cupboard. "How you get any writing done at all is something that has always amazed me, and I had no idea that you had two invalids to look after as well as running the house and coping with the children," O'Hea wrote to her.[19] To the four boys could often be added a fifth, Nick Tait, whose parents lived in Ceylon (now Sri Lanka). He would come to spend weekends and holidays at Court Farm with his school friend Andrew. Ursula had assistance from Peggy, from Peggy's sister Rita, and from a succession of Icelandic girls who came to help care for Mabel. Even so, without a proprietorial command of the household, or the ruthless allocation of her own time, Ursula could not have written so much, while continuing to cook, maintain a showpiece garden, care for others, organise her famous children's parties, and play a leading part in village activities.

The autumn of 1952 had been busy but frustrating for Ursula's career. The illustrations for *The Binklebys on the Farm* look perfunctory compared with those of its predecessor. A story to be called *The Chinese Goose* was abandoned at an early stage. Then, after researching falconry for what was planned as another full-length historical novel, Ursula started, in January 1953, to outline the plot of what was to become *The Noble Hawks*. She got no further than a synopsis of the first seven chapters when the story seemed to sink beneath the weight of its accumulated information.[20] Meanwhile, Walter Harrap was pressing Ursula to produce illustrations for a new edition of *The Good Little Christmas Tree*. As a result, work on *The Noble Hawks* was set aside.

With the artwork completed and the prospect of the last of the four boys going to boarding school, new projects tumbled over each other to find release. The first of these was in response to the Rev. Marcus Morris, founder of the adventure comic *Eagle*, who wanted to launch a new title at Hulton Press for a younger audience and had asked Ursula for ideas. She suggested the title for the magazine, *Robin*, and what was to become one of its most popular strip cartoon characters, Woppit. With her letter she sent a stuffed bear with a footnote explaining that she created him for one of her boys when he was aged two, and that he provided its name by trying to ask "What is it?" Morris liked what he thought of as her "miniature Sir Galahad," but got other artists to provide the pictures, which he admitted departed a long way from the author's originals, and very much resembled E.H. Shepard's drawings of Piglet in the *Winnie-the-Pooh* stories. "I don't think this matters very much as they were not as far as I know consciously an imitation," he added. So much for copyright concerns in the 1950s. Every Monday from 28 March 1953 young readers followed the adventures of the little bear, Mrs Bumble, Mokey the donkey and Tiptop the scarecrow, that were often witty improvisations on life at Court Farm. Mrs Bumble, like her creator, organises an Easter egg hunt, while Woppit helps with domestic chores and learns about animals and gardening, including the revelation that rice pudding, although good for him, is less effective when fed to plants. Ursula provided the short text in batches of episodes until 1961, when the magazine's editors took over the script for another six years.[21]

Woppit was however to achieve his greatest fame beyond the pages of *Robin*. The little bear never had the mass appeal of Andy Pandy, the BBC puppet who appeared on its front page, but in 1955 Merrythought Ltd, a small company at Ironbridge, Shropshire, brought out a Woppit soft toy. Sales were low, but one found its way to Donald Campbell, the world land and water speed record-holder. Mr Whoppit, as Campbell called him, travelled to publicity appearances and sat in the cockpit on all his record attempts, including his final run on Coniston Water in the Lake District in 1967. At 300 mph, the nose of Campbell's boat *Bluebird* rose. "The water's not good ... I can't see much ... I'm going ... I'm on my back ... I'm gone," were the pilot's calmly spoken last words as the vessel somersaulted and plunged into the water. Campbell's body was never found, but rescuers recovered the mascot floating on the surface, wet but unharmed.[22]

Legacies from spinster aunts and those without children of their own had helped pay for the education of Ursula's boys at Cheltenham College. Although each of them went on to find enjoyable out-of-doors careers, none was academically gifted at school, and Robin brought home particularly critical reports. The boy needed encouragement, his mother seemed to conclude, for soon after delivering the first episodes of Woppit to *Robin* magazine, she set to work in the spring of 1953 on *The Secrets of the Wood*, the story of one Robin Johnson who moves to the countryside, learns the habits of birds, and with another young boy bravely defends their nests against attack by vandalising youths. Ewart Wharmby of Brockhampton Press had been impressed by the Binkleby books, and had been looking forward to reading the first three chapters. When they arrived in July, he was disappointed. "Although the story is original and pleasantly wholesome, the writing becomes a little pedestrian and the story is completely without the delightful flashes of humour and imagination of the Binklebys," he wrote.[23]

Meanwhile, O'Hea had been complaining to Walter Harrap about his refusal to pay an advance for the new illustrations for *The Good Little Christmas Tree*, or to pay royalties twice a year. At Court Farm, Mabel's health had deteriorated to such an extent that for the first time Ursula felt she could not leave for the usual summer holiday at High Winds, so Peter took instead his friend, drinking companion and fellow car enthusiast Paul Mogford. Rita had left for a job in Cheltenham. *The Noble Hawks* lay untouched for months, and *The Secrets of the Wood* had been rejected by Brockhampton in fairly uncomplimentary terms. For the first time in her life, Ursula confessed to a feeling of depression. O'Hea wrote to her in August, "I am so very sad to hear that you feel so frustrated about your … work. … I know the summer is a difficult time for you to concentrate on writing, but I do hope that soon you will get over the bad patch." A month later, her colleague Phebe Snow expressed her concern: "I was very distressed by your last letter as it seemed to me you were in a state of great despondency and I do realise how extremely difficult it must be for you to find the time to do any writing at all."[24]

In the circumstances, it is remarkable that in just a couple of months, September and October, Ursula produced one of her liveliest, funniest and most carefree books in exactly the style that Wharmby had been looking for when he praised the "bubbling inventiveness" and the "rich character" of Mrs Binkleby. Relations with Moray were not particularly happy at the time, so there was an ironic resonance that the new title should be called *Grumpa*, and that it should celebrate all the irascible playfulness and outrageous sense of fun that her rather cheerless father now lacked. When he is not leading his grandchildren into mischief, he is pitting his wits against them, hiding his birthday cake, trying to lose them on a fishing expedition, or burrowing out of the tool shed when all the time the key was inside. The critic from the *TLS* was enchanted. "This Grumpa," he wrote, "[is] tetchy, autocratic, a little vague as to his grandchildren's names … Alternatively bullied by them and bullying them … he nevertheless stands the indulgent, impenitent patriarch most children will recognize."[25]

Ursula finished *The Secrets of the Wood* the following January, with a dedication to Robin and a friend, and an uncharacteristically tendentious close: "We've got to learn how to live in [the wood] so the birds will like to live there too." Despite O'Hea's continued sniping about Harrap's "niggling ways," she was probably happy to place one of Ursula's less impressive titles.[26]

The author at first turned down Harrap's suggestion that she should provide the illustrations, but not because of earlier arguments about payment. Her mother was approaching death. In a letter to Alan in February Mabel described James skipping around the room while reading *The Twins and Their Ponies* and talked of lost relatives, but of her own suffering wrote only that she was confined to her room. Three weeks later, when Moray wrote to his son, thanking him for his birthday present – a recklessly extravagant gift of foie gras – he mentioned that Mabel could only lie in bed "trying to bear the pain," that she had lost her appetite and would have to move to a nursing home. She died five weeks later, on the Sunday before Easter.[28]

Mabel's "long and weary dying" affected Ursula in the short and long term. There was immediate relief, which later she would consider in the context of her own life. "One of life's revelations to me has been acutely remembering the childhood agony of even contemplating the loss of a parent, at the same time as one was longing to be free of those same loved parents forty years later. ... One never quite sheds the guilt of one's frustrations," she wrote in retrospect to a friend. She told Alan how it was "awful to have mother in so much pain for so long, but one gets used to anything, and though one was utterly thankful when she ultimately died, the relief was so short compared to the sense of loss, which surprised me."[29] The experience was one she was determined not to pass on to others. Among talks that Ursula continued to give when in her seventies and eighties were some about growing old. She would ask for her listeners' understanding of the young, and said of herself: "I shan't go to my family because I had my parents with us for nine years, and I think it is too great a strain to put on the next generation."[30]

Chapter 14

"A little masterpiece."

Letters from fans arrived at Court Farm from all over the British Isles, from Europe, Australia and South Africa. Sales of Ursula's books reached a peak in the late 1940s, helped by serialisations on *Children's Hour.* The audience for both books and the serials naturally included pupils from the red-brick village school on the small square beside the lychgate of Beckford church. When the head teacher asked Ursula to read one of her stories in person, she was only happy to oblige.

There seemed some irony in the fact that the once reluctant schoolgirl should now delight in talking to schools. In fact, from the time in 1933 that she took her drawings of stoats and weasels to a primary class near North Stoneham, and showed its pupils how to identify trees by touching and smelling their bark, she had discovered a talent for capturing schoolchildren's attention by what she said as well as what she wrote.[1] As an author she made dozens, possibly hundreds of such visits. The apparent paradox can be explained by her understanding of education, particularly primary education, as a means of liberating imagination, rather than of accumulating facts. Some things needed to be learnt, certainly, but more about kindness to others and the beauty of nature than about dates and irregular verbs.

Beckford was the first of four schools in the district of which Ursula became an active governor. She presented copies of her books and came to read them. She made embroidered cushions for reception classes and hobby horses for sports days. She invited the children to her parties and Easter egg hunts. She gave pupils their first taste of American chewing gum when she handed out a packet to every child.[2] The affection was mutual. A few months before the school closed, its favourite storyteller returned from a long trip abroad to find that pupils had prepared a Welcome Home reception, including an album filled with drawings of their favourite adventures of the Little Wooden Horse. It remained among her treasured souvenirs for forty years.

The popular governor was invited to join other boards, at nearby Bredon, like Beckford now closed, and two in Evesham. Typically, those in which she had taken the greatest interest took pupils of lesser academic abilities, the County Secondary which then tended to admit children who had failed to get a place at the town's Grammar, and Vale of Evesham School for children who would today be described as having learning difficulties. Its future head teacher, Emlyn Matthews, remembered her "with great warmth and admiration" from times when young people with severe learning difficulties were only just being accepted as educable. "She spent a good deal of time in the classrooms and loved to read to the younger children. She contributed a great deal to the life of our school and its significance in the community," he said.

For some of the time that Ursula was associated with the County Secondary, Catherine Wallace was the deputy head. She remembers her as "an excellent governor, a very, very caring person, and particularly interested in the less advantaged children." At the end of Ursula's long service as a governor Michael Duffy came as headmaster, determined to abandon the school's rigid streaming. He was already a fan of her work – *Adventures of the Little Wooden Horse* was the favourite reading of all five of his children – and he was soon grateful for her support against more conservative members of the board.

> In those days it was quite enough for many of the governors to come and have a nice lunch once a term. But Ursula was genuinely interested in what I wanted to do and encouraged me in it. … I liked talking to her. She was a genial spirit and was interested in anything that would defeat the awful finality of the eleven-plus. She shared my feeling that those [who failed the examination] should not be written off.

Other commitments forced Ursula to resign as a governor in 1971, but she continued to support what had by then become a High School, by providing a bursary for pupils to go on outward bound courses. For at least twelve years, she paid for beneficiaries to go climbing, canoeing, and fell trees, after which they would write to Ursula describing their experiences. Or occasionally failed to write. One later headmaster explained that the boy had "benefited to the full. We have tried to persuade him [to write] but clearly he is not that sort of boy." Usually, however, letters arrived with comments like those from a lad whose course at Fort William in Scotland "made me build up my confidence in getting to know people, made me realise that I could attempt anything and possibly succeed if you try hard enough." His sponsor must have thought it money well spent.[3]

Fellow governors at Evesham included councillors, magistrates and the wife of a retired colonel, and it was probably through them that Ursula learnt of a local charity, the Disabled Servicemen's Handicraft Association.[4] As a result she made an extraordinarily generous gesture. She devoted her entire proceeds from the book commissioned in 1955 by Richard Hough at Hamish Hamilton to the organisation. The story was chiefly inspired by the Association's work, but a little also by events at home, where she demanded of herself and her boys that they respond with fortitude to any adversity or periods of dejection. *Goodbody's Puppet Show* tells how the eponymous wounded old soldier is carried home, unable to walk. In hospital, a kind lady – if not Ursula herself then someone very much like her – has taught him to sew and to make animals from felt and rags. Eventually, however, he discovers an unlikely alternative means to make a living, by setting up a puppet booth on top of his invalid carriage. A rival Punch and Judy showman is so filled with admiration that he drops his opposition and even, improbably, starts attending church with the Goodbodys. After farcical adventures, all ends happily with the puppeteer invited to visit American GIs in hospital to show them what can be done with a little imagination and much determination. He promises to bring back lots of chewing gum.

Ursula expressed doubts about the book to her agent. Her letter has been lost, but O'Hea's reply suggests that she found it difficult to find the right tone to deal with the serious theme of disability in what was commissioned as a humorous story for young learners.[5] What emerges is an optimistic assumption of what individuals can do for themselves, whatever the circumstances, and however unrealistic that might seem in real life. On a more superficial level, *Goodbody's Puppet Show* offers observations on what the author regarded as proper behaviour.

Mr Goodbody is a war hero, and so a man to be admired, even when he clouts two fighting dogs with his fist. When his wife objects to the story of Punch, "a wicked old man – beating his wife and dropping the baby about," he drops the show to perform his own funny story. The new play is a great success, but at a party he finds the children badly behaved, partly because "their kind hostess was too patient with them" and thinks "how he would have loved to wallop some of those young rascals." In fact, a few loud words from the former Sergeant Major bring silence, then apologies from the young hooligans. Discipline prevails.[6]

Many who knew Peter, with his service background and intolerance of unruly children, would see points of similarity. Neighbours called him "quick-tempered", "stern-faced", "strict", "abrupt", "austere and not a great mixer." Barbara Marsh played on the farm as a girl and noted, "He would call and the boys immediately went running." No compromises were made for outsiders. As chairman of the village youth club, of which Barbara acted as a young volunteer secretary, he expected to have the minutes "written up and on his breakfast table the next morning, verbatim, or else." All contrasted his personality with that of his wife. "She was an exceptionally nice lady, with no airs and graces," said another villager. "She was one of us. Peter was quite different."[7] O'Hea visited Court Farm and reported that she thought Peter was a bit of a bully. When James accidentally set off fireworks, she felt sufficiently confident in a letter to Ursula to describe Peter's over-reaction as "horribly callous."[8]

Despite the close friendship that Peggy developed with Ursula, she remained on poor terms with her employer's husband, and each of Peggy's children found him intimidating. "Mr John was a difficult man to talk to. He frightened me," said Stephen Tandy. He had a paper round and hated the long walk to Court Farm in case a supplement was missing and he got an angry ticking-off. Stephen's sister Elaine described Peter as stern and distant. "He avoided children and would burst in and ignore them if they were there," she said. It was around 1956 that she had her own run-in with him, when she was cycling to school. "Mr John was coming down the hill much too fast in his sports car. I was coming up the railway bridge, and he swerved. When I came home, my mother asked if I had an accident with Mr John. I said it wasn't me – I was too terrified." On a later occasion, Robin allowed Elaine to borrow his father's tent. She returned it the following morning after spending a night on Bredon Hill with a girlfriend. "Mr John was furious – not with us for spending the night up there but because the tent was muddy and we had borrowed it. He was a very stormy person."

Marilyn Monroe had caused a longer rift with the Tandy children. They were the only boys in the village with whom Robin was allowed to mix. He and Roger were great friends, and, in 1955, the pair went pea-picking with the intention of swimming later at the outdoor pool in Evesham. It was raining. Far more inviting, when they arrived by bus, was the cinema showing *The Seven Year Itch*, and although they were underage, the trio managed to get into the Saturday matinee. They said nothing, but Ursula, of course, realised that Robin's swimming costume was still dry. Roger was sent for. "How dare you do this? How dare you?" shouted Peter. Roger did not have the courage to go back to Court Farm for a month.[9]

Even Ursula had to admit that her husband was "not a patient kind of man." She told her friend Faith Jaques, who disliked his manner, "He is a bit aggressive on the surface. Most people think he's a tyrant at first and lots are scared of him, but afterwards nearly everybody finds him very funny and endearing and he has mellowed in middle age. It suits me well as life's a perpetual challenge and I'd have been bored with a placid man – we remain deeply in love after 35 years and simply hate each other now and then."[10] When Luc Perrelet came to stay with his wife in April 1956, Ursula told him proudly, "Since our marriage, we can both say we have never looked at another person." It might have seemed to many an odd assertion about Peter, who started to notice girls when they became attractive young women, who with his drinking mates followed a particular barmaid from one pub to another, who went for bachelor weekends to Paris with a friend, and became a regular reader of *Playboy* magazine. "Flirty", "a ladies man", "a bit of a spiv", said those who knew him quite well. There was, however, never any hint at infidelity. "I doubt it went any further than flirtation," said one. "It was nothing serious."[11] Was then his wife's claim wishful thinking, or an admonition? James saw it as neither, but as a statement of trust. "She was a great believer in good, not of the gooey type, which she found in her man. She knew he would never let her down. She would rely on him and he had confidence in her assumptions that good would survive."

The John boys were each were given daily chores, fetching milk in a half-gallon can from the farm, lighting the Aga water heater, or feeding the chickens and chasing them into their sleeping quarters to move their heavy ark every other day. The dinner table was the court of etiquette at which children did not speak unless spoken to.

Conversation over breakfast was sparing with those who had broken the rules. Robin in particular found it difficult at times to accept Peter's authority, but all four regarded more fondly, or remembered more generously, the figure that revealed only his stern face to outsiders.

"Within ten years of marriage, father was commuting 40 miles a day to a desk job he hated, and responsible for a house that demanded total commitment and practical application," James said. "He grew vegetables all year, kept the boiler going 24 hours a day, the paraffin stoves alight, the plumbing from freezing, the roof from leaking, the cars repaired, the chickens keeping us in eggs, and the grass cut. Father had a house full of young males and he was determined to keep them in order. I am not surprised that he might have been short-tempered at times. Because he was socially insecure much of the time, he could appear intimidating and aloof, but within the family and amongst established friends, he could be extremely charming and entertaining. He was a very good father who would have done anything for any one of us if required. Both our parents were incredibly strong-minded. Neither would give in to the other. If she started to think she could bully him intellectually, he would bring the table to a standstill by saying, 'Don't do that again.' He didn't have her imagination. He did not mean to be rude. He was very aggressive outside but a pussy inside. She was the opposite way round, and for subtle forms of discipline, where manipulation and guilt were most effective, mother was without equal."

Contact with other boys in the village was limited, and misdemeanours brought groundings that further limited their freedom. There was a quiet, but firm authority, which could not be challenged with questions about the running of the household. Children's parties, running wildly and joyously, could be halted by a peremptory command as soon as roister threatened to turn into riot. But Ursula's chief device for keeping order among the boys was the custom of Sunday Surprises – small rewards such as a chocolate biscuit that would be given for good conduct each week, or withheld for misbehaviour. Other sanctions included early bed, or being banned from a Saturday morning shopping trip. Andrew explained: "We all knew we were very lucky to have the parents we had. Mother had great lateral thinking when it came to disciplining her own children. She dreamt up this amazing system which worked like magic. Over the years we would anticipate and value this and withdrawing Sunday surprises individually or en bloc had a great effect."[12]

In March 1956 Ursula told Curtis Brown that a manuscript of *The Noble Hawks* was finished at last. Typing and revisions took another three months. It had been her most protracted and longest work, one for which she had conducted the most research, from reference books and among experts. She had even cultivated the support of a teacher at Cheltenham College, who kept two hawks in an outbuilding.

It became James's duty to take dead mice from Court Farm for the birds, an uncomfortable arrangement for both as pupil and master regarded each other as incapable of teaching and incapable of being taught.

Ursula was hoping both to reach older children and to achieve serious critical recognition, but when Smallwood returned the typescript to O'Hea, it was to suggest major changes. The agent agreed. "I longed to be able to write to you disagreeing heartily with Norah ... but I am horribly afraid that I agree with her entirely. ... Knowing how you feel about prestige at this particular moment, I do urge you to stifle your sobs and do the work on the book, for I am sure it would prove worth while." Ursula agreed to make substantial cuts, and instead of despatching one of the principal characters, the squires' leader Edward of Lentwardine, to his death, she despatched him to the Crusades instead.[13]

It is clear from the outset that the book will depart from the constantly fast-moving, episodic style of her most popular works. It opens in a scene of sylvan contemplation.

> Under the trees the small blades of autumn grass stood upright, or shivered for a moment at the underground passing of a mole. The boles of the beeches, circled by undergrowth stood surety for the peace within this wood.

Yet a hundred feet above the ground, the boy Dickon and a falcon lie breast-flat, watching each other, in one of the most gripping and fascinating passages that Ursula ever wrote. The book tells of the rise of the yeoman's son to become a falconer, against the claims of more nobly-born rivals. The descriptions of training falcons in the harsh days of the fourteenth century are absorbing. The narrative can move slowly as a consequence, but such intervals alternate with realistic and highly exciting episodes such as that in which Dickon is lowered over the cliffs in a basket, or in the final battle of the squires' falcons to catch herons. The author seldom created incidents as compelling, or characters more plausible than Dickon or the admiring but resentful Gareth. Publishers liked the episodes, but found the overall story somewhat tame and slow. It was not until May 1959, six years and four months after the author wrote a first synopsis, that the novel was issued, without illustration, by Hamish Hamilton.[14]

To the author's disappointment, *The Noble Hawks* failed to receive the attention she hoped for, nor was the book as she would have wished. Addressing a conference in 1972, she applauded the growing realism in children's stories and lamented that she had been forced to reprieve Dickon's fellow falconer. "The fact that my publisher and my American publisher insisted that he remain alive in print, makes not the slightest difference to my [original] story. I feel a slight contempt for the published version," she said.[15]

In such circumstances, it was not surprising that for her next book Ursula returned to familiar popular themes: a variation on *The Twins and Their Ponies* in which the hobby horses are given something of the spirit of their little wooden cousin. After finishing revisions to *The Noble Hawks*, she wrote *Hobbie* in less than four weeks, and it shows. The story, about the abandoned hero who follows his owners to the seaside, has moments of humour, applied with an even greater leap of illogicality to horses with just one stick for propulsion and digestion than it had been to the Little Wooden Horse with his body and four wheels. But the book has accidental shortcomings too that the author declined to correct. As O'Hea pointed out, Hobbie sets off with four other hobby horses made from socks left hanging on a clothes line, but arrives with twelve, his only explanation being that he collected them along the way. And when naughty children from another family steal the horses' legs, Hobbie says they cannot use new ones for some time, although they were perfectly able to do so at the beginning of the story. At its end, Hobbie declares, "I'm going to live happily ever after," a commonplace conclusion to a rather commonplace and backward-looking story. Brockhampton accepted it immediately.[16]

Hobbie typified most of Ursula's little heroes with iron wills to be steeled in the heat of adventure. What worked in fiction was to be practised in life in adventure and travel. When, in 1948, Nora Unwin's brother Philip arranged a house-swap with a family in Norway, he had invited Ursula on the grounds that she could talk to possible translators of her work. Robin and James, aged four and three, had missed the trip to Iceland the previous year, so she took them and Rita. After a rough sea crossing, when all had been sick, the group arrived at their holiday destination where the boys were able to impress their mother by "being brave" – Robin by threatening to jump from one of the old houses, James by submerging himself in the sea up to the chin.[17] As they grew up the boys were encouraged to join the scouts and go camping. Andrew and Hugh went sailing with Peter, capsizing several times and swimming to the bank of the Avon. When he was thirteen, Andrew travelled back to La Forclaz with Paul Perrelet's grandson, François. Holidays at High Winds, although offering rugged exhilaration, were also exercises in stoic resilience, to which Robin and James added the distinction of cycling the 180 miles to get there when they were twelve and eleven years old. Such exploits were preparatory for the greater challenges that Ursula had in mind for her boys.

In 1953 Ursula had enrolled all four of them in the British Schools Exploring Society, founded by the surgeon on Captain Scott's last expedition to the Antarctic,[18] to develop the character of boys in extreme conditions. Two years later Andrew was selected as one of a group of fifteen- to seventeen-year-olds to go to Newfoundland for six weeks, living under canvas and fending for himself. Hugh and James later went separately to Finland, and Robin to Norway where his potential to demonstrate leadership skills was somewhat restricted by being flown to hospital after a boiler exploded in his tent.[19] All four found the experiences exhilarating and life-changing

– a description justified by the fact that all were to work abroad, mostly in the great outdoors.

While the three older boys earned independence quickly, James had it thrust upon him when he was twelve years old. Robin had just transferred to the senior college at Cheltenham as a boarder, and it was decided that James should board too, even though he was still in the junior school. It was clear that he was expected to toughen up and not be like the young Francis in *Jockin the Jester* – a "petted, spoiled boy, still missing his mother's caresses."[20] Thus began one of the unhappiest periods of his life. "I get sudden bursts of home-sickness and loneliness all through the day," he wrote between lessons. At night, he sat by his window, and each time he saw the lights of a car turn into the drive hoped his parents were coming to collect him. When they failed to do so, he made his own way home several times. There were hugs not reproaches when Ursula met him at the door, but he was always returned within the hour. Though the episodes had the desired effect, they left a lasting impression with James:

> Mother always assured me that I would have become spoiled at home on my own, but I never quite bought that. As boys we were expected to keep up, and frankly she expected all her boys to be the same age at the same time to make the house run properly. She never had a school playground experience, and had no idea what trauma it was going to school. She was a very good mother – but she and father wanted life on their terms and not ours. I was the youngest and they had the first sniff of freedom and couldn't wait, but who could blame them after all those years of parents, carers, nannies and four sons?

He had a further lesson in self-sufficiency when he travelled home from Switzerland alone when he was fifteen. Arriving back in London he expected to find someone to meet him, but when no one appeared he caught a train to Evesham and then a bus to Beckford. Ursula was out and Peter was surprised to see him. They had forgotten it was the day he was to return.

Curiously, while the John boys' horizons of adulthood were expanding, so was their mother's view of childhood, as seen from the somewhat elevated position of Court Farm. The children who played tricks on Hobbie and his friends were rather grand, fond of riding real horses, and like those who poked fun at Ursula and Barbara when they were young. Only in *Pretenders' Island* and *The Secrets of the Wood* had Ursula's principal characters included problematic children from ordinary households. The reader learns little about the backgrounds of the evacuees or the housing estate children that might have contributed to their disruptive behaviour. But in at least a dozen stories from *The Moonball* onwards, such children assume central roles, following similar expeditions after difficult upbringings: through trouble with the law or authority, to finding the love and encouragement of a caring adult, and finally, through their own striving, to achieve a happy homecoming, usually accompanied by lots of milk pudding or eclairs.

While Hugh was spending July 1957 in Lapland and Andrew was working on a cattle ranch in Ontario, Canada, Ursula was sometimes sitting on the public benches at Evesham juvenile court hearing about the wrongdoings of young offenders. She would frequently hear about the fractured homes from which they came and the lack of a mother's love or a father's control. Into the "light, whitewashed room" with "beams arched across the ceiling like the bows of a boat" came a succession of young offenders, shoplifters with a fondness for Woolworths, and burglars most likely to break into their own youth clubs.

In August, armed with such sad examples, Ursula started writing *The Moonball*, featuring Freddie the Nipper, whose father has left his mother, and who now lives unhappily with his sister Norma and her resentful husband.[21] Freddie has "nothing of his own … no father, hardly any mother, no bicycle, or holidays or even new clothes. No wonder if he picked up something they all discarded and took it home to keep," a principle he extends to stealing sweets and cigarettes, and cheating customers on his paper round. Befriended by a probation officer, the lad appears before sympathetic magistrates "like a sick sparrow, rain-bedraggled and passive with lost hope." He seems to welcome being sent to an approved school, "for boys like me – what haven't – got – any Dads to wallop them."

If the story appears to have a saccharine ending, one should take into account the compassion with which the author was offering the medicine. Freddie wanders into a Sunday school, which he has not dared attend because of his poor clothes, then along a railway line, where he narrowly escapes being hit by a train. A plate-layer saves him and gives him a good hiding. It is his father, who takes him home, to find a pot of tea on the table. Freddie's parents argue, but make up. Home wallopings prove harder than approved school, but his mother is always there when he returns from school, and "between being loved by God, Mum, Norma and Dad … Nipper did not feel a tagger-on any more."

The Moonball is really two interwoven stories, for Freddie's fate is determined by the strange object of the title: a strange creature like a gentle furry hedgehog, but without eyes, mouth, nose or legs that exercises beneficent, supernatural power. Ursula experimented with writing science fiction on only one other occasion. Some time in the 1950s she drafted the plot of *The Hen and the Egg*, a short satirical drama in which Great Britain and the Soviet Union seek to colonise a planet, one by sending a hen, the other an egg.[22] If *The Moonball* is also to be classed as science fiction, it is of a very distinctive style. Like that of C.S. Lewis, it affirms the presence of a force for good, albeit one that delivers only the smallest miracles, but it is charmingly antiquated, in a world of old-fashioned biscuit tins and linen chests with lavender bags. Above all it is absurdly funny. The Moonball polishes off lamb cutlets and secretly adds more of them to the charwoman's shopping list, knocks over a magistrate's ink-pot, and despite a lack of eyes and limbs reads the newspaper and tackles the crossword.[23]

The typescript was finished by Christmas and published the following year by Hamish Hamilton, with a dedication to O'Hea. Hough sent it first to a Justice of the Peace to check passages about the juvenile court.[24] Others also took note. A year after publication, the author who had described the work of the juvenile court and its probation service with such sympathy was herself appointed as a magistrate.

Ursula had never felt more confident in her writing, when on New Year's Day 1958, within days of finishing *The Moonball*, she started writing the plot of what was to be one of her best and most successful titles, with the most memorable of all her opening passages:

> One August bank holiday afternoon a little shipwrecked cat called Mackenzie was swimming for his life towards a desert island, pursued by eight hungry sharks. ... The sharks took their time, swimming slowly – one coming up behind the other, ready to take his comrade's place when tired. 'Take your time, my friend!' they seemed to say to the cat Mackenzie. 'Swim all afternoon and we will eat you for tea! Or swim all evening, and we'll have you for supper!'

The inspiration was probably an "intelligent, attractive, friendly, bad-tempered and imperious" tabby called Timmy Willy. Peter used to take business contacts to the stylish Greenway Hotel outside Cheltenham, and when the owners told him they had kittens for sale, the family went to select one. James remembers the visit. "One male stood out as having the most character. Ursula was immediately drawn to it and it became very much her cat. She thought it had Siamese genes, on account of its amazingly feisty temper and haughty demeanour. It was everything she wanted in a cat."

The synopsis of *The Nine Lives of Island Mackenzie* was finished within a month, and the typescript by the end of February. Washed up "like a small, soaked hearthrug," Mackenzie finds himself on a desert island with Miss Pettifer, a woman of equally indomitable spirit – apart from a fear of cats. Gradually his nine lives are used up: he jams the jaws of a crocodile with Miss Pettifer's case, is swallowed and disgorged by a snake thanks to a dose of Miss Pettifer's medicine, and stuffed into a cooking pot by cannibals.[25] His reluctant companion at first plans to drown Mackenzie but mercifully relents and gradually grows to admire his generous nature, even tolerating his behaviour when he grabs and eats a hummingbird. After fleeing a forest fire, the two companions comfort each other in a cave, where Mackenzie carves an eighth notch to mark another life lost. Guns sound. Captain Jupiter, on whose ship they were wrecked, returns. All are saved. He proposes. "Love me, love my cat," says Miss Pettifer, and he does.[26]

O'Hea was delighted with what she read. "Mackenzie is one of the most delectable characters I have met for a very great many years. He walked straight into my heart on the first page and will remain embedded there for all time," she wrote. Her only suggested change to the text was that Ursula might modify an episode in which Mackenzie is nearly lured to his death by mermaids, which seemed to her fantastical and out of key with the book's realism. The incident was turned into a more dream-like sequence in the final version completed at High Winds. O'Hea also liked the author's drawings, although she agreed that the portrayal of Mackenzie could be "a little less stylised." Chatto & Windus decided not to use them, but their reasons could not have brought Ursula greater satisfaction. Smallwood had given the typescript to her chief reader, the future Poet Laureate Cecil Day-Lewis, already an established author of adult and children's novels. On the basis of his enthusiastic report, she decided to commission the distinguished Edward Ardizzone to provide the illustrations for a "pretty staggering" fee.

Mackenzie – called Montmorency in the author's first draft but renamed after the flamboyant author Sir Compton Mackenzie – was to reappear as Balthasar, Mississippi and Menelao, as the book was translated into German, French, Italian, Dutch, Norwegian, Danish and Swedish. The BBC adapted the story for television as episodes on *Jackanory*. Anne Wood did the adaptation for Yorkshire Television; a company in Copenhagen staged it with grotesque life-size puppets. *The Guardian* described the book as "a winner. ... Mackenzie is to a large extent humanised, but the author has tried hard to make him catlike as well." Streatfeild, who chose it as one of her recommended Christmas books in *Elizabethan* magazine, wrote to her friend complimenting her on "a little masterpiece ... exquisitely written and imagined."[27]

Ursula, it seemed, was approaching the prime of her life and of her career. The appearance proved cruelly deceptive. She had spent several holidays in the Highlands of Scotland, the most recent of them in the spring of 1958. In February, immediately after the completion of *The Nine Lives of Island Mackenzie* she started thinking about a story to involve the Loch Ness monster. She got no further than the first chapter. Moray had moved out of Court Farm after Mabel's death, first to a rented cottage, then to Oxford. He returned to Beckford for short periods, but relations were difficult, and his health was deteriorating. Some time after his eighty-first birthday in March, he suffered a further stroke and required constant nursing. As he sat alongside a nurse on the edge of his hospital bed, he was convinced they were both fishing in the Avon.[28]

Ursula had also felt unwell for some time, and in June travelled to Cheltenham General hospital to receive the worst possible news. She was suffering from a malignant cancer of the colon and her chances of survival were not good. Ursula told at least one friend that she expected to die. She told her surgeon that if an operation were to leave her seriously incapacitated, she would not wish to regain consciousness. She believed this helped persuade him to adopt an extreme course. Meanwhile, there was work to be done. In July, Ursula took the oath to become a Justice of the Peace, and produced two extra Woppit stories required by Hulton for its *Robin Annual* – a "rush job" reluctantly passed on by O'Hea, "when I know how distraught you must be." *The Nine Lives of Island Mackenzie* had yet to appear in bookstores when, on 26 September 1959, his creator underwent the operation on which her own life depended. On that day she was unsure of the success of either.[29]

Chapter 15

———

"Stitches in a sweet tin."

Moray died in Winchcombe hospital, Gloucestershire, on 25 October 1959. Barbara came for the funeral. Alan, by then living in Denmark, stayed away because he "felt awkward."[1] Ursula was still in a private ward of the West Block of Cheltenham General, too ill to attend. She had come through the operation safely; only the third colostomy to have been successfully performed there. But recovery was to take four months in hospital – helped, she swore, by the thinnest sandwiches of diaphanous cucumber sent in by an elderly spinster friend – followed by six weeks at home under the charge of a nurse.

As news came from Curtis Brown of the success that *The Nine Lives of Island Mackenzie* was achieving in Britain and abroad, Ursula's strength was slowly returning: physically and spiritually. It was an experience she later referred to sometimes when writing to others about bereavement, as when she wrote to Stanley's son David on the loss of his mother.

> [It is] funny how death the executioner loses all his horrors later in life ... When I was so ill that one's filthy nothing body was almost being shed like a worthless rag, I realised that the ME in one was stronger than ever and something quite apart that had nothing at all to do with physical death.

She learnt to admire the young nurses who came shivering on cold nights to offer an extra blanket or a hot drink, and stopped to chat until perhaps a bell sent them rushing to the adjoining male ward. Ursula returned a favour when a confused old man was admitted. He had left his hearing aid at home and two young nurses were becoming frustrated in their efforts to find out what he wanted. Ursula wandered across and showed them how to make an ear trumpet from a rolled-up newspaper.

One wonders to what extent they were appreciative. Perhaps they were more so if they read the poem that their patient composed for amusement. The verse, written at about this time, is undated, so any reconstruction is fanciful, but it is pleasant to imagine a copy being passed around the post-operative beds, or being read aloud to sympathetic souls as once Brownies had heard their leader tell stories around the campfire.

> Let's creep into a corner, dear, and talk of operations,
> Let's perorate in private on our pains and perforations,
> Let's talk of our transfusions and enumerate our stitches

And allocate our ulcers, which are what and which are which's.
I'll ask the lab to render me my late peritoneum,
And make my marble mantelshelf a medical museum,
With stitches in a sweet tin, and some tissues (adipose),
And little odds and bodkins in regulated rows.[2]

For the next two years, Ursula wrote little. Even her correspondence virtually ceased in 1960. However, in September of that year, she did complete a new book *Miss Bellamy's Tiger*, which O'Hea immediately sent on to Smallwood without having read it. When she did so, she must have been dismayed, for Chatto & Windus's files show that two days later the typescript was withdrawn at the author's request "as a result of the agent's criticism."[3]

The work that O'Hea found unsatisfactory probably re-emerged in amended form four years later, in 1964, when Harrap published *Johnnie Tigerskin*, the name given by two boys to the rug owned by their great-uncle Mr Bellamy. The tiger-skin is dragged into their adventures at a zoo, and is later used to foil a raid on the post office. By the time that the plot was reworked, the author had, as a magistrate, seen into the unhappy circumstances of many individuals coming under her kindly scrutiny. Another of the characters does indeed get into trouble with the police, trouble for which her parents are blamed. "All that money, and she's left alone morning, noon and night," says Bellamy's landlady. By the writer's own standards it is an unremarkable story, except perhaps in one related regard. Bellamy and his tiger-skin come to live in Apple Street, which "sounded friendly, homely, countrified and domestic, as if every home stood in a little orchard and every landlady were a retired farmer's wife with a loft full of Cox's Orange Pippins. … But he had lived too long to suppose this were true." This final remark is hardly an outright submission to world-weariness, but not the slightest hint of such a sentiment was ever expressed in the long springtime of her earlier career. The *TLS* called the story "delightfully original" and noted that no moral was pointed, and the troublesome girl remains unreformed.[4]

Ursula's creative powers recovered slowly. Hulton decided in the autumn of 1961 to provide its own scripts for Woppit, and eventually the very domestic bear was replaced by one from outer space. There followed a series of humorous, well-written, but mostly unremarkable books of modest thematic range, delivered, in contrast with the effulgence of the period before her illness, at the rate of one a year. The first, *Battle of the Billy Goat*, later re-titled *Beware of This Animal*, was delivered to O'Hea in March 1962 together with the author's own gloomy assessment of its merit. O'Hea and Hough nevertheless liked the charming, if slight, story of Bounder who causes havoc in Wood Bantering, a village rather like Beckford, until captured by brave George, thanks in part to his skills as a scout. *High Adventure*, written two years later, is a short tale of a boy stuck up a tree with the cat he has chased away from garden birds. One might not believe the twist that the animal would not have harmed them because he was brought up with a budgerigar, but he is a very credible cat, who assumes that his would-be rescuer is responsible for the thunder that rolls while he approaches.[5]

Between the two, Ursula had completed the more substantial *O for a Mouseless House*, the only title since *Mackenzie* in which O'Hea succeeded in attracting the interest of Chatto & Windus. In the battle of the church mice against their larger, sinister cousins, Ursula returned to near top form, and to territory familiar from its opening sentences. When Gilbert, the vicar's nephew, arrives in the village for a holiday, he pushes open the faded door of the neglected church, sniffing "for the fragrance of old prayers pressed out of kneelers, for the echo of hymns clinging to high, dusty places – all mingled with acrid hints of withered flowers, of Sunday schools and mice." There is a protracted battle between the groups of mice, enlivened by the intervention of Samson the cat, who eats a peace envoy, and an invasion down a chimney to take possession of the church, before bells – and bats – celebrate its deliverance and a restored congregation. Meanwhile, down below, in pews and choir stalls, the church mice resume their ageless task of putting the place to rights. As if celebrating her confidence in the work, the author includes a small acknowledgement to Beatrix Potter, when Gilbert sees the church mice polishing and repairing, and recalls his first affection roused by "the tale of the mice who sewed a coat for the tailor of Gloucester."

Smallwood sought and obtained a few cuts to the typescript, for artistic and economic reasons, she explained, and accepted the author's "really delightful drawings." "I had no idea that she was such a gifted artist," she told O'Hea. Mary Crozier in *The Guardian* called it a "funny and charming book; with some recklessness it mixes the human and animal worlds and gets away with it triumphantly." Streatfeild told Ursula it was "a heavenly book which I have adored reading and looking at. ... I doubt if anyone has ever drawn mice better" yet, she added, "even your skilled pen is incapable of making a mouse look really bad for, curiously enough, though one hates them in the house all mice have an endearing quality."[6] Was it a compliment?

By the time that *O for a Mouseless House* was published, the author and her husband were in New Zealand visiting Robin who had emigrated. A lot had happened in the John family since Ursula had come out of hospital.

Moray had left a total of nearly £16,500, worth around £675,000 at today's values. One third of this went to Ursula and the remainder to Alan, according to the wartime agreement between the sisters. Andrew had returned to England from Canada and, in August 1962, married Elizabeth King, daughter of a wealthy steel manufacturer. The following June, Ursula was introduced to her first grandchild – another boy, Ben. Hugh had joined the RAF and in September 1964 he too was married, to Susan

Smallwood, whom he had dated since schooldays.

Ursula and Peter had paid for Robin's journey to New Zealand. In September 1962 they took him to Southampton Water and watched their nineteen-year-old son sail out of the harbour to the other side of the world on the *Johann van Oldenbarenfeld*, an "awful old boat" which caught fire during a later voyage. None of the boys achieved academic distinction, but the headmaster of Cheltenham College seemed to take particular pleasure in finding new ways to express Robin's level of performance. "He hits a hockey-ball extremely hard: I hope he puts equal energy into his work. There should be no disguising of the fact that his position is grimly low," he wrote.

In a house more concerned about scholastic success there would have been difficult moments as end-of-term reports were read out. This, however, was a household with parents more concerned that their children could cope with life than that they should enter university. Ursula's paternal grandfather had dissipated intellectual and material gifts, and she had come to associate academe with the dependency and intellectual self-indulgence of Moray and Alan. For Peter, a Southey literary inheritance counted for little when he had to support a widowed mother, a brother lacking ambition and a sister lacking means. He didn't think much of a chap with a degree but who could not change a spark plug.[7]

Robin's final report concluded: "He prefers the world to see things as he does. ... He must expect some clashes of interest." This observation would have been no surprise to his father, as Robin increasingly resented the greater freedom that his elder brothers enjoyed. "Father's natural character was very self-controlled, and he expected the same of his sons," was his laconic summary.[8] As for the wider application of his energy desired by the headmaster, this seemed most likely to be noted the further the field of activity was from the classroom or from home. The highlights of holidays to the shores of Loch Ness were the fly-fishing expeditions with his mother. The dedication in *The Secrets of the Wood* to her most reclusive son proved prophetic when Robin contacted his Unwin cousins in New Zealand saying he wanted to come out to work in forestry. By the end of 1963 he could report that he was loving his job, and having a great time fishing and shooting wild pigs and deer.

Peter had retired in 1963 with the closure of the Gloster Aircraft Company, and when a local vacancy for Worcestershire County Council arose the following May, he stood as an independent. His opponent, in an area where council seats were rarely contested, probably did not have the advantage of such a determined electoral machine. "We all canvassed and rushed about taking people to vote," Ursula reported. Result: C.S. John 668, V.R. Russell 112. In September, in the full council elections, he was returned unopposed. Seven weeks later, he and his wife set off to fly via New York and San Francisco to meet Robin in Christchurch. It was a great arrival. Robin was waiting, "looking so big and brown" and with news from England of the baby that Elizabeth had been expecting when they left. It was a girl at last: Sophie Louisa.

Apart from the grossly overweight bags, which had meant books and clothes being returned to the car with James at London airport, Ursula had planned the trip carefully: two months in Canterbury district on South Island with Robin and descendants of Stanley's late brothers William, Sidney and Cyril, followed by a few days on North Island. All along the route, meetings had been arranged at schools and bookstores, which she found were doing good business with *Hobbie, Grumpa, Adventures of the Little Wooden Horse*, and *The Nine Lives of Island Mackenzie*. In the audience of one of the school visits were Sidney's granddaughters, Ruth and Judith Miller, and their brothers. They were delighted, not only because their famous relative had come to talk, and not only because they were given the rest of the day off school. For Ursula had researched her private visits as much as the semi-professional ones. At their home, she unpacked presents that matched perfectly each child's main interest – ballet shoes for Ruth, a signed copy of *Beware of This Animal* for Judith who loved to write, a large green propelling pencil for their artistic elder brother, and a wind-up mouse for the younger.

By Christmas there were five thousand extra miles on the clock of the rental car that Peter had hired. Ursula found time to spend at a magistrates' court, where she was unimpressed by the speed with which cases were heard and summarily despatched. She also visited a home for girl offenders, which depressed her. More than half were of Maori descent and many absconded. They "haven't yet settled well into civilised life and are lazy and shiftless in society, but one feels they might not have become delinquent children in their own way of life. It is sad," she wrote of her visit.

Ursula's diary is filled with records of birds and flowers, of magnificent mountain views that reminded her of Scotland, and of mundane domestic activities that seemed a continuation of life at Court Farm. With Betty, her cousin Desmond's wife, she decorated a tree and an old people's home, and made floral decorations for the church. She got busy in the garden wherever she went. She made Christmas cakes and the celebrated eclairs. She also spent hours fishing with Robin, ten at one stretch, and often at night. It was, in a sense, a way to catch up on time they had not spent together before, when he was away at school, and the closest form of communication that both enjoyed. There was, nevertheless, more to be said.

On their last day, before boarding the ship that was to bring them slowly back to England, Peter and Ursula had the last of many talks with their son about his future. She noted in her diary: "We felt very happy about him having given him some pep talks which he took very well. It is easy for a young man to lose ambition when so much here is to be had without effort and we feel he misses the opportunity to make friends among people who will inspire him rather than mere boozing pals, but people seem to like him and are ready to help him, so he ought to be all right if he keeps a sense of self discipline at times."

It was another clash of interests, but one that Robin was now in a position to decide for himself. He remembers the "heavy conversations" that took place. "I think both Mother and Father were a bit taken aback by the unfettered attitude applied to life in this part of the world which persists today, thank God. We were given a tremendous start in life with two devoted and strict parents. I knew they were right in a perfect world, a high standard was expected and I acknowledged that, but whether it was relevant to the way I led my life was probably why I was in New Zealand in the first place."

At 5 p.m. on Saturday, 9 January 1965, Ursula and Peter were on the deck of the *Rangitoto*. As its siren sounded, the vessel set off from Wellington harbour. Teenage New Zealanders, going to England for the first time, talked of "arriving home." Passengers threw streamers to be caught on the quayside below by those who ran alongside the ship until the tapes snapped. Last to snap was a rope made of nylon stockings that stretched for 200 yards until the umbilical broke. In the golden light, Ursula felt "an acute heartbreak at leaving this lovely country. ... Over and above the kindness and beauty of scenery it has a kind of gallantry."

Two days out of port, Ursula settled down in her spacious cabin to begin another book, about a boat, a happy one. Catching the Maori cadence of the name of the ship on which it was written, she called it *The Cruise of the Happy-Go-Gay*. The route took the vessel past a tropical island densely covered with jungle and palm trees, with dark tunnels through the mangrove – so like Mackenzie's island "I could have charted it" – on past the peaks of Bora Bora to Papeete in Tahiti. Yet seldom can the writer have had so few distractions after that. She was dismayed at being asked to join the captain's table, shared with two elderly Americans from Florida, and irritated by the bitchiness of a community forced to share six tedious weeks together. A fancy dress evening brought welcome relief, or at least the making of outfits did, as passengers discovered Ursula's skills with a needle and sewing machine. Orders rolled in for a turban for one, a bowler hat for another, which took most of a day, and a falconer's costume. Peter went, appropriately enough, as a racing driver and Ursula dressed herself as a monkey, with a barrel organ filled with earrings to jingle merrily when she turned its handle.

By the time that the ship passed through the Panama Canal, the first half of *The Cruise of the Happy-Go-Gay* was written. But the strain of the long journey home, especially the last days when the ship was tossing in heavy seas, put a strain on Ursula's health. In March she returned to hospital for a fortnight, followed by a week in bed with influenza. O'Hea did not receive the manuscript until May, and when she did so, she was unhopeful about placing the book because of its whimsical tone. Parts were enchanting, "but so many children's publishers these days have depressingly got their feet very firmly fixed on the ground," she wrote. Her pessimism proved unfounded, for after changes suggested by the publisher, it was accepted by Hamish Hamilton.[9]

The book sets upon its journey with all the gaiety of the departure of its mother ship from harbour, and makes an immediate appeal to the hearts of its young female readers.

'It is a tragedy for nieces to be bored,' Aunt Hegarty wrote. ... 'Send them to stay with me, bringing warm underclothes designed for danger. Do not send their brothers with them. I detest boys.'

Thus the author with four sons and a grandson jocularly dismisses the male sex, and introduces instead five nieces led, in a double tribute to the granddaughter she had not yet seen, by Sophie and Lucy. In Victorian times ladies stayed at home. Not the indomitable explorer Hegarty, who dons her Admiral's hat and buys an old steamer. The party, having loaded essentials like bull's eyes, a goat, a kitten and paper doyleys, set off to find adventure, together with one extra long-lost niece and her stowaway brothers.[10]

Ursula put aside the manuscript about halfway through the story. "I had the nieces with Aunt Hegarty afloat on the high seas in the paddle boat with pirates on the tail and not an idea as to what was to become of them, although I knew there were to be buried treasure and cannibals before the end," she later told a group of aspiring writers. "That is when you have got to ride it out somehow, and sooner or later the story gets the bit between its teeth and gallops on leaving you nothing to do but follow."[11] The second half, which does not quite match the humour of the first, with its charming mix of the everyday and the nonsensical, had to wait until well after the author's return, and was not completed until Ursula spent a week at High Winds in October. It depends mainly on the discovery of the Paradox Islands, and its entertaining chief, who may or may not be a cannibal, who has been to the Houses of Parliament, and values his Queen Victoria mug more dearly than his treasure.

John Cushman Associates of New York agreed to publish an American edition. When its editors asked for substantial changes, Ursula resisted. She did eventually provide an alternative ending in which the pirates repent, but stoutly British references to the Union Jack and Queen Victoria remain. "Over and above the normal Americanising of it they want to do such extensive alterations that it will hardly be my book at all and I'm sticking my toes in," she told Alan. "There is a growing trend with publishers to re-write authors' books for them and I think it is a dangerous one if it goes beyond a certain point. But one hates to jettison a good contract. ... The question doesn't arise in England. I don't mind a certain amount of changes in translations but to alter the whole character of a book is another matter."[12]

After her long absence, followed by illness and a period in which Peter also was unwell, the resumption of duties in the magistrates' courts, of church activities, and the return of obligations as a hostess to the un-dammed stream of visitors[13] seem to have left Ursula relatively little time to focus successfully on her writing during the remainder of 1965 and early 1966. In September 1965, Smallwood rather firmly dismissed her latest work *A Book for Ben*, now lost, as "static and monotonous." "Oh dear, how difficult it is when a favourite author doesn't come up to scratch," she told O'Hea. In November, Ursula opened a sale of work at Beckford church. For the occasion she made eight brightly-coloured hobby horses in felt with coloured broomstick legs and scarlet wheels. They gave her the idea for *The Silver Horse*, a simple Christmas story about the toys, here made by "Mr Tandy," which was rejected by Chatto & Windus but accepted for an anthology by Eileen Colwell.[14] *The Beauty Queen* might also have remained as a very short story for young readers, possibly in *Girl* magazine, had Rosemary Garland not asked for a longer version. Soon, re-titled as *A Crown for a Queen*, it tripled in length, outgrowing anything she might publish in a Hulton magazine. Jenny, chosen as the queen, loses the borrowed crown in a stream, and she and her friend become trapped in a shed after recovering it. Not much else happens, and although it is a charming tale of childhood friendships, little would have been lost if it had remained in its original form. What did however make the book special was the decision of Marion Koenig at Hamish Hamilton to commission Shirley Hughes to provide the illustrations. With Hughes' training in life drawing, and Ursula's ability to create lifelike young characters, it was an ideal match.[15]

Ursula was looking forward to a couple of clear months after travelling to Iceland in December 1966 for the marriage of Barbara's son Vifill. Her recent titles had been undistinguished, and O'Hea reacted cautiously when Ursula told her she was working on something quite different, possibly an adult novel. It was clearly causing problems, and when *The Prisoners on the Island* arrived a few months later, neither writer nor agent was happy and it was temporarily abandoned.[16] In the meantime, however, somewhat against recent expectations, O'Hea had opened a package from Ursula to find one of the finest books she ever wrote, perhaps the very best.

Ursula had been seeking new audiences. Searching for new environments to explore, she had struggled with longer plots that failed to find their natural course, or were really extended short stories. Now she had been tempted back to the familiar and well-loved territory of *The Three Toymakers* and *Malkin's Mountain*, and, as a consequence, had produced the final and most impressive volume of the series, *The Toymaker's Daughter*. It quickly developed its own momentum. Like the others, she explained, it was "so enthralling to write, the kind of book you merely transcribe onto paper as if it had been in being for a long, long time."[17]

The Toymaker's Daughter makes no pretence at being an adult novel, but with the confidence to develop already well-established characters, Ursula comes closest in her career to creating mature, contradictory personalities in a world of moral complexity. Anders has grown up since *Malkin's Mountain* and now has children of his own, but it is in the redemption of Malkin and Marta that the author creates the most moving climax to any of her novels, and the apotheosis of the series that had been hinted at in the closing lines of the first volume. The action is dramatic from the moment that an eagle drops Marta, the wind-up doll who claims that she wants to be good while unable to resist a compulsion to play tricks. A teacher's inkwell is filled with black beetles; a cow delivers chocolate instead of milk. It is in fact only when Malkin, old, infirm and blind, loses his power over her that she breaks the metaphorical spell of self-destructive behaviour, and decides to return to his side of the mountain to look after him. Marta has become like a real child, who has learnt to love her father, and in a poignant final scene the families are reconciled. "Kindness isn't a thing you carve out of wood," says Malkin as he sits contentedly with his daughter and Anders' children who have come to stay.[18]

Harrap had taken an option on potential further titles in the *Toymaker* series, but by 1967 had lost interest. It was nearly twenty years since *Malkin's Mountain* and tastes had changed. O'Hea wrote to Ursula after reading the typescript, "I love it, but I have to tell you that I think many publishers may consider it 'old-fashioned' which in their vocabulary is pejorative. ... I may have to break down some barriers." The barriers, if any, proved insubstantial. Within a month Marion Koenig had accepted the book for Hamish Hamilton's Reindeer Books list. Shirley Hughes was again the chosen artist, and the partnership proved so successful that two years after publication Reindeer brought out the full Toymaker series with her illustrations.

Stanley Unwin, who had done so much to encourage his niece's early career, never had a chance to read what might be regarded as her greatest book. He was taken ill on holiday in Switzerland, and died on 13 October 1968, a week after its publication. "He was so dear and thoughtful among all his preoccupations and always so interested in us and in the family," Ursula told his widow Mary.[19] Stanley's help had been wide-ranging, but despite the trouble he had taken to help place her titles with others, Allen & Unwin had published nothing that she had written apart from *Grandfather*, dedicated to his father. Business was business, and from Ursula's point of view there was a reticence to approaching her uncle, for obvious reasons. It might seem significant, therefore, that her next two books published after Stanley's death should appear with the Allen & Unwin imprint, but in fact discussions had already taken place with his son Rayner.

Ursula had finished writing *Mog* on holiday in Menorca in January 1968, describing it as a novel for children aged ten to thirteen, "linking them to the lives of an adult world, slightly caricatured but not entirely untrue to life." It tells the story of two large, middle-aged twin sisters who look alike, dress alike and even eat the same food – listed at great length – in order that neither should lose a pound and thus become more alluring than the other. Mog, the more spirited of the two, organises a greedy day, a wicked day during which a hideous vase is smashed, a beautiful day, and so on. Along the twisting and occasionally confusing way, they look after

Margaret, whose mother is expecting twins, switch identities in the magistrates' court, and sabotage the cars of their visiting suitors, an Admiral and a vicar, when they mistakenly suspect burglars.

The author did not want the story to go into the Reindeer Book series, and O'Hea did not think it right for Harrap or Chatto. Ursula admired Roald Dahl's *Charlie and the Chocolate Factory*, recently published by Allen & Unwin, so suggested that the typescript might be sent anonymously to her cousin. The agent agreed to send it, but only on condition that Ursula was identified as the author. "Selling a book by Ursula Moray Williams is one thing, and a book by an unknown author is quite another. I am sure that what you had in mind when suggesting this was the avoidance of any possibility of nepotism, but would you like to think again?" she wrote. In June, Rayner offered a contract for the "splendid" book, and, unaware of Ursula's liking for the Dahl book, suggested commissioning its illustrator Faith Jaques. He was happy to let the text stand as it was and did not request any changes. The author did nevertheless make one change. The book had been dedicated to Noel Streatfeild, as indefatigable and resolutely cheerful a figure as Mog herself. Unfortunately, the manuscript included a line that the stout heroine "went on the stage before she married." Ursula took it out. As she explained to Rayner, "Noel was on the stage, and as she's fat I didn't want the risk of hurting her feelings. She isn't Mog at all, in fact."

The publisher's main concern was to find a transatlantic partner to offset the high cost of the lavish production. Meredith Books had published American editions of *The Moonball* and *The Cruise of the Happy-Go-Gay*. When its juvenile editor Gloria Mosesson invited Ursula to lunch in London, Ursula promised Rayner she would "put a circle round the earth to fetch the precious herb and squeeze the juice upon her."[20]

"Quite frankly, we don't want to lose you to another publisher as Morrow lost you to us," Mosesson told her guest over smoked salmon and Coca-Cola at the Savoy. "But anything so specialised as *Mog* might affect your prestige with people longing for another *Moonball*."

The episode proved an entertaining distraction. Ursula had never expected *Mog*, with its "purely British and rather personal humour" to have any appeal in the US. If America did not want the book, or if she did not want to make the radical changes required for an American market, she hoped that Allen & Unwin might produce it in a more modest format, as she delicately told Rayner. So it was to be, with Jaques's textual illustrations and a simple jacket.

While on holiday in Menorca, Ursula had watched the Festival of the Three Kings, who come in from the sea and ride through Mahon on horseback, followed by carts filled with presents for good children, and coal for the naughty. She quickly turned it into a short story *Three Kings Came Riding*, but despite rewriting it for Barbara Willard's anthology *Hullabaloo*, it was ultimately rejected.[21]

Four months later, another holiday was to contribute the idea of her next book. Ursula and Peter took his sister Jo to Austria for two weeks to celebrate her sixtieth birthday. Ursula was feeling wonderfully fit. "In spite of being so ill in 1960 I can walk almost indefinitely and climb, and got quite frustrated by the slowness of my companions," she told Alan. So while she walked to the mountain-tops, they took chairlifts, and when all returned, she still had the energy to start writing a story, partly based on the history of the converted barn in which they were staying. There was something about the mountains in Haute-Savoie and in Switzerland that had inspired much of her best writing. Austria was no exception.

The noise of plane engines, the rattle of guns had ceased, and an enormous quiet rose from the forest and mountainside below as John Harding dropped slowly out of the sky towards the trees.

The bold opening of *Boy in a Barn*, with the parachute descent of the pilot shot down over Austria, leads into an exciting adventure that switches confidently between wartime and Harding's return on holiday with his family twenty years later. His son James is given the chance to stay longer, but when he is accidentally stranded alone, he has to fend for himself and stays in the barn that sheltered his father. The language is evocative – "Chalets and barns huddled like sleeping cattle" – and there are fond references, as if for validation, to happy memories of Switzerland, such as the scene of painters of the mountainside. As in *The Toymaker's Daughter*, however, it is the changes wrought in the two main characters that give the book its emotional and moral appeal. An apparently mad old woman, who mistakes the boy for his father and locks him into the barn, is actually suffering from dementia and reliving the time when she sheltered the pilot from capture. But the book's defining moment comes when the destitute hero, sitting by a waterfall, sees the wind carry off his last one hundred schilling note, and the last of his food roll off a parapet. James, son of John (the names are no accident), is ready to despair but faces his trial of resolve and proves himself a "fine English chap ... never say die" sort of fellow. Ursula had originally intended to dedicate *The Nine Lives of Island Mackenzie* to her son: "For children with stout but tender hearts, especially James." It was possibly not the type of public statement about himself that a 14-year-old boy would have greatly appreciated. He was ten years older now and engaged to be married, so *Boy in a Barn* appeared with the simple inscription "To James and Rosemary."[23]

It was, however, a holiday in freezing surroundings, not sunny Menorca or Austria, that witnessed the opening of a new chapter in Ursula's life. In January 1970 she stepped off a train at the tiny station of Haltwhistle, to be driven to Featherstone Castle where the Puffin Club had just started its first ten-day "Winter Whoopee." Many of the youngsters attending would remember the storytelling, the games of make-believe, the plays and picture-making as the beginning of lifetimes surrounded by books. For Ursula too, the event acquired a symbolic significance. She arrived on the first day of a new decade, one that was to bring great personal distress, but through which she would be sustained in part by the example of what she found among the young Puffineers at a rather gloomy castle in Northumberland.

Chapter 16

———

"There's Nuffin' like a Puffin."

The appointment in 1961 of Kaye Webb as editor of Puffin Books had surprised the sorority of children's book editors. Under its founder Eleanor Graham, Puffin had, for twenty years, enjoyed a virtual monopoly in paperbacks for children, and many expected her protégé Margaret Clark to take over. Webb was then editor of *Elizabethan*, a monthly magazine where she had formed a club to encourage contributions from its young readers. She had published work by leading writers and illustrators of juvenile fiction, but had no experience in book publishing. Within a year of joining Puffin, however, she acquired rights for J.R.R. Tolkien's *The Hobbit*, *The Hundred and One Dalmatians* by Dodie Smith, and P.L. Travers's *Mary Poppins*. For a time Webb discouraged other publishers from bringing out their own paperbacks by promising to take a guaranteed number of their titles. Thanks to her seemingly inexhaustible energy and marketing flair, sales quadrupled in four years, although commercial success seemed a secondary concern. "In an ideal world, no-one would try to make money out of children's books," she declared. "We are making literate human beings."[1]

Graham had already published a Puffin edition of *Adventures of the Little Wooden Horse*, which she had been one of the first to recognise as a classic. With a reprint due in 1963, Harrap approached her successor about taking paperback rights for other titles. Webb chose *Gobbolino the Witch's Cat* and asked Ursula to shorten the original, which had been unavailable for twenty years. In fact, the abridgement was made by Webb or one of her assistant editors, for O'Hea noted that *Gobbolino* had been "truncated" but added, "if Kaye Webb sells it well, I will forgive her."[2] The change involved the removal of four chapters about the sea captain's daughter, during which the hero turns himself into different animals and becomes invisible. The section, which also includes a rather sickly romance, reads like a traditional fairy story, out of keeping with the rest of the work. As a result, apart from the loss of a lively few pages involving a parrot called Pericles, the omission of the entire episode produced a better book. O'Hea's forgiveness should have been swift. It was in this shorter version that *Gobbolino the Witch's Cat* became a bestseller, reprinted twenty-six times in twenty-three years, broadcast by the BBC, and issued on gramophone discs read by *Pinky and Perky* narrator Jimmy Thompson.[3] O'Hea had tried to get Webb to take The Nine Lives of Island Mackenzie. She never did, but Puffin published another six of Ursula's titles without significant changes.

Webb's most celebrated achievement was the creation in 1967 of the Puffin Club, and with it *Puffin Post*, which together aimed to encourage children to choose their own books. "Books have to go through five lots of adults, the editor who chooses, the traveller who sells, the bookseller who buys, teachers, parents. The whole point of the club," Webb said, "was to cut out one or two sets of grown-ups."[4] In the first issue, she told her readers, "If you choose wisely, you can share adventures which leave you gasping, conversations which keep you fascinated, you can discover how people think, why they behave as they do."[5] The quarterly magazine provided fun too with its backwards codeword "Sniffup", silly jokes – "What's got a big mouth and is covered with flowers? A hippypotamus" – and amusing, useless information: "You can roll a hibernating dormouse across the … table without it waking it up." There were many common references between Webb's ideas and Ursula's, which harked back to their childhoods. "I shall always be grateful to my mother," wrote Webb in words that Ursula might have expressed verbatim, "for the way she shared books with us, encouraged us to talk about them, made good things in them fun that we all enjoyed together and understood so much better because we shared."[6] Another coincidence was the use of the title Puffin itself. A year before the launch of the Club, Webb had arranged the recording of a song called "There's Nuffin like a Puffin", unaware of the similar verse in Ursula's pre-war book. "I wish I had known about your Puffin verse before," she wrote. "It would have been gorgeous to have included some of it."[7]

Webb was a dynamic force. When she asked, "Oh darling, you will do it, won't you?" it was hard to resist. Artist Shirley Hughes remembered: "She was very hyper, very persuasive, always getting you to do what she wanted."[8] Not that Ursula required much persuasion to become involved in a club that was soon spreading its enthusiasm for children's books among 44,000 members. She was drawn into judging Puffin competition entries, and when the magazine organised a competition for twenty children to win a week's holiday in the Wye Valley, Herefordshire, Ursula suggested they all came to tea.

One of those who went, on a sunny September day in 1968, described what happened as the high spot of the holiday.

> We found the [other] group huddled excitedly in the kitchen. A beautiful white-haired lady, as old as my grandmother, was building a perilous construction of wine-glasses, a tray, and real, unboiled eggs. Just as we entered the room, she gave the tray a hefty clout. There was a sound of chinking glass and frightened gasps, but when we felt brave enough to open our eyes again, we saw with amazement that there wasn't a trace of omelette mixture to be seen. The eggs had dropped uncracked into the glasses, and absolutely nothing had been broken. .... I wondered if my mother would let me experiment with the family glasses if I told her I was only following the

example of a famous writer.[9]

The ebullient Webb ungenerously described herself as "the fattest Puffin," based upon the Fat Puffin character, who eats too many doughnuts. In fact, it was her personality, rather than her ample figure, that was larger than life. Small, with thick, plum-coloured curls often offset against a bright pink blouse, and usually wearing her Puffin Club badge, she attracted and welcomed attention. Open-hearted, creative, sparky, shrewd, seemingly always keeping two steps ahead of chaos, she and Ursula immediately took to each other. "They got on like a house on fire," Andrew observed. "They both gave top performances when they saw each other." James remembered a "very warm relationship. They respected each other. Kaye was hyper-active, and mother saw that as a bonus." On a visit to Court Farm, their chat went on too long for Webb to catch her return train in comfort, necessitating a telephone call to Evesham railway station and a dare-devil drive by Peter. It ended with Webb running over the ice-covered footbridge, bags clutched in both hands, while a patient train driver glanced back at the "Very Important Person due to attend a board of directors meeting when she gets to London."[10]

From Puffin's base, in what resembled up-market Nissen huts near London airport, Webb and her enthusiastic staff had started to organise meetings at which members could meet authors. They planned a party in aid of the Save the Children Fund at the Over-Seas League at St James's Street on Friday, 3 January 1969. After seeing how Ursula had entertained the Puffineers that summer, Webb invited her to attend, adding, to confirm the light-hearted nature of the event, that the children would play "Pin the Beak on the Puffin." To Ursula, a genius at organising games at home, this must have seemed tame stuff.

Parties at Court Farm had become legendary. Children at Beckford primary looked forward to her annual Easter egg hunt, held just before the holiday. It was one of the major school events of the year, so all arrived in their best clothes, irrespective of what lay ahead. First there were stories from Ursula in the kitchen, decorated with chicks and rabbits, then the "hares and hens" races across the lawn, with contestants choosing either to have their feet tied together or hopping on one leg. After sandwiches and cakes came the hunt itself. The children were given ten minutes to improvise bird nests from whatever they could find, then were allowed to swarm freely over the garden, up trees, among flower beds, along a stream, to find the hidden chocolate eggs and put them in their nests. There were "pie-rats" too, lurking in bushes and waiting to be caught, and to work off remaining energy the youngsters were allowed to knock the heads off the now drooping daffodils. The event concluded as Ursula stood on the terrace and flung Smarties in every direction, to be pursued by screaming children in frocks, shirts and short trousers no longer as clean or well-pressed as an hour previously.

For the children of friends there were regular "crazy teas" with the delicious opportunity to do things that normal table manners forbade. Instructions were drawn for every mouthful. "Share this with the dog." "Eat this without using your hands." "Sing a song while eating this." There were hobby-horse gymkhanas, Red Cross parties, and gypsy parties for which the large chest in the nursery provided a vast array of oversized dressing-up clothes. Suitably attired, the gypsy boys and girls could enjoy "rabbit pie" on which a real crust hid sweets below, compete in clothes peg races, or in "Move along please," devised with blithe innocence by Ursula, in which they tried to fool policemen. Local favourites included Halloween parties, for which Ursula made inverted half orange toadstools set over burning nightlights. The table was set with a gingerbread house, made from cake stuck with sweets and almonds, and with brightly-coloured jellies set in orange segments. Giant spiders hung from the trees, whose sparkler legs burst into life as the children went home, each carrying a lantern they had made, each with a mask, and with a small gift chosen from a witch's cauldron.

Older boys, aged up to eleven, could enjoy a Brave Deeds party, the programme for which occasionally alarmed parents. To reduce their anxiety, but more "to add to the spirit of the evening," a bucket of water and a First Aid kit was always on hand, as the young men competed for military awards in feats such as grabbing Smarties from a bucket filled with holly leaves. Games included "Burnt mouth, burnt fingers," in which baked potatoes were taken straight from the oven and, protected only by a paper napkin, the winner showed the cleanest potato skin after five minutes. Playing with matches was also encouraged in a contest to light three matches, one from another, and hold them as long as possible. There were trials by water as well as fire. In *Children's parties (and Games for a Rainy Day)*, based on her experiences, Ursula explained, "True heroes can display their courage by submerging their faces in a basin of water, while a timekeeper counts the time they can stay submerged."

By collecting her party ideas, and setting out advice to parents organising similar events, Ursula revealed much of her philosophy about the bringing up of children that went beyond the exigencies of an hour or two of entertainment. "Mother took an awful lot of trouble preparing and organising," James said. "She seemed to delight in imagining what a young child found stimulating and intriguing." What mattered was not just the time required to disguise a vacuum cleaner as a dragon that sucked up offerings, or to turn a shed into a witch's cave, but also the principle of making children use their own senses and draw on their own abilities. Winners received small prizes, and while she arranged that every child went home with something, there was no automatic distribution of gifts to all. The allure of an Easter egg hunt, for example, was that "however small the hidden egg its impact is enormous if it is found 'all by myself'."[11]

She sent the manuscript of *Children's parties (and Games for a Rainy Day)* to Webb, with suggestions for the London event. Her ideas for a detective party might make a suitable theme, she thought, but Webb wrote back: "I wish we could organise a game with blood and soot clues, but with 200 children it would be a bit difficult." She did however take up the idea of turning the hall into a fairground. Ursula took charge of a group of twenty-five boys, and with authors Michael Bond, Leon Garfield, her friend Noel Streatfeild and others signed dozens of autographs. At teatime all children were given ten tokens to spend at the fair as they chose, on hoopla, skittles or to have their fortunes told by Madame Aikarti (bearing an uncanny resemblance to writer Joan Aiken), who predicted reading lives filled with adventure.[12]

When Webb bumped into Ursula by accident at Paddington station one night a few weeks before Christmas 1969, she bubbled with compliments about what a great success the gathering had been, and mentioned the first winter holiday that the Puffin Club had arranged, to be held at Featherstone Castle, Northumberland, for ten days from Boxing Day. William Mayne had agreed to attend as the resident author, but the following day Webb wrote to Dearest Ursula: "I know it's simply not practical to ask you to come up to Featherstone, but if you had time to send the children a letter or a telegram … it would be very exciting for them to find it on the notice board. Better still if you could ask them a riddle and they could spend part of their holiday puzzling out the answer." Ursula took the hint and caught the train.

The holiday came about through Chris Green, an energetic former teacher who had founded Colony Holidays, specialising in countryside breaks for children aged nine to fourteen. He wrote to Webb, describing his use of Puffin titles in the training of assistants. They met, and over lunch agreed on a joint venture that was to last ten years. The venue for their first holiday was Featherstone, a former boarding school owned by the altruistic John Clark, a magistrate keen to break down social barriers and encourage children from the big cities to appreciate the countryside. For Green and Webb, the choice was a gamble; unlike their previous, independently organised holidays, this was to be held in winter, in the far north of England. When the fifty youngsters arrived, temperatures had dropped to the lowest in Northumberland for thirty years. Webb had persuaded Leon Garfield to write a play for the youngsters to act, but it was a scary plot, and with darkness falling by 4 p.m. and imaginative eleven-year-olds hearing the weather howl around the battlements of the old castle, the idea was dropped. Green and Ursula also had to contend with the challenge of working with a whirlwind of changeable direction.

On the night that the children arrived, Webb wanted Featherstone to look like a fairytale castle, so while Green went to the station, she turned on every light. The consequence was similar to that of her impact on some lesser colleagues. The effect was marvellous for thirty minutes until all the fuses blew. So stories were told by candlelight. Disaster turned to triumph.[13] The experience gave Green a suitable introduction to working with Webb on holidays and at exhibitions for a decade.

Holiday monitors at Featherstone, who had worked hard to get their charges calmed down and into bed, were horrified to see Webb breeze in after lights out, to laugh and chat, and hand out sweets after they had brushed their teeth. A matron who decided it was unwise to give aspirin to a child stood aghast as Webb intervened. "Poor darling, have some of mine," she said. Green summed up the experience:

> [Webb] was a complete genius as Editor of Puffins, and the Puffin Club was another massive achievement. However she was very difficult to work alongside. She would decide something, tell you to go and do it, then change her mind and tell someone else to do the opposite. Everyone who worked with her was regularly infuriated, but forgave her anything since she was such an inspiring head of the organisation, and her objectives were totally honest, unselfish, child-centred and educationally exciting.[14]

On arrival, Ursula had been required to fill out a Puffin passport:

Eyes: *Grey.*
Hair: *Off-white.*
Shoe size: *Seven.*
Special virtue: *Enjoying life.*
Special vice: *Inability to concentrate on more than one thing at a time.*
Special phobia: *Having enough time to myself.*
Personal motto: *Chalk it up to experience.*

Favourite childhood book, food, colour, smell, word, sound, song and poem were recorded as: *The Secret Garden*, smoked salmon, pink, outdoor wood fires, courtesy, curlew's song, "Skye Boat Song" and *The Changeling*. If she couldn't write, she would like to be a gardener, and to a question of how she might use £1,000 she wrote "launch a scheme for providing a Puffin bookshelf for every children's ward in the country." Having described her arrival at Featherstone on New Year's Day as her "most thrilling moment," the passport was stamped.[15] Over the next five days, she plunged into activities and games, swabbed floors, hunted for puffins in the woods, told stories by firelight, and got cramp from drawing Gobbolinos in autograph books. She dressed children who played parts from Alan Garner's *The Weirdstone of Brisingamen*, and revived them with smelling salts when they fainted. She "had a fantastic time and enjoyed every minute," although she confessed the castle had been as cold as North Stoneham House. Despite the frustrations shared with Green, she appreciated that what Webb was attempting with the Puffin Club closely corresponded to the values presented in her books. After the holiday, Webb described the liberating experience of the children spending time away from families that had ascribed fixed personalities to them. She likened the situation to novels for older children that often featured crises that arose after parents had been called away. "Whatever the ramifications of the plot, the basis of the story is children left to their own resources, and of course coping magnificently."

Such sentiment was central to Ursula's next book based directly, too directly it transpired, on the holiday in Northumberland. It arose from a misunderstanding. Webb had probably told her how marvellous it would be if she wrote a novel about the Puffin Club itself. Ursula took that to be a commission, or at least a strong indication that she would publish one. In March she told a friend she was "terribly engrossed" in finishing the book. It was, she said, "an unlikely episode ... but Kaye Webb wanted me to make a book out of it." Writing it had been almost as much fun as the holiday itself, she said.[17] Ten weeks after leaving Featherstone, she posted *Castle Merlin* to Webb, with a copy to O'Hea.

As in Garner's book, spirits of the past pervade the present. Susie, the heroine, flies north in the corner of a chilly railway compartment on January 1st, to a castle with a dungeon, close to Hadrian's Wall, to join a holiday club where authors tell stories by candlelight. An interest in falconry links a visiting woman writer with a long dead ancestor, who reappears to Susie as a ghost. A mysterious prisoner is discovered. Thereafter matters become more confused. Spirits, one explains, are "just a little bit of one's essential being, caught in a ray of time."[18] Characters flit in and out of focus, sometimes acting in the past and present at the same time. Susie's time away from home gives her confidence, an absconder returns to his Borstal with new resolve, and the visiting author goes off to write her story. It was not to be one of her best.

Susie was not the only one bewildered by what went on. A report by a Puffin adviser highlighted the difficulty of mediaeval ghosts talking with modern children, but the problem was more fundamental. Ursula told simple stories extraordinarily well, but here it seems that the author's usual judgement has been submerged by the enthusiasm of the newly recruited acolyte. Its message, about the liberating value of reading books, seems as muddled as the time periods in which it is set.

In April 1970, Ursula went to London, again at Webb's invitation, for the Puffin Club's birthday exhibition. It seems to have been the usual frantic, but enjoyable affair, with no one on hand to greet her when she arrived. Webb wrote apologetically: "I really feel furious at being so disorganised ... I know it is my perpetual state ... I should have been there to greet you. However, you are perpetually forgiving and understanding and I just have to rely on that." It made matters worse that, when they found time to talk, Webb delivered her depressing verdict on the book. "We have come to the conclusion that it is really and truly your remark that it 'wrote itself after Featherstone' [that] is the answer to what is wrong. I just think you must have gone at it too hard to work out the plot and the Puffin Club could be getting in the way." In a letter, now lost, Ursula apologised for seeming "money-grubbing," and Webb admitted that she remembered a conversation in which it was mentioned that Ursula might write about the club, although "I didn't realise I'd been so brash as to actually ask you to write a book about it." It did indeed seem an unlikely, formal commission, but Webb nevertheless sent her a cheque for seventy-five guineas, adding that she would hate there to be any shadows on their relationship, which she valued very much.[19]

O'Hea too had reservations about the book, and found herself in the unwelcome position of having a novel to offer to publishers about the activities of another publisher that had rejected it. When it came back from Chatto & Windus, with a discouraging note from Jane Birkett, she suggested, almost apologetically, sending it to Rayner Unwin. Perhaps he genuinely liked the book, as much as he professed, but his cleverly worded comments hint that his acceptance of the book might also be seen as a family favour, not necessarily to be repeated. Sales of *Mog* and *Boy in a Barn* had yet to earn their advances, he told O'Hea, and he was very anxious to be assured that Ursula was not letting him have the books just because he was her cousin. The message was understood. It was the last of Ursula's books that Allen & Unwin were to publish, but after all the fuss, Webb later decided to issue it as a Puffin paperback after all.

As if to show that the episode had caused no hard feelings, the Puffin Club party that Ursula organised at her home not long after completing *Castle Merlin* was one of the most elaborate she ever devised. Nearly fifty children were singing as they tumbled out of the bus from their holiday site at Malvern Abbey for an evening of Arabian Nights entertainment. Peter, dressed like a sheikh, rode up and down the avenue of cypresses on his motor-mower. Webb, in flowing robes, was his first passenger. In "eerie moonlight" the children wandered around an Eastern market lit by candles, acted and mimed scenes from *Omar Khayyam*, and watched snake charming and the Indian rope trick performed by William Mayne and Ursula operating black cotton in the shadows. "It went like a bomb," she reported.[20]

Throughout the 1970s, despite personal setbacks and duties as a magistrate, Ursula continued to organise Puffin parties, attend holidays and the book days that caused traffic jams as children queued down the street to meet favourite authors. In 1974, Webb published *The Line*, four stories about a chemical formula that enables a boy to miniaturise everything and everyone around him, and turn them back again to normal size. Ursula had written them for *Puffin Post* and it was the first time that an author had seen her work go from the magazine into book format. The work was dedicated "to Kaye Webb with love," and the compliment was returned when Ursula was asked to become the first Honorary Life Member of the Puffin Club. She returned to Featherstone, and became President of the Newcastle upon Tyne branch, urging its organisers to attract many new members, just as "when one puffin moves off the ledge another takes its place."[21]

On a sunny day in August 1978, Ursula was one of the distinguished guests invited to an unusual burial in the grounds of Penguin headquarters, near Heathrow airport. Webb, concerned about the possibly deleterious effect of television on young readers, had put together a time capsule that would celebrate the revelatory world of the best – or as she put it "nicest" – children's books of the past century, among them *Gobbolino, the Witch's Cat*. The occasion, formally recorded by the British Museum and others, was devised to help revive an activity that "heaven forbid, could have fallen into disuse," by the time the container was opened. So Ursula watched with particular interest as TV astronomer Patrick Moore performed the ceremony, after which a flowering cherry was planted on the site. Webb talked of a new golden age of children's fiction, but Moore's words were largely drowned out by the roar of Concorde overhead. Others had their say too. Young Puffineers had written accounts of their lives that now lay wrapped in protective foil, and many authors had bequeathed pithy messages to posterity to be interred with their books. Ursula was one of the contributors. Later she wrote to Webb: "Funny to think of those books sleeping under the soil on the hill at Harmondsworth. What kind of world will read them in 2078? Books are a tremendous responsibility, aren't they? They simply <u>must</u> influence a lot."[22] But what message Gobbolino carried into the next world, alas, is not recorded, so the curious must wait until the capsule is opened.

The following spring, Webb reassured Ursula that contrary to rumours, she was not planning to resign completely, but would reduce her work toward the end of the year "and perhaps just concentrate on the Club." Her retirement was announced officially in a letter sent to Ursula on 12 November, addressed by the editorial director of Penguin Children's Books simply to "Dear Author/Illustrator/Friend in general."[23]

Ursula wrote to Webb some days later describing how she still drew "great breaths of fresh air" from what she and the Puffin Club had achieved, and recalling happy party memories together:

> All those eager little faces and dear Noel sitting fatly in a corner signing autographs ... and you rushing off to Tewkesbury to pinch that tarpaulin from the fire station for the children to sit on ... and all the occasions of swarming happy Puffins with you dashing about ... like what Peter called a blue-arsed fly dispensing such love and interest and inspiration.

Webb carried on as editor of *Puffin Post* for a couple of years, but then "the powers-that-be decided it's time the younger ones took over." The two women's friendship and visits continued for another fifteen years, apart from Puffin Club exhibitions that both attended. But Ursula's relationship with Puffin was never the same. An electric current, that positively charged all it touched, had been turned off. Penguin Books were entering the Thatcherite age, and Puffin would henceforth be more orderly, more businesslike. Duller.

Chapter 17

_____

"It's our book and we're both in it come rain or shine."

Ursula and Webb continued to write to each other until a few months before the latter's death in January 1996, and long after either could comfortably make the journey between London and Beckford. Their long association typified Ursula's ability to turn professional colleagues into friends, notwithstanding the fact that often they were in positions to criticise or reject her work. The same was true of her relations with illustrators, over whose interpretation of her text she had little control, and who in later years were often called upon to replace her own artwork used in original editions.

With the exception of *The Adventures of Boss and Dingbat* with photographs by Peter, each of Ursula's first fourteen books included her own illustrations. For more than thirty years, they appeared in her own titles, once in another writer's work, and in numerous diaries and sketchbooks kept for her own amusement, or given to relatives. Watercolour sketches of Annecy, with their delicate shading and assured draughtsmanship, show a considerable talent in a seventeen-year-old. Five years later, for *Grandfather*, she produced brilliantly dramatic linocuts in monochrome, ideally suited to the austerity of the snow-covered mountains. Among them, the small broken body of a fallen climber at the foot of a cliff face remains as arresting an image as any that ever appeared in her books. Yet such examples of artwork, more likely to be appreciated by adults than by children, are as rare as her attempts at adult fiction.

Ursula never seriously attempted portraiture. The closest she ever came to a self-portrait was when in Switzerland, in 1934, she posed for Paul Perrelet and Barbara. On a page in Ursula's sparkling cartoon diary, in which she recorded incidents of the holiday, she depicts herself three times – as the sitter, and as the smiling face emerging on both artists' easels. The contrast between her humorous watercolour sketch and Barbara's and Paul's serious canvases might serve to characterise the diverging ambitions by that date of Ursula and her sister. For *Kelpie*, *Sandy-on-the-Shore*, and *Elaine of La Signe*, Ursula provided numerous small drawings, particularly impressive in their naturalistic depiction of horses and ponies, but it was Barbara who provided the more detailed full pages.

Although not quite as talented an artist as her sister, it seems likely that Ursula could have earned a living as an illustrator had she chosen to. As early at 1927, when she added daily headings and margin jottings to her Girl Guides camp diary, there are indications of the techniques she would employ: convincing depictions in ink with hatched shading of animals and birds, caricatures of adults, figures in silhouette, and the Guides themselves in lively poses as they set up camp. Each of the styles was developed to suit the character of the particular title being illustrated. Cut-outs on black backgrounds particularly suited stories about the mountains. In *Jean-Pierre*, colourful fairies and goats dance around the head of the androgynous hero against a plain blue skyline cut by snowy peaks. The artist recycled the goats and fairies in some of her Brownie books. With *For Brownies* and *Adventures of Anne* she started to add drawn outlines and interior detail into the larger pictures, giving them the glowing effect of stained glass, but for *The Good Little Christmas Tree* she returned to the severe discipline of relying on scissors alone. As pieces of handicraft they are considerable achievements, but the difficulty of cutting out tiny details and the limitations of colour printing available at the time required a large and expensive publishing format.

In their first lessons at Petersfield, the twins' nanny Elsa Mueller had taught them how to draw stick people, and the emaciated Gothic knights and long-nosed old ladies that peopled Ursula's early sketchbooks reappeared in fantastical stories like *The Pettabomination*. Favourite characters popped up repeatedly in Darwinian profusion. The Pettabomination himself, a squat beetle-browed creature, was surely descended from the baby dragons that Ursula depicted in her Brownie fairy tales, and might have grown up into one rather like Norah Shaw's *Vermilion* which Ursula had illustrated. An indolent sub-species even makes a brief appearance among the original drawings of *Gobbolino*.[1] The greater the improbability of the stories, the more extreme the caricature could be. Conversely, everyday events suggested a more restrained style. As with her writing, it was in rather domestic contexts that Ursula produced some of her most entertaining artwork, much of it unseen except by members of her family. Between 1932 – when she hiked through the Black Forest with Alan – and 1936, she sketched five splendid books of cartoons, the last of them unfinished, that also recounted her holidays to Switzerland and expeditions such as the Land's End car rally. The humour is of everyday events: staying in youth hostels, encounters with slugs, bugs and German sausages, crowded sleeping arrangements, plunging into hot chocolate for breakfast, or Peter's sneezes upsetting shelves at a shop.

Even in these private diaries, however, the skills of one trained in life drawing classes are evident. In the cartoons, Ursula and Peter contort their torsos in exaggerated fashion for comic effect to light a campfire. In work published later, their poses are replicated, now perfectly proportioned, as Grumpa digs under his tool shed, and a girl lies watching Icelandic ponies. With sufficient time and the right choice of subjects, Ursula celebrated her talent for figure drawing in images bursting with energy: the Binkleby boys bursting a balloon, a spread-eagled horse from a milk dray, or a boy crashing into a dustbin on his bicycle. Even the sleeping mice in *O for a Mouseless House*, the last of her books to include her own illustrations, seem to twitch as they dream.[2]

It was therefore no misfortune that *Adventures of the Little Wooden Horse* was the first of Ursula's titles to be given to another artist. Of all her artwork, that for books with inanimate subjects, such as *The Twins and Their Ponies* and the later *Hobbie*, were the least successful. The prospect of selling *Adventures of the Little Wooden Horse* to American publisher Lippincott may well have been a factor in George Harrap's decision to commission Brisley. Her *Milly-Molly-Mandy* stories with their fanciful evocation of an English rural childhood idyll had been popularised in the US by the *Christian Science Monitor*. With little more than the glance of an eye or the turn of a tail, she gave the hero a feisty spirit. Ursula justly called her work "superb,"[3] but it cannot have entirely convinced Eleanor Graham when she was planning the first Puffin edition twenty years later. Perhaps by then it appeared like a perfect image of an unchanging world that had since changed profoundly. Perhaps it was simply a question of fitting the drawings more exactly to the paperback format which favoured small horizontal images at the start and end of chapters, although most of the originals could have been accommodated well enough, and Brisley was still very active.

Whatever the reason, Graham decided to look elsewhere, and was quite particular in what she required. Roughs by Judith Brook showing the Little Wooden Horse with separate head and neck pieces were rejected. "She is allowing herself to be too whimsical. The little horse is a tough, valiant little creature, and needs a strong simple line which will allow an effect of great activity within the limits of his material," she told Margaret Clark, one of her editors. "It needs humour and vigour, NOT pathos. I've a feeling we want someone who understands action better ... It should be a lively adventure story, not a little fairy tale."[4]

Clark then wrote to Peggy Fortnum, whose work she had seen for Michael Bond's *A Bear called Paddington*, shortly to be published. Clark enclosed a copy of the story and a few Puffins to show the general layout. It is not clear whether she sent a new copy of the typescript, or more probably the Harrap original, as no changes had been made to the text, and two or three of Fortnum's illustrations were to show striking similarities with Brisley's. Perhaps overall they lack the charm of the earlier versions, but what they added were new perspectives, tangential lighting in place of Brisley's rather flatly illuminated scenes, with their limited depth and restricted range of shade. Graham, however, remained dissatisfied. She questioned what she saw as disparities between Fortnum's drafts and the text. "The little horse is rather a noble little creature, noble and honest and persevering, and very brave. Don't you think she has drawn one a trifle too hag-ridden? She has got the feeling of movement exceedingly well, but will you try to convey to her the need to express also that kind of personality," she told Clark.

Fortnum, whose relationship with Bond, or at least his agent, proved acrimonious, did not give in easily. "I will remember your comments when I continue to work on the illustrations," she immediately replied to Clark. "Actually he is rather hag-ridden poor creature – and has the most frightful experiences, all through the book (so different to Paddington who spends his life eating and having a wonderful time) but I will try and find the parts where he looks more cheerful." Graham was still unhappy when the drawings arrived six weeks later, and noted fourteen specific objections, mostly concerning the design of the toy horse himself, and particularly the reference to Uncle Peder unscrewing his head and popping coins down the hole in his neck. In fact, the sketches had followed exactly Brisley's example in showing the toy with a neck and head as flat as a board, the same as in the toys that Ursula had seen hanging outside the Bradley store in Petersfield. Fortnum made the neck "a little more vague" in some of her drawings, while pointing out that the reference to the screwed head was "according to the toy experts, a technical error." When Clark wrote yet again requesting changes to the cover, she replied regretfully that she was "now rather tied up with other work." Six of Fortnum's illustrations, those with which Graham was most unhappy, were dropped. When a decade later Hamish Hamilton wanted to use the remainder in their own edition, Webb described her as, "a very tricky lady" who "agitates enormously" about the use of her drawings.

Ursula too disliked the cover – later replaced with one by Pauline Baynes – finding it too sombre, especially she said as the book was often the first that children read for themselves,[6] but as was customary the selection of illustrator and the subsequent discussion about the suitability of the artwork had taken place directly between the publisher and artist, with little reference to the writer. After the original publication of *Adventures of the Little Wooden Horse*, and while Ursula was balancing writing with the duties of a young mother, the task of illustrating her works was given to others: Jack Matthew for *Peter and the Wanderlust*, Mary Shillabeer for *Adventures of Puffin*, Brisley again for *Pretenders' Island*. Wildlife artist Eileen Soper's work on *A Castle for John-Peter* in 1941 possibly helped her to become Enid Blyton's illustrator for *The Famous Five* novels.[7]

Starting with *Gobbolino, the Witch's Cat*, Ursula resumed responsibility for illustrating her own work for the next sixteen years, so she may have been disappointed when Norah Smallwood hesitated over using her "stylised" drafts for *The Nine Lives of Island Mackenzie*. If so, the mention of Edward Ardizzone, who had recently won the first Kate Greenaway Medal for the most distinguished contribution to children's book illustration, immediately overcame any dismay. She told O'Hea: "I really am glad Mackenzie has crawled into a friendly lap at Chatto & Windus and feel sure they will treat him well. Pictures are of paramount importance. Do you remember discussing Ardizzone? … I would go to any terms to get him, sharing a royalty, foregoing an advance or anything that was not absurd – just for the fun of having him do it."[8] Despite pleading that he was fully booked with work until the following March, Ardizzone accepted the commission after reading the typescript.

Adrizzone worked on *Mackenzie* at about the same time as Fortnum was having her troubled correspondence with Puffin. In contrast to Graham, it is unlikely that Smallwood did much more than leave her artist to it. The results seemed to have pleased all. Critics, particularly in the US, praised his inimitable style for capturing the spirit of the story. Ardizzone himself talked about encouraging the imaginative cooperation of the child and not making everything explicit. The best view of a hero, he said, was a back view.[9] To the untutored eye of this writer, his illustrations are executed with a brio that can occasionally reduce Mackenzie to a background smudge, but Ursula seems to have been delighted. From her bed in Cheltenham hospital, where she was then still desperately ill, Ursula wrote to Smallwood that "the expression on M's face is pure genius. I can't imagine how Ardizzone has got inside a cat like that." Ursula wrote only once to Ardizzone, thanking him for what he had done, but seems not to have received a reply.[10]

Over the coming years, a large number of illustrators worked on her books and short stories. Rarely did the writer influence the choice. "One has to accept, usually, the pet artist belonging to the publisher," she commented.[11]

In 1988, when Walker Books were planning to re-issue *The Good Little Christmas Tree*, Anthea Morton-Saner, who succeeded O'Hea at Curtis Brown, wrote to Julia MacRae at Walker stressing how important the title was to the author, and saying she wanted to be sure she would be "really happy with the pictures." Nevertheless, MacRae chose Gillian Tyler as the artist, for whom it was a first book commission, and of whom Ursula knew nothing. To her annoyance, it appeared with Tyler's dedication and without her own. The author nevertheless wrote to Tyler, saying how much she liked her work, although privately she thought them pretty but unmemorable compared with her own original cut-outs. When the then struggling artist explained that she had taken more than a year to produce the highly detailed artwork, Ursula advised her about Public Lending Rights, and happily agreed to share such revenues equally.[12]

In many publishing houses, an artist would normally communicate with a writer only by sending roughs of characters for approval via the firm's children's book editor. Glenys Ambrus, who worked on *Bellabelinda and the No-Good Angel* of 1982, found it easy to imagine and portray the characters from Ursula's descriptions in the text. Sometimes, however, author and illustrator would speak on the telephone, as illustrator Gunvor Edwards recalled:

> Just hearing her voice cheered one up a lot, a real storyteller's voice I thought. Imagine how exciting to make friends with Aunt Hegarty [*The Cruise of the Happy-Go-Gay*] – the exact voice of authority our own children needed – and *Tiger Nanny* with her carrycot just like our own baby Tamsin's, who grew up to be a real fan of *Gobbolino* and *Spid* [1985]. We had a feeling of excitement

awaiting the arrival of the next of her books. She kindly invited me down to her place, but we never managed to get together.

One who accepted the invitation was Tor Morisse, who travelled from Sweden in September 1986 ostensibly to talk about what was to become Ursula's last title, *Paddy on the Island*. From the moment that he arrived at Evesham railway station, however, it was clear that this would be more of a holiday than a business trip.

> It was like a reunion of old friends … It was quite a trip back to her cottage in her little Renault, with her blind in one eye, and pointing in all directions, gesturing and talking. Then we had a stroll in the garden, and sat down with a toast of whisky for a chat. After a while she felt a little tired. 'Please excuse me, Tor, it's time for my afternoon nap, but feel free to wander over the premises and I'll see you for dinner.' And what a dinner it was. She was a magnificent and remarkable person.

He and his family continued to visit regularly. "That old house, the nursery and the garden have always stayed in my memories like a perfect dream," his daughter Py fondly remembered, "but I was always petrified when she picked me up – the world's worst driver."

Ursula was not beyond inviting illustrators to visit or stay, even when she was aged eighty-nine and unwell. Paul Howard had been commissioned to produce colour pictures for the Kingfisher 2001 editions of *Gobbolino, the Witch's Cat* and *Adventures of the Little Wooden Horse* and sent two versions of the latter, one with a flat front, the other, eventually adopted, with "a bosom," as Ursula described it. She loved the finished books, as many young relatives and friends discovered that Christmas, and told him so, but their letters also exchanged bits of family news, and although Ursula could no longer accommodate visitors, she assured Howard she could put him up locally if he came to show her his other work. "Her letters exuded a warmth that made you feel special," he said. "She was always complimentary and remains to this day the author that I enjoyed working with the most. She always seemed to be someone who was eternally young at heart and optimistic in outlook."

Ursula formed friendships with many of her artists, among them Shirley Hughes and Faith Jaques. One lasted, albeit on a fairly casual level; the other, more intense, did not.

British publishers had started to appoint children's editors in the 1950s, and the advance in offset-litho presses in the following decade had strengthened their role. Full-colour printing was still expensive, but due to the high volume of initial waste that it generated, the greater the print run, the lower the unit cost became. Publishers therefore were starting to seek partnership agreements in the US and Europe, and for this the required standard of illustration was consequently raised. In a very small way, the effects could be seen in Ursula's work – after *The Nine Lives of Island Mackenzie*, and the interruption of her career by cancer, she was to illustrate only one of the twenty-eight volumes that appeared under her name during the rest of her career.

Like Ursula, Shirley Hughes had studied life drawing, and with the additional knowledge of theatre design excelled in drawing chubby, real flesh-and-blood characters at moments of domestic drama. "I knew that drawing real children in action, in a naturalistic style, was my strong card," she wrote.[13] With her success in re-illustrating Dorothy Edwards's *My Naughty Little Sister* stories, she seemed the perfect designer for the stage on which many of Ursula's stories were set. That *A Crown for a Queen* avoids soppiness owes as much to her finely judged drawings – with the heroine Jenny a familiar tousle-haired figure – as to the text. Commissions for other titles by Ursula followed: *The Toymaker's Daughter*, re-issues of others in the series, and for *Bogwoppit* published in 1978. When Hughes beat her deadline for the Toymaker titles by three weeks, the author appreciated her efforts so much that she suggested to O'Hea that she might pass on more of her royalty share. Her agent told her that this was not a good idea.

When they met, Hughes was struck by Ursula's "impressive" appearance – "quite large, with white hair, dressed rather well in a slightly arty way." She was struck even more by her animation. "She was confident, an old hand, very established and hugely thought of, but particularly pleasant, very nice and very generous." If they talked about Hughes' illustrations, however, it was after they had been completed, not before. She explained, "You don't get anywhere by meeting an author socially, and this can get in the way. You work from the text and get far more from what they have written. The author doesn't know whether to say how they think a character looks – and anyway that's not a help. You are like an actor – you just have to get into that part."

Jaques had just illustrated *Charlie and the Chocolate Factory* by Roald Dahl when Rayner Unwin suggested her for *Mog*. Apart from the superb craftsmanship that also made her a regular contributor of black-and-white drawings to magazines such as *Radio Times* and *Strand*, the artist was known for her meticulous research. Appropriately, the only suggestion that passed between illustrator and author, via publisher, was technical. Jaques noted that the text described Mog and a child riding on a moped, and pointed out that a moped with its engine at the back, could not carry a passenger. Did she mean a motor scooter? Ursula made the necessary change.[14]

While Jaques was working on *Mog* for George Allen & Unwin, Ursula added her support to an approach from Evelyn Edwards at Chatto & Windus for Jaques to illustrate her next book, *Johnnie Golightly and his Crocodile*, despite Ursula's privately expressed reservations that Jaques could be too serious and lacking a sense of humour.[15] The story tells how Johnnie's landlady Mrs Minneapolis (Roy Griffin, whom Ursula's former nanny Rita had married in 1957, was in Minneapolis when it was written) is polishing the furniture, and while brushing the teeth of Johnnie's pet crocodile, is accidentally swallowed. The indomitable lady, for ever cheerful, issues her sensible instructions from inside its tummy, in order that she might be released without herself or the insouciant reptile getting hurt.

The project seems to have gone well enough, despite Jaques lamenting how difficult it was to draw crocodiles. Ursula wrote, as usual, to tell the illustrator how much she enjoyed her work on both titles, and how she hoped that Jaques would collaborate on her next, a picture book to be called *A Picnic with the Aunts*. They began to exchange long letters, six pages or more, not just about publishing matters, but about their working methods, about the frustrations of making money from writing and illustrating, about growing up, and about their families and cats. Jaques revealed that she had known Alan at Oxford – not well apparently because she thought he was Scandinavian. In an early letter she lamented sacrificing so much of her life to look after her now demented mother. Ursula wrote back sympathetically describing her own experiences, and repeated an earlier invitation to stay at Court Farm. Jaques came in February 1971, bringing Jane Birkett from Chatto & Windus on this first overnight visit, to talk about *A Picnic with the Aunts*.

The short story tells of six boys who, taken for a picnic on an island in a lake by their six aunts, become bored by supervised games and good behaviour. They abandon their elders and run wild on the shore. At the climax, the aunts swim back to take them home, their curious bonnets marvellously preserved, while the youngsters sob, thinking their aunts have drowned. The unusual plot had a curious history. It almost certainly came from a treasured portrait of the six Spicer sisters (Mabel's mother and her five aunts) photographed in spectacular millinery in 1907 at Mabel and Moray's wedding, and re-imagined perhaps at Stoneham lake. A first draft, entitled *The Prisoners on the Island*, was improbably aimed at older readers, and a revised version had been intended for a "bad boys" collection of short stories by Eileen Colwell, before it was decided that it best suited the picture book format.

Jaques, who had accumulated a huge reference library of historical costume and architecture, must have revelled in the commission. Ursula suggested slight modifications to her drawings, including one of a horse-drawn charabanc to resemble the open cart in which she went for a picnic when she was seven. Jaques visited at least three times during 1972, on the final occasion bringing a copy of the finished book, "For dear Ursula, with thanks for a story I loved so much; working on it was sheer pleasure all the way." Within a fortnight, Ursula had sent her another short story, this time even more directly based on memories of Stoneham, *Grandpapa's Folly and the Woodworm-Bookworm*, and although the artist said that pressure of work meant she could not finish it for two years, the author was prepared to wait. The setting comprises a library with imitation books, a domed hall suitable for roller skating, a music room and grounds with a lake that freezes. The plot, which seems secondary, is a confusing one involving a woodworm who cuts words from books to leave a message for the grandchildren. The words so neatly extracted by the little creature were to be printed in red by the publisher so that actual readers could decipher his message too. Ursula posted photographs of the old mansion to her illustrator, as well as a sketch of the hall, and a description of the library and staircase. "I am not at all worried about likeness, it's the period that counts," she wrote.[16] They might have talked more freely face-to-face, but by the time that Jaques set to work, the two were no longer on speaking terms.

The two personalities made a combustible compound. Andrew said of his mother:

> ... she could take the legs from almost anyone at a stroke by being so totally, unorthodoxly rude. If she did not entirely approve, she might give an indication of just what she was thinking. The older she got, the naughtier she would become. A comment would mortify the strongest of personalities. 'Shut up, let me talk,' she would say. That's how she controlled things.

According to James, she had little experience of the commercial world in which individuals had to push themselves forward to succeed. "Mother liked people to observe unspoken rules – don't be boring. People might irritate mother if they talked too much." Jaques was garrulous. That quality no doubt helped in her role as a redoubtable warrior on behalf of more timid colleagues in the Society of Authors.[17] Hughes remembered her as a superb artist, a forceful and quite prickly personality, and an unsung hero in the battle to include illustrators in Public Lending Rights, but quite difficult to get on with.

Things went badly from the moment Jaques got off the train in July 1973. Jaques talked constantly about personal worries, and about troubles with her mother. Ursula seemed on edge, the more because her guest had brought her dog and took him upstairs to her bedroom. Relations were strained. To escape, Jaques went off to walk around the church, and longed for the weekend to be over. After three days, they parted coolly. Ursula was not one, however, to give up on a friendship easily, and two days later wrote to Jaques hoping to restore the previous state of affairs. Her purpose was cloaked, as it were, in a small subterfuge, for she sent a raincoat which, she said, her guest had left behind. If the gesture was honestly meant, however, it was not the most delicately managed.

Enclosed with the coat was a book, Radclyffe Hall's study of Sapphic love *The Well of Loneliness*, and a letter both jaunty in tone, and offering a measure of contrition. Ursula and her sister had both found the book "fascinating and a wonderful picture of such a subject," and "so compassionate," she wrote. "You will like the riding parts. I still don't know what lesbians <u>do</u>." She apologised for being snappy, but crucially went on to her "dear generous clever and intelligent Faith … you do pack more words in a minute than anyone else and we just can't get a word in edgeways. … You said your mother was a compulsive talker. I would have been if some years ago someone had not told me, 'Ursula don't talk so <u>much</u> and so <u>fast</u>. People don't like it'."[18]

A note came back. "Dear Ursula, I'd sooner forget the whole thing," it begins, then predictably goes into a tirade of vituperation, the tiny italic handwriting crammed across a horizontal page, without margins, and with more crossed out words as it progresses. Ursula had delivered "a string of absolutely slashing remarks," and had "a surprising ability to hurt," it said, and concluded that it was best for both not to have much contact, and never to meet again. Jaques, who never married, returned the book unread, with the coat which was not hers.[19]

She continued to work on the book, and raised points about the smallest details, such as the type of brush that Mabel had used for applying beeswax to the furniture. In answering them, Ursula tried to revive her familiar chatty tone, relating for example how several people had walked out when Roald Dahl had recited a "very crude and grubby" sex story at a book festival she had attended. She also told her artist, "It's our book, and we're both in it come rain come shine." A few months later Jaques gave her the original painting of the cover design, signed "with love and fond memories."[20] The reconciliation had come about, however, only as a direct result of a greater misfortune.

Chapter 18

"My darlings, you have been so sheltered, you cannot possibly know how they live."

The children who attended meetings of the Puffin Club were very different from those with whom Ursula was becoming increasingly involved in her own community. The former selected themselves by an enthusiasm for books; the latter were usually characterised by a limited capacity to read anything. Through her work as a magistrate, often on the juvenile bench, she had built a close working relationship with the head teacher of a school for children classed as educationally sub-normal at Malvern. When the similar Vale of Evesham School opened, she was appointed in January 1969 onto its board. English teachers and librarians told her of their frustration that most stories that their pupils could read contained subject matter that was "too babyish" to interest them. Within a few days of taking up her official role at the school, she wrote to Smallwood proposing a series of books for backward readers.

As it happened, Ursula had written *Terry's Tree*, a delightful story for a Puffin anthology about to appear in aid of the Save the Children Fund, which suggested some elements of the style that older but poorer readers might engage with. Terry, who suffers from cerebral palsy, is four, "bright as a button inside his head," and makes his brothers laugh when he thinks Christmas trees are silver and grow in Woolworths. They take him instead to a plantation where he chooses one by hanging a silver ball on it. Terry hopes to see it grown bigger each time the boys return, but by the time they come finally to collect it, all the trees have been stolen, and the boys have run into a little trouble with the police. The story appeared in a "collection of happy ending stories especially written by your favourite authors to help children with no happy ending in view." Accordingly, it is the policeman who saves the day, telling Terry that the Mayor had chosen his tree for the Town Hall – and there, to his delight and amazement, in the square, grown much larger, is the great fir, with a ball just like Terry's. Or not very different.[1]

Ursula wrote the story in the first person – one of very few occasions she had used that format since *Grandfather* – taking advantage of the loving insight of an elder brother to describe Terry in lively, simple language. Ursula planned to develop the style in a new series of short stories, written with short words in short sentences, each on a new line, and with the distinctive feature that the last page could relate to almost any point of the adventure – like a happy ending on demand, to which the bored or emotionally disturbed child could turn for comfort. She thought of each book as being "exciting and slightly poetic – [with] repetition, vision, with very rarely a long and difficult word that is an interesting word – like 'panorama' that a child would recognise in a sudden flash in quite a different context."[2]

Smallwood responded enthusiastically and within a fortnight Ursula sent the initial three stories, one of which had already been seen by the Malvern principal, who recommended it for boys aged ten plus with a reading age of eight or just below. With the project being handled by Chatto & Windus's Educational division, the author found herself writing for a specialist market for the first time since her books for Brownies, and for a much more exacting one. Editor Geoffrey Trevelyan sent the stories to teachers who tried them on their classes and reported back on the results, mostly but not always favourably. It would not be the only occasion when educators would try to tell the writer how to write. "All three stories need *considerable* revision to make acceptable in my view," wrote one. "I am doubtful about taking on stories for a *specialized* market written by someone other than a reading expert." For Ursula it was a slow and irritating process, during which she completely rewrote some items, and changed details in others. One exchange about the story *Traffic Jam* concerned the best way to grab a swan – by the neck or around the body. Tevelyan described how his neighbours had manhandled an injured bird into their car. Ursula responded with the story of the swan on Overbury Estate that survived for several years after having one broken wing amputated. She solved the dilemma by having two policemen seize the animal using both methods.

The protracted discussion does provide a greater than usual degree of insight into the author's selection and treatment of subject matter. She continued to discuss the project with Norman Moore, headmaster of the new school, who advised her that early teenage girls were the worst catered for, but that their interest was instantly awakened "by anything related to babies, boyfriends, weddings and clothes!" Moore also supported her use of the first person, which Ursula had employed for all the stories in order to stimulate the involvement of her young readers, but for which she had been criticised. "Writing in the third person is stultifying for this kind of work, for one thing one is almost completely cut off from colloquialisms," she told Trevelyan. To satisfy her professional critics, she tried to recast the narratives in the third person, or at least said she did, but gave up.

———————

During this period, in the early 1970s, Ursula was "bursting with ideas," sometimes writing an entire story on the kitchen table in the morning, and returning after midnight to answer points from her publisher. She seems to have submitted eighteen in all, of which fourteen appeared in four small volumes issued, after much head-scratching, under the title *Hurricanes*. This, it was thought, would appeal more to ten-year-olds than Ursula's earlier suggestions of *Kangaroo* and *Terrapin*. Some of the themes are familiar: a troublesome goat, an imitative parrot, and a variation on an episode about a disastrous Pancake Day, which had already been used in *Goodbody's Puppet Show*. Others suggest the writer's own biography: a story of baby twins, a dramatic account of volcanic eruption in Iceland, and in particular the story *Out of the Shadows* of the apprehensive young bride referred to in an early chapter. The range of storylines, however, is wide, from a gripping story of a dog sled team trapped in the Arctic, to pigeon racing. Bearing in mind the background of some of her potential readers, there is a story about the son of a Jamaican bus conductor, and tales of boys with delinquent tendencies and soft but not sentimental hearts. Ursula's long experience of reading to groups of children, and her habit of building longer works from individual episodes rather than from one grand design, had made her particularly adept at the short story. Little gems such as *The Fire and Old Tim Taylor* and *The Wild Goose* would surely have earned greater recognition had they not been written in such staccato style, appropriate and effective for its particular audience, but rather off-putting for other readers.

Other short stories continued to appear here and there, such as in anthologies by Noel Streatfeild and Barbara Willard, and in *Puffin Post*. The best were usually enlivened by that spiky humour with which one can visualise the author drawing in a live audience of young children like fish on a line. What little girl, uncertain about her own looks, could not both laugh and be comforted by *The Story of a Plain Princess:*

> …[who] was not plain ugly, which is often nice, especially with a smile. She was ugly ugly. Back, front and sides, in fact ugly ugly ugly. Inside she had a kind, warm heart, but how was anyone to know that? She never smiled, or tried to be anything but ugly. … The knights who came to fight for her were ashamed to wear her shabby favours on their armour at the tournaments. The dragons who came to eat her, didn't.

Of course the princess finds love and happiness, which make her pretty. But after her wedding – with plain bridesmaids – she doesn't change her shabby habits, wearing her wedding dress "outside out in summer and inside out in winter," until her chimney sweep husband gives her a new one after twenty-five years.[3]

By comparison, many of Ursula's longer works written around this period are of comparatively lesser interest. It was almost as if, after the frustration of *Castle Merlin* and the highly functionalised writing of the *Hurricanes* stories, she wanted a return to the familiarly flippant. Certainly, *No Ponies for Miss Pobjoy* is one of her oddest, most regressive titles, with its high jinx in a girls' school on the South Downs. Certainly, not many of those backward readers were ever likely to read a sentence like: "If the fees were up again Daddy would have expostulated at once, Frances thought."[4] Like some prolific composers, Ursula reworks old ideas, her leitmotifs, the pony that gets stuck in the house, the donkey that starts backwards, and throws in a few ideas that have been hanging around looking for employment – an archaeologist and even an ancient Stoneham-like water pump.

O'Hea disliked it. "You have touched me on a very raw spot by using animals who talk, Black Beauty notwithstanding," she wrote after a disappointing weekend with the typescript. "I adored Mackenzie so much because he was a thinking cat and not a talking cat. … I also felt the children were universally so against Miss Pobjoy that it became rather unpleasant." There was even an attempt to kill the head, which the author removed, together with the equine dialogue. None of Ursula's books are without vivacity, or closely observed details of life's detritus, but despite rewrites over the next three years, this one remains as flaccid as its main point of invention on which the plot turns – when the pony-hating headmistress trades in an Aston Martin car for a horse of the same name. After its eventual publication in 1975, Ursula described it as a satire. It seems unlikely that many ten-year-old girls would have appreciated it as such.[5]

Ursula had just turned sixty when she started writing *The Kidnapping of my Grandmother*. If one accepts her previous book a little reluctantly as a satire, there seems little doubt that this one was intended as an allegory, with someone like herself as the main character. On her birthday, the lady in question leaves her flat in "Rue Perrelet," Paris, and is kidnapped while scattering sweets. Her kidnappers, orphan children, demand toys and books, especially their favourite about a little wooden horse. All foil a timely if unlikely raid by real bandits, and rather than seeing the dirty, savage-looking, fag-smoking but dear youngsters sent to an orphanage "like caged sparrows," Grandmother installs them in her house, telling her initially aggrieved grandchildren: "My darlings, you have been so sheltered, you cannot possibly know how they live." The unidentified *TLS* critic said the enchanting book rose "triumphantly above both realism and moralizing," and was "full of humour and charm, and the kind of effortless artistry that is as rare as it is satisfying."[6]

The comments must have been gratifying for this grandmother on whose time so many other children had claims. Increasingly, she had to be mindful also of looking after Peter, who seems to have suffered a mild heart attack in the spring of 1971. Partly as a consequence of this she stepped down as a governor of Evesham High School, although she remained on the board at Vale of Evesham next door. Court duties were also time-consuming, not only as a magistrate at Evesham, but in meetings with probation officers and social workers, and in lengthy cases at Quarter Sessions in Worcester that sometimes lasted from 10.30 a.m. to 5.30 p.m. for seven consecutive weekdays or more. In addition, after her years as an ordinary magistrate, Ursula was about to become chairman of Evesham Juvenile Court. Had she not been a writer, it was a job she might have been born for.

Evesham was not an area that entertained many serious criminals, apart from those on occasional nocturnal outings from Birmingham. The young man who rode naked through the town, the one who peeped through a neighbour's window, and the splendid "Anonymous dog in collision" were enough to make headlines in the local newspaper. Market gardeners were wise to watch their sprouts before Christmas. Young offenders were charged mainly with vandalism, like the boy who kicked in the windows of a telephone box after watching a Kung Fu film, vehicle theft (from lorries to milk floats), or petty theft. Those not dealt with on the spot found themselves in a large courtroom next to Evesham police station, with its high metal windows illuminating the magistrates' bench at the top. From 1972, when Ursula stepped up to become chairman, they would look up slightly to see a soberly-dressed figure in a black suit and a pale blouse, her silvery hair tucked under a small black, close-fitting hat that was not compulsory for women magistrates, but was required by local custom.

Cases could take some time. Ursula always sat alongside a male colleague and usually one other magistrate, and frequently called them into the retiring room to discuss privately the background of the young person awaiting their decision. One of the magistrates was John Johnson. He recalled:

> She would never rush into making her mind up. She would listen to what everyone said, and by the time you had heard her two-pennyworth, you often changed your mind. She talked about a lot of children suffering from poverty, seeing others enjoying life when they should be, and about the construction of the family, but she would also say, 'You can only help those who want to help themselves.' She was exceptionally good at delving into the background. 'Let's have a look at what his family is,' she would say, so a back light driving offence could take an hour.

John Darlington regularly attended the court as a prosecutor, yet he welcomed a new generation of magistrates who did not necessarily accept police evidence without asking questions. "I always felt with Ursula John and others of her kind that they were thinking of nothing else but the case, trying to find the right solution. Thank God for magistrates like Ursula," he said. "I'm no softie, but I want criminals to have a fair crack of the whip." From the press bench, Hilary Sinclair often heard the chairman make her concerns clear in the open court.

> 'You cannot always judge the person – you have to look at the background,' she said, and often she was giving a long list of mitigation that the defence solicitor should have given. But she used to get stuck in on the old domestic courts when couples came in and started arguing together.

The work, Ursula confessed, could be "gruelling" in extent and intractability, but what she took closest to her heart and gave her the greatest anxiety, particularly in her first year as juvenile chairman, was the search to find the best outcomes for seemingly ungovernable and often unhappy young offenders. One traumatic and salutary experience came when a mother made such an outcry at being parted from her son who was being sent to a remand home for three weeks. Ursula and her colleagues were upset for days. Later, they were told that during the entire period the woman neither visited her son, nor sent any message. The governor reported that the effect on the boy was crushing.

As a magistrate she became familiar with penal institutions for all ages, and saw the germ of adult criminality in the upbringing and treatment of offenders when they were young. Family circumstances "count so much in a child's development, being sure someone loves him, and enough not to let him down. Some never get enough all their lives and pay society out as a result," she wrote after visiting a long-term prison, where she found "the sense of sheer isolation from the outside world … terrifying."[7]

A year after becoming chairman of the juvenile bench, a speaking invitation gave Ursula the unusual opportunity to explain her views explicitly. She talked about the harm done unknowingly to children, so spoilt and indulged at home that they were likely to receive twice their share of knocks in the world, but most of all she talked about the factors that brought so many young people to court. "Broken homes, homes where affection has broken down, are so prevalent behind all delinquency," she said.

> I feel that children in trouble, prisoners, and all delinquents, need kindness as a lock needs oil. Of course, they need punishment too, and oddly enough they are the first to recognise it. But we go on loving our own children when we punish them. … Over and over you hear it said: 'Nobody thinks of the victims!' But it isn't true. The victims do get kindness and sympathy automatically as they well deserve, and they cannot have too much, but the delinquent does need it too.

The 1971 Guardianship of Minors Act had given much greater responsibility to social workers who knew families intimately and could advise about health, marital and educational difficulties. With the "simply admirable" Probation Service, they had changed the atmosphere in which magistrates adjudicated. "Mind you we do consider kindness to be one of our functions, and when you hear cases criticised as differing wildly in penalties from each other, don't be too hasty in condemning the Bench," Ursula told members of a local Mothers' Union.

> Behind each case the quality of mercy is also at work: how many children are there in the family? Will the wife suffer unduly from a heavy fine? … Kindness does beget kindness. We now call our old approved schools community homes, with a significant suggestion of family affection and atmosphere. We are slowly, oh so slowly, turning our prisons into something more humane than the relics of the mediaeval oubliette we have known for

far too long.[8]

One of those probation officers with whom Ursula worked was Audrey "Andy" Moore, who learnt to admire the new juvenile chairman immensely. She now lives in a pretty Cotswold village far removed in every way from those of County Durham where she was once a police sergeant. A lurcher bounds toward visitors through the small hallway. The sofa is covered with teddy bears and a large Winnie the Pooh, all getting on a bit. It's not clear who comforts whom. Surrounding her are half a dozen large portraits of her dogs, all of them once unfortunates, abandoned or adopted from rescue shelters, rather like many of the sad human cases who passed through her hands, but with a far greater likelihood of redemption. Moore sits in front of the fire, with her leg on the coffee table to ease an aching joint, and remembers Mrs John fondly, out of the court as well as in it.

> I had to see someone in Beckford late one evening and she said I should pop in for a drink after the call. I went up and she had made the most marvellous three-course meal served on the long refectory table in the kitchen, all set out with crystal and silver. I was so taken aback, I felt like I was dining with the Queen, but that was just like her.

What did she remember best of her work as a magistrate? "Her smile," Moore said. "She was a lovely lady, a very caring person. She wanted to know the whys and wherefores in the nicest possible way, and did not like sending people to prison. She was prepared to listen to what the probation service said, and she got her way with other magistrates because she had a lot of feeling for people. Whoever chose her to be a magistrate did the best thing in the world."

Most cases on which Ursula was called to pass sentence were minor, but she used the occasions to comment on wider issues in the lives of those facing her. Speaking firmly, but quietly, in a voice that scarcely reached to the back of the room, and with kindly eyes directed at the young person at the front of the court, she told vandals of the trouble they brought "to themselves and their parents." After fining the father of a boy who had accidentally broken a windscreen, she advised the miscreant to get a spare time job to repay him. A youth caught shooting rats on the Avon was urged to take up fishing. A fifteen-year-old playing truant after the school leaving age was raised to sixteen, was told, "You are not the only boy chafing at the new law, but … it is your right to be educated, and only a fool throws his rights away."[9]

Occasionally there were cases, which for all their essential sadness, brought out a more appealing side of human nature. One such concerned a tramp who had been stealing bacon, and might have got away with his crime had not the acute nose of a passing policeman detected the smell of rashers being fried under the Avon bridge. The man had a long record of theft, but seemed unusually upset at being sent down for a month. "It's not the sentence, your honour, it's my dog," he said. "We'll look after his dog," the Chief Inspector broke in, and the man went off quite cheerfully. The dog spent a comfortable month in one of the policemen's houses before being reunited with its master.[10]

No doubt away from the court, Ursula's appreciation of the absurd could also be indulged with the unlikely explanations sometimes offered for juvenile misbehaviour, as in a short poem aptly called *Trick Cyclist*.

We took my little brother
To a chap called Sikey Ike,
'Cos he ran a pussy over
On his little three-wheeled bike …
And when the talk was over
Very gently Sikey said –
"Why run poor Pussy over?
And make poor Pussy dead?"
"I though it was a cow pat,"
My little brother said.[11]

During the early 1970s, although court work was demanding, it seems to have made little difference to Ursula's determination to support writers' seminars, book fairs, visit schools, and judge children's writing competitions around the country, including one for the BBC with 4,000 entries. At Tewkesbury, not only did she assess stories written by local children , but also dressed their authors as the Pied Piper and rats, which looked "quite ferocious." A nativity play written for Beckford primary had to be revised at the last minute because no one could find a donkey quiet enough.

It was, nevertheless, something of a relief in December 1971 to sit down in front of her smallest audience, and one of her most attentive. The entire assembly of the little school on the island of St Agnes in the Isles of Scilly, just four pupils, knew her books well, she reported with satisfaction after her visit. Ursula had regularly interrupted holidays to call in on local schools, and her appearance on this occasion also came during a short break that she and Peter had arranged after "an exacting summer."

They would previously have gone to High Winds, but its condition, always spartan, was deteriorating. Other members of the family used it less often, and its owner had asked to quadruple the annual rent. The lease was surrendered. For twenty years, Ursula had spent writing holidays on the Pembrokeshire cliff-top, the most westerly promontory in Wales. There must have been a fascination in the remoteness of the location, as much as in its wild character. Peter had loved long drives – his idea of a proper day out had been to pack the family into the car, motor down to somewhere like Seaton, and, after a five-minute stroll along the Devon sea front, pack them in again for the journey back. But for Ursula the attraction lay in the seclusion of favourite destinations such as High Winds, the northern Highlands of Scotland, or the Western Isles that felt like they were "miles off the map."

Appropriately enough, the hotel they had chosen was the Bell Rock, St Mary's, which claims to be the most southerly in England. After spreading her writing across the oval dining table at High Winds or the large refectory table at home, it was a little constricting to clear a space on the dressing table, but she was "full of ideas." Also, as Robin had moved from New Zealand to Canada, Ursula and Peter were planning to travel there the following year to meet him and his wife-to-be, so this was an additional reason that she was working "extremely hard to earn some money and trying to get 3,000 words written every day." By the end of her ten-day stay, she had set down in longhand around 15,000 words – about two-thirds – of *Tiger Nanny*. In January she took the typescript to O'Hea in London, carrying gifts as usual – a dozen large brown eggs, a bouquet of Christmas roses, and a pheasant. The book was rejected by Chatto & Windus, where Jane Birkett felt the writing "seemed to lack Ursula's usual wit and exuberance," but taken instead by Ian Aitken then at Brockhampton Press.[12]

The story is packed, almost to excess, with adventure – a film star, a hijacking, a baby prince, castaways, and a revolt of rebels armed with guns, poison and a tranquiliser dart. Yet however exotic the scene, the ordinary rules apply, or at least those of which the author would approve. The children speak as children do: "[You] look just like puddings. I shall eat you … only I know you will taste disgusting. … I'd rather eat a frog." And Tiger Nanny reforms the unruly by teaching them courtesy and respect. In a neat overturning of life, the youngest boy goes to sleep without his fluffy toy, and although Tiger Nanny thinks him too young to go to boarding school, he insists on doing so. A happy ending is assured when the film star has twins.[13]

Despite the author's faculty at writing quickly, from 1972 she wrote relatively little by her normal standards for the next two years. There was an uncompleted adaptation of *The Three Toymakers* for a planned production in Iceland, *Grandpapa's Folly and the Woodworm Bookworm* at just over 2000 words in length, and a few short stories, including those published as *The Line*. Even the revisions of *No Ponies for Miss Pobjoy* were not completed until the summer of 1974. Undoubtedly, the principal causes were the greater responsibilities of the juvenile bench, and what appears to have been a generally increased workload as a JP in court and at meetings and conferences. There were also family factors.

Aunt Ella, now ninety-three years old, had been ill for some time. Ursula continued to call in at her home during trips to London, but when she did so in October 1973, for what would be the last time, her "dearest and least demanding aunt" was unable to understand what was being said to her. Two weeks later she died. Ursula, who never attended the funerals of those she loved, stayed away from the cremation. Closer to home, Peter's sister Jo, who had moved to a village five miles from Beckford, had started a sudden decline into ill health. Until only a short time earlier, the former concert pianist had continued to give piano lessons, but within a short period her tall figure appeared frail, her face matching the pallor of her grey wig. The humour that lightened her rather stern features seemed to drain away. She looked a little lost and dependent when Ursula came to do her gardening.

Jo probably realised that there was a limit to the amount of help her sister-in-law could provide, for at the same time Peter had also been feeling unwell, and exhausted even by walking along the lane to the village. At the close of the year, Ursula wrote to Rita, her former nanny, explaining that she hoped to do a lot more writing in 1974, but first she needed to help with redecorating. "I can't let Peter do it all alone," she wrote. "He has been pretty tired lately and goes to bed about 6 p.m. I hope it is only Christmas and the end of the bad cold he had, but he does seem to have lost a bit of ground this year. But after all he's two years off 70, and so long as he enjoys what he can do, it is all right." By February, he did not seem to have shaken off the malady.[14]

Chapter 19

————

"We have been so happy ... Wasn't it wonderful?"

Richard Calver drew back the curtain across a window of the large guest bedroom at Court Farm late on the morning of 10 March 1974, and caught his breath. Inches of snow had fallen overnight, and as it was Sunday they lay unsullied by footprints or tyre tracks across the lanes and fields that stretched away toward the Malverns. From his high vantage point, it was a magnificent and unexpected sight, a picture of beauty and peacefulness to take home as a memento of his first, happy visit to the aunt who had been so generous to him. His parents would love it too. He reached for his camera.[1]

The family friendship went back generations. It was Richard's grandfather Sidney Unwin who had brought Ursula's parents together at Bedales seventy years previously, and Sidney's daughter Helen had remained among her dearest cousins. As godmother to Helen's son Richard, Ursula wrote to him regularly, often offering advice that might help him "cope with the world at large." After he complained about the frustrations of school life, for example, she sent a long letter, pointing out that "many outdated rules would be so much better changed," but that if older pupils like Richard got away with protests, the younger ones would emulate them without being "mature enough to view such issues in the wisest way." He should "spare a spot of sympathy for the senior staff ... who have to go on and on and on, poor devils, coping with advancing ideas." And if despite all this, "you are going to be rude, be clever and always do it politely." It was typical that she should choose to dedicate to him, in June 1965, a book like *High Adventure*, with its model of a gutsy boy doing a good turn.

In Richard's case, Ursula had the intense additional pleasure of witnessing the development of his exceptional musical talent. She listened to recordings of him playing the piano and organ, and travelled to Harrogate to hear him sing with his choir. The ten-year-old cherished the visit as much for the bag of fish and chips that they shared in the street afterwards as for the interest that his godmother had shown in travelling so far for the performance. Ursula had regularly sent gramophone records to her godson – Benjamin Britten was a particular favourite – or money to buy them. She was full of praise when Richard gave up a summer holiday to take a manual job and earn pocket money. "People do respect a man who isn't afraid to dirty his hands," she told him, well knowing his inclination toward intellectual rather than physical pursuits. But when in 1973, Richard confirmed his intention to try for the Royal College of Music, she determined that a special gift would be in order. "If he is going to be a professional musician," she told Helen, "he had better hear some of the best musicians before he enters college." Better still, it should involve a trip to Europe, and for that Ursula would pay the entire cost.

In March 1973 Richard was delighted to open a letter from Ursula containing a cheque. "I have stretched it to £60 to help you take a fortnight, but that will have to include your next birthday, which I'm sure you will agree is fair," she wrote. "Let me know what you fix up. I have never been to Salzburg or Vienna so shall be very interested and even envious." Richard recalled: "I didn't know any Continental festivals apart from Salzburg, so I picked that one. It was all done through an agency. It turned out I had chosen the most exclusive and expensive one. I wasn't a huge opera fan before that, but it was absolutely brilliant."

He wrote with descriptions of the concerts: the staging of the *Barber of Seville* by the Salzburg Marionette Theatre, a sublime *Marriage of Figaro* conducted by Herbert von Karajan, and one of the first, and few, performances of Carl Orff's grim *De Temporum Fine Comoedia* (A Play at the End of Time), again under Karajan and which featured elderly singers suspended from the ceiling. But the letter could not do them justice. Richard was bursting to tell his stories in person, especially as he could be sure of a most attentive listener. "My main memory is of her always being interested in *me*," he said.

He hoped they could meet in London the following February, when Ursula was due to attend a BBC television recording of *Tiger Nanny for Jackanory*, read by Pat Hayes, but her busy schedule of meetings with publishers and agents made this impossible. Would he like to come instead for a night or two to Court Farm during half-term? She would pay his fare. It would be his first visit to the house, and as if to encourage him to take up the offer, she wrote at greater length than usual about its charms.

> Down here it is spring and I love it madly. They say one's life goes in a kind of circle and you gradually go back to liking and being what you just were – well I was crazy on being in lovely scenery and with wildlife and beauty and having a lot of time quite alone (I don't get much of that!) and a lot of reading, and both Peter and I find we don't want to go away much any more, and are not even planning for a summer holiday. We love this place so much.[2]

There was another attraction for the eighteen-year-old. Richard knew little about Ursula's husband beyond an association of him with fast cars that he knew from his favourite childhood book, *Peter on the Road* (originally published as *Peter and the Wanderlust*). They had never met, and Richard was curious and hoping to get to know him. It was to be an exciting introduction.

On the evening of Saturday 9 March, Richard arrived by train at Cheltenham to find Peter waiting for him with his top-of-the-range 3-litre Ford Capri GTX LR. He was "inordinately proud" of it, and keen to show what it could do. They took the longer route home, up the M5 motorway, where for the first time the impressionable teenager experienced the thrill of travelling at 100 mph. Then it was tea and back into Cheltenham for all three to see *Day of the Jackal*. They loved the film, and as Peter drove home, Richard could reflect on the start of a perfect weekend and look forward to the next day. Ursula had insisted that he should bring his camera. She needed more press photographs, she told him, and could pay him properly if any of his portraits were used. She was full of praise for the slides he showed after supper of his trip to Austria, and it was agreed that she would sit for a portrait session on the Sunday.

That day, Richard woke a little late, shortly after 9 a.m., unaware of the heavy snow that had fallen during the night. He dressed, opened the curtain, and was pleasantly astonished. At first, there seemed to be no one about. He took picture after picture – the fields and pathways merging into smooth contours, the branches bending under the clumps of white. Then he noticed Peter. He saw him briefly, behind a wall, in the courtyard leading to the log store, and then he was gone. "He disappeared downwards. I thought he had slipped, but a couple of minutes passed and he did not get up," Richard recalled. He ran downstairs, out through the front door, and found Peter lying in the snow. Richard ran to fetch Ursula from the house, then to summon help from the neighbouring farm. Together they carried him inside, but by then it was too late. The heart attack, which Ursula had feared for the past three years, had been fatal. Peter had stopped breathing in the few seconds that Ursula cradled him alone. He was sixty-nine years old.

It was one of those moments that when confronted by catastrophe, Ursula would demonstrate her steadfastness, of faith perhaps, and care for others. "She was very calm. She was collected and didn't lose control. Ursula seemed to be more concerned about me – worried that I would be all upset by finding him," Richard said. In the midst of death, there is life, even – as revealed by an importunate image that penetrated the consciousness of a widow's mind – humour. The family cat watched as the farm workers laid Peter's body on the couch before leaving. "Frankie just longed to go and sit on his chest, and I knew how tickled he'd have been, but I couldn't allow it because the police would have been so shocked," she wrote.[3]

Later that day, Ursula wrote a long letter to Barbara, then on a long holiday with the seventy-nine-year-old Magnús in Tenerife.

Richard … luckily saw it from the spare room window, as had he lain there I would always have thought he might have been calling me in vain, but he knew nothing. … Poor R. such an awful shock for him. I keep thinking how *splendid* for Peter, no illness, such a happy spring. He agreed a few weeks back that he no longer resisted the thought of dying but decided like me that it would be quite nice. … He used to say he'd hate to leave it all behind but he was getting tired and the doctor said it was angina. No pain ever, so lovely. I couldn't have borne to have left him alone if I'd died first … I couldn't have let him feel like this. We have been so happy and so lucky and loved each other so much and so dearly. I think the worst part will be having no-one to need or give so much love to, it's so different to one's love for children or friends.

As Richard sadly departed, the house filled with close family members; Andrew, Hugh, and James with their wives, and Peter's sister Jo, with whom Ursula had not always been on the best of terms, but who was "so good and brave and natural." Robin was due to fly from Canada on the Tuesday. Now there were practical matters to be seen to. "Peter was so good at it all, our accounts, the house repairs, the cars, the machines. I shall learn all I can and be as independent as possible but obviously the future holds no colours. I shall just make as good a job of it as possible to fill in the time left," she told her sister.

But as the awful day subsided, Ursula looked for a time of solitude and peace.

I'm longing to be alone and quiet … Today has been exhausting and a century long. But I'm quite all right really. I can adapt to almost anything and we have been so happy. I'm so grateful for it all, only I do want him back so badly. I don't think anyone knows how utterly loving and good he was to me. … I really am so thankful we had 38½ years. Wasn't it wonderful.

In the following turbulent days, industry offered an outlet for Ursula's overflowing emotion. Dozens of letters of appreciation were written to those sending letters of condolence, and in them she could define the remembrance of Peter's parting. One of the first people to whom she wrote was Helen Calver, reassuring her that Richard's presence had spared her additional pain. "One can never believe there'll be any colour in life again, but that is the weak and selfish side of one's horribly human nature," she wrote, "because everything I've prayed for has come true, Peter didn't become too old and ill to enjoy life, he did go suddenly without realising it, and he did go first. I just couldn't bear to think of him being left alone and feeling this sense of loss. So really I'm deeply grateful – we have had such a lovely time together, so much love and happiness." She was finding it hard to sleep, and it was 4 a.m. the following morning when she wrote also to Alan. The suddenness of Peter's death, she said, was "such a wonderful coup de grace and what I'd hoped for, as he was slowly losing ground, but still able to enjoy himself and the garden, but no longer long mad motor drives or travelling. Of course one never expects it to be 'now' but only 'to-morrow' and I'm cut in half, but I was prepared and so very grateful for all the love and wonderful happiness we have had. You and Barbara never saw his best side … but he was incredibly good to me, always, and spoiled me so."

Ursula and Peter had agreed not to attend the other's funeral, more because of her aversion to such events than any strong feelings on his part. "I have a horror of all funerals," she wrote to Alan years later. "Having seen so many die, and Peter so suddenly, I know how utterly <u>nothing</u> the body becomes and have no feeling for it at all." Accordingly, while the boys went to the cremation service, Ursula stayed away.

She did attend a "short, cheerful" memorial service two days later, conducted by a family friend, Eric Cordingly, Bishop of Thetford and formerly a vicar near Cheltenham, with verses read by Peter's four sons. James gave the final reading, one of Ursula's favourite texts from Philippians: "Finally, brethren, whatsoever things are true, whatsoever things are honest, whatsoever things are just, whatsoever things are pure, whatsoever things are lovely, whatsoever things are of good report; if there be any virtue, and if there be any praise, think on these things." Then, after the others had departed, on a fine evening a week after Peter's death, Ursula and Robin climbed the path running from the side of Court Farm to scatter his ashes at the top of Bredon Hill. There was, she wrote, "a gorgeous sunset westward over Wales, and in the east the misty spread of the Cotswolds under a blue sky." Larks were singing, flocks of plovers were tumbling, and above their heads was the vapour trail of an aircraft, an appropriate tribute, it seemed, to the departure of her adored pilot.

Chapter 20

"The room was full of bogwoppits, stamping, jiggling and dancing to the music."

Peter's death ended the breach with Faith Jaques, who wrote to Ursula as soon as she heard about the tragedy. The relationship was never again quite as unreserved as before, but Ursula wrote back, immediately and with "much love," perhaps finding in a fellow artist someone to whom she could express her feelings more completely even than to relatives. "One does feel completely unreal – cut in half, just searing agony, physical almost, and now an odd light-headedness," she wrote. "It's the small poignancies that get you – the garden coming so rapidly awake. I look at the polyanthuses that have come into flower since Sunday and nearly cry aloud 'Why can't you bloody little things wait?'" Already, four days after Peter's death, Ursula was "determined to be perfectly efficient and independent and not a misery to myself or anybody else." When the world had "stopped reeling, and we're both more used to the idea of the half emptiness of Court Farm," she suggested that Jaques come again. "We'll neither of us feel self-conscious or attempt to be anything but ourselves."[1]

For months Ursula's letters are full of references to her loss. She missed Peter "terribly," and felt "like a shell," but the practicalities of life quickly squeezed any space for self-pity out of her correspondence and her daily existence. In a typical week in July, she organised a garden party as President of the local Women's branch of the British Legion, held a hobby-horse gymkhana, and hosted a meeting of the village play group. The visit by Jaques had to be planned around a talk to a club for the elderly and a tour of a prison, not to mention "gruelling" court work that could last until 6.45 p.m. with only a short hour for lunch. "No tea these days – nobody cares. I bet our clients get one. One does get very tired, and we've lost two clerks of the court through overwork and strain," she complained. Magistrates could claim for lost working time and travel costs, "but on a rural bench like ours nobody ever does." Her diary included judging a literary competition and presenting prizes, trips to London to see O'Hea or for recordings of *Island Mackenzie* and *Tiger Nanny* at the BBC, duties as secretary of the Parochial Church Council and the Mothers' Union, the usual hospitality at home, and at least four scheduled book talks in the autumn. One of these talks was to the Federation of Children's Book Groups 'Witches and Wizards' event at Bolton. It involved an "awful journey – four changes and stood the last hour in the train," but Ursula was rewarded by the wonderful reception she described to Webb. "All kinds of possible witches, paintings, models, mobile scenes, thousands of children, far more than they expected, lots were turned away after queuing for ages in the rain. I've never signed so many autographs in my life." The insouciant young fan she liked best, however, was "the small and grubby boy who demanded a signature and then waved it in my face saying idly 'What's it for?' 'Your guess is as good as mine,' I replied."[2]

Ursula had been writing hard during the winter of 1973, especially after Christmas, despite the difficulties caused by the miners' strike and the three-day working week imposed by Prime Minister Edward Heath from January. During power cuts, she sat in the cold kitchen wearing thick jerseys and sheepskin boots, finishing a second draft of *No Ponies for Miss Pobjoy* for Chatto & Windus by candlelight. Even then, it seems the author was asked to make further revisions to satisfy Gloria Mosesson, now junior books editor at Thomas Nelson, New York which was publishing the American edition. Norman Thelwell, Fortnum and Jaques all turned down the art commission before it was taken up by Pat Marriott, an illustrator unknown to Ursula. Jaques reassured her, "Marriott does not do much because she married well and went to live in a splendid manor house in Wales. She only does books she likes and will be much better than I for Pobjoy."

Thus *Miss Pobjoy* found a happy ending. Not so the new book which Ursula was working on at the time of Peter's death. *An Author in the Garden* was surely not the most appealing title of a children's book that she had ever devised, and this unpromising start proved to be a portent of what was to follow. The writer sensed as much before it was finished. By February, she was having difficulties with the ending. "Possibly I went for it too fast," she told Jaques. Whatever problems Ursula was facing, the events of 10 March must have drained her enthusiasm to find their resolution, but not apparently exhausted her determination to do so, for less than four weeks later, O'Hea received the completed typescript. She enjoyed the story of Melanie Medrose and Veronica Flyweed enormously, and it made her laugh a great deal, she reported, but clearly the denouement had not been sorted out. The agent called it "confused," and complained that the "delightful" Flyweed lost the reader's sympathy as soon as she was revealed as a plagiarist of Medrose's titles and plots. O'Hea thought it worth another try, but conceded, "I can see you are not in any frame of mind at the moment to look at it again."

Spring was in any case the season when Ursula's attention normally turned to her real garden. It was about an acre in all. The house looked out across the a broad path lined with herbaceous borders and straddle stones, past the circular rose bed toward the orchard of apples and plums, the small copse that Peter had planted after his retirement, the vegetable plots, and the stream where they had both built a small stone wall now suffused in flowers. It was, literally, a garden of remembrance, of consolation, and of considerable labour now that there was no longer Peter to charge across the grass on his latest, beloved mower. Long before the accustomed return to writing in the autumn, however, a new crisis had arisen.

In August or early September Peter's sister Jo had suffered a stroke. Ursula planned to take her to St Mary's, Isles of Scilly, for a recuperative week, rather against friends' advice. Jaques was worried about the extra stress involved. "Can you be a bit ruthless and avoid it if possible?" she advised. "I simply don't think you have to have another burden on you just now – you've soldiered on marvellously … but it takes its toll somewhere along the line – such a massive change in your life can't be dealt with just by keeping busy for a few months." In the event, it was Jo who had felt unable to cope, so Ursula went instead with her friend Freda Williams. The pair got on well, and Ursula enjoyed revisiting the little school on St Agnes, but nevertheless the trip was not a success. Ursula felt bored and homesick, and memories of Peter were never far away, especially when she visited a cemetery containing the graves of those who had died in the many wrecks off the islands. In her notebook she jotted down the legend inscribed on the gravestone of a Captain William who had perished in a storm: "To live in hearts we leave behind is not to die." She was glad to return home, and was talking about writing again. "If I had something like … a challenge I might begin to write again," she told Jaques. "It's there but it won't come out."

Any hopes were quickly dashed by weeks of "hell." Jo had a nervous breakdown and Ursula felt obliged to take her in for a fortnight, then for a further three weeks when she walked out of a nursing home. She confided in Jaques, whose mother had also just gone into care, with despair and some anger at having to cancel at the last minute a conference speech as a result. Having Jo at Court Farm "nearly killed me," she wrote.

> She just sank down into letting me do absolutely everything for her, even empty her beastly slops, and some days I couldn't get her up at all. She had got over her stroke and the doctor said there was no reason not to move about. Finally the psychiatrist said she must go into hospital and have therapy and be made to wait on herself a bit. He was quite firm about it – so I took her yesterday. I know she won't like it but quite frankly I don't intend to be a nurse housekeeper for the rest of my life. The boys are most concerned but none of us can see much solution – Peter would have said, 'Drop her in the middle of the Sahara.' But you can't completely let her go. If only I were really fond of her, but I never was. … There is a lot on – courts, book talks, a lot of hospitality. People are marvellous but I had to cancel and cancel all last month [and] felt awful. I knew not everything was under her control but my word how people do betray their natures in this kind of illness. … Luckily I was sorry enough for her always to be kind though people said I ought to have been firmer, but the only time I blew her up it was disastrous and I wished I hadn't so you can't win.

In December Ursula told Jaques, "I think writing is coming back and I shall get on to it after Christmas. Nothing like having a spot of frustration to start up the cogs and ideas are coming back." O'Hea "gave a whoop of joy" when she heard that her client would start again in the winter of 1974. But the troubles with Jo continued to engulf plans to resume writing.

Jo's physical and mental collapse was rapid, painful and distressing. Ursula too suffered a recurrence of colitis, almost certainly brought on by stress, that made her ill throughout December, but she visited Jo almost every day in hospital. In January she was told that there was nothing physically wrong with Jo, who "just won't try to help herself," but by March she had suffered a thrombosis and had her left leg amputated. "It was a ghastly shock – it jerked her back from neurosis into real physical suffering." Unconsciousness, infection, regained consciousness, and another stroke followed. The release that Ursula called merciful came in April.

When Peter had died, Ursula had told Jaques that she hoped her life would last as long as her husband's, for another six years in effect, "since it can't end now." A year later, the tone of her letters had changed. "I certainly don't sit and mope," she told her friend.

> I work and work and enjoy the garden and go out an awful lot, and make things, and laugh, and enjoy the family, and just about behave as usual, quite easily, also sleep well and eat well and the days fly by. But if anybody said would you like to relinquish life here and now this minute, I'd say Yes! And that isn't because I'm unhappy. I've just had all I want of it and it has been so wonderful that I'll live all the rest quite adequately until released. ... One should be capable of making a decent job of it, but I do hope for not too long. One can't help resenting the weeks and months rending one away from Peter and driving him into the past.

By July, no writing had appeared. "There's a block somewhere though I know writing is still under the surface," she wrote to Alan, but added, "Or is it? It will affect my income, but I haven't many needs ... and can always cut my coat according to my cloth." By the time that her letter was popped into the wall box at the Post Office down the lane, another was already on its way to her from O'Hea announcing her intention to retire a little early at the end of the year. She had worked for Curtis Brown since 1929 and had represented Ursula ever since Stanley Unwin had recommended their services. "I certainly hope that the fact that I am no longer an agent will not mean a loss of contact with you. I regard you more as a friend than an author – although a very important author," she wrote. Her "nice" successor, she said reassuringly, had been both a publisher and an agent. The news must nevertheless have come as a blow. O'Hea had been her confidante as well as her representative, and however pleasant and qualified, her replacement was male – unusual in the world of juvenile fiction – and Ursula's junior by nearly thirty years. She travelled to London for O'Hea's farewell party in December 1975 but was unable to exchange more than a few words in the mêlée either with her agent or with Mike

Shaw, whom she met for the first time. What happened next is not clear, but within three weeks Ursula was flying to Iceland after a call from Magnús. By the end of the year, Barbara was dead.

Few letters between the sisters have survived, making it difficult to assess their relationship. Their husbands' temperaments and interests could not have been more different, and Magnús's rather reclusive character made Barbara's long physical isolation seem the more distant. Barbara's own personality and interests had also been radicalised since leaving what she thought of as the stultifying atmosphere of her youth. She had become a well-known figure in Iceland where her anti-American views and widely-reported opposition to the Vietnam war apparently made the British ambassador quail. As a feminist, she resented being left literally holding the baby "by virtue of my sex" when Magnús and Vifill went on an expedition, leaving her grandchild at home. "I do not consider that the joy of bringing up a child is all-satisfying to any artist of creative ability," she told Alan. "A man artist's enemy no. 1 is the bourgeois way of life demanded by his mate – and a woman artist's enemy is the old fashioned egoism of the male regarding domestic chores and expecting woman to be the one to make the sacrifice." As a professed Bohemian she confessed, "People have to be a little bit unconventional to be really congenial to us." As an atheist, she found during occasional visits to London that the "sanctity" of those around her aged aunt Ella drove her mad.[3]

After years of doing fairly poorly paid portraits of children, Barbara had won commissions for decorations of public buildings in Reykjavik in the 1950s. Since then she had designed postage stamps, held exhibitions of her engravings in London, America, Rome, Romania and Scandinavia, sold wall panels in Mexico, and successfully exhibited three times in Paris, where she supplied hangings in Icelandic wool for designer Pierre Cardin.[4] Ursula seems not to have been particularly well-informed about her sister's career, telling Alan, who wanted to write an obituary, that she did not know when or in which countries she had shown her work. Nor does she seem to have been aware of the seriousness of Barbara's condition, until close to her final days when she was admitted to hospital with pancreatic cancer. The illness had progressed for the best part of a year, but if Barbara knew the prognosis when she visited Court Farm for the last time in April 1975, she seems not to have mentioned it. When Ursula eventually learnt the truth, she was just a little hurt that her sister had not felt close enough to confide in her. Hugh was on an RAF exercise at the time and was stunned on his return by the news of his aunt's death. He had "no idea she was so ill."[5]

While Ursula was at her bedside, Barbara rallied briefly, enough to talk with a last show of vitality. Her sister did not remain for long. In a fearsome blizzard that reminded Ursula of the snow in which Peter had died, and perhaps of the storm through which Barbara had struggled for a fateful meeting thirty-one years earlier,

Vifill drove her back to Reykjavik airport. She did not return for the funeral. As with Peter, this had been a mutual agreement with her sister, she explained to the family.

Ursula remained deeply fond of her sister. The sisters grew apart in outlook and disposition, but never broke the intimate bonds of childhood. How else was it possible that twins should appear in no less than twenty-two of Ursula's published works, always – except in *Mog* – as children? In a late, unpublished story, *Our Little Ancestor*, she even contrives a third identical twin by having a family portrait come to life. Ursula asked to continue to write "now and then" to Vifill, not one of the world's most assiduous correspondents, because it was "almost unbearable not to be able to write to Barbara." She did not expect to hear back, she told Alan, who did attend the funeral.

Ursula spent the next fortnight with influenza, "stumbling round in a kind of daze … trying to carry on as if nothing had happened as I did when Peter died. It's the only way to bear it really but it tears one apart inside and I hate waking up in the mornings," she wrote to Alan. After all the blows, however, a renewed determination was asserting itself. "I can and will bear it. Nothing will ever get me down [the words were underlined] … and the one thing I must get back to is writing just as soon as I can." When she wrote again to Vifill at the end of January, she was finding it "very hard work," but had made a start on a new book.[6]

For thirty years it had been Ursula who had often come to comfort those in trouble in and around Beckford. At her time of loss, it was the turn of many local friends to support her. In the process, the mutual affection and respect between writer and villagers combined in happy coincidence to break through the creative block. For she had, in fact, already written a short story, in November 1975, for a local charity auction, possibly in aid of Beckford church. The subject matter was close at hand – the churchyard at the bottom of the lane, and the supposedly haunted grounds of Beckford Hall next door, a favoured, but strictly off-limits playground for the more daring local youngsters. The story, later published as *Family Feelings*, uses variations of local names, including "Stephen Griddon," an amalgam of Rita Griffin's son Simon, and Peggy Tandy's son Stephen. While researching a school ancestry project, the Griddons and their rivals meet in the churchyard at midnight. As a joke, one dresses as a ghost, but all are genuinely scared by Granny Woodford [the elderly Betty Woodward lived next to the churchyard, to which there was a connecting doorway] arriving spirit-like in her nightgown to investigate the commotion. Writing the story had "broken the jinx," O'Hea told Ursula.

A new title that she was finding "very hard work" was probably *Lucy Lollipop*, about a witch who doubled as a crossing attendant, and which she brought to her first serious meeting with Mike Shaw in June 1976. Apart from her early opportunistic ventures with the Girl Guides Association, Ursula's writing had never been guided by commercial acumen, and she had rarely discussed the proposed subject matter of her books in advance with Curtis Brown or potential publishers. Shaw said he found the story "charming," but author and agent seem to have overlooked the difficulty with the cost of colour illustrations. This would need to be offset by a transatlantic agreement, and a British lollipop lady would be unfamiliar to American readers and buyers as Jane Birkett at Chatto & Windus pointed out.[7]

There was little time to prepare an alternative version, for Ursula had started another book and wanted to complete it before November when she was to make a second trip to New Zealand, to where Robin had returned with his Canadian wife. On this occasion, the writing seems to have gone without a hitch, perhaps because the idea for *Bogwoppit* came from North Stoneham, but unlike *Grandpapa's Folly and the Woodworm-Bookworm* it allowed her imagination full rein. The spirited young heroine, Samantha, goes to live in a large house in the middle of a park, with familiar features including a pillared portico, a terrace, even bat droppings in the attic and a rust-stained shabby lavatory. But this time, the inspiration came, deliciously, from the cellars and drains below. Ursula was back to top form. The language is sharp – a zip fastener hangs "like the discarded backbone of a kipper" and the action moves quickly, especially in the climactic rescue of Lady Daisy Clandorris from a sewer. The Bogwoppit itself is one of the writer's most memorable creations: a cuddly toy come to life, furry and feathered, fluffy, funny, lovable, crafty as an owl, but dirty as a rat. The entry of a pack of his fellows is vivid.

> There came a tearing, wrenching noise as a loose bit of panelling fell out of the wainscot. In another moment the room was full of bogwoppits, stamping, jiggling and dancing to the music, their small wings flapping, their large feet slapping on the stone floor. Samantha giggled at their swishing tails and waving wings, half-amused, half nervous at their numbers, but they seemed to be wholly friendly and delighted with her, crowding round her legs and rubbing affectionately against her ankles.

The plot is, however, quite unsentimental, for dozens of the creatures die in the drains before Samantha and the remaining Bogwoppit achieve a happy ending of sorts.[8]

Much of the action is observed by Mr Price the plumber, who, as critic Isabel Quigly noted, has the enthusiasm for drains that "Dr Muffet felt for spiders." Consequently, the book's credibility was "based on an iron precision … a consistency that applies in everyday life, follows you into fantasy … and does not, whatever the circumstances, let you down. … You have simply to accept one premise; the rest follows with total logic and exactness, and with a kind of merry lunacy that's good … for the often prim literary sensibilities of the young."[9]

Ursula recommended that Shirley Hughes provide the illustrations, which Morton-Saner said captured perfectly the creature's "ferocious cuddliness." Nothing came of the artist's idea to interest a toy company in making bogwoppits, but she did receive one of several that Ursula made herself and distributed to friends. They usually arrived in boxes, resting on tissue paper, and with air holes to let them breathe in transit.[10]

The five-month trip to see Robin and his new Canadian wife, Terry, in New Zealand – which began in November 1976, and included stops in South Africa, Australia and the US – was relatively uneventful, at least in terms of Ursula's writing. Publishers' agents and sponsors had arranged interviews, book signings, and visits to schools, bookshops and libraries. So many had been arranged for what was to be a short stop-over in Australia, that Ursula cancelled some engagements, causing annoyance all round. Matters improved in New Zealand. Talks went well and her works were well known. Ursula was captivated by Dorothy Butler, a mother of eight children, who had started selling books at her home when they were small. By now, her shop in Auckland had grown into what Ursula called a "children's literary paradise." Naturally she found many of her own titles on its shelves.

Most of the earlier weeks, however, were spent visiting relations. Ursula's diary lists at least twenty-five Unwins at a Christmas lunch. She also met with old acquaintances such as Sheila Weir, a New Zealander whom Ursula had met and befriended at Overbury ten years earlier. Weir had found herself and two daughters facing eviction from her tied cottage when her marriage to a local farm manager broke down. Ursula had made complete Viyella layettes (nighties and vests) with hand embroidered herringbone stitch for the girls. When she needed help, Ursula also loaned her white convertible Morris Minor, sent a cheque for £70, and "a really nice set of underwear." "I think you need these because I hope you have a nice young man," she told her.

Weir, a teacher, had returned to Nelson, where Ursula was due to talk to her primary school. She remembers her plane coming into the tiny airfield, with its old shack of a terminal with buckets to catch the rain. "I saw her coming across the field, beaming. She was so together. When she opened her bag at our house, on top of all her things were her gardening clothes and secateurs. 'I need to make myself useful here, not just sit about,' she said."

Ursula came prepared to work during her sojourns in New Zealand. There was babysitting (which she hated), housework (which she undertook willingly), and cooking, dressmaking and gardening (which she loved). Ill health would not get in the way. Several times during the holiday, Ursula confessed to her diary about "awful" discomforts caused by her colostomy. On the first occasion she seems to have worked it off by digging a ditch.

There were potentially two highlights of the holiday. Ursula slept through them both. Terry was expecting her first child, and its grandmother had arranged her programme so that she would be there up to the time of the birth. The baby was still delaying its appearance at the maternity hospital when Robin came into his mother's bedroom at 2.30 a.m., and stayed to talk for an hour "so appreciatively and fondly" of Terry, of his upbringing, and what Ursula called "training" at home. Robin had been for a night out, Ursula had been unwell, and both were tired, so neither heard the telephone ring at 4 a.m. It was a neighbour who came in the next morning to say she had heard the party line ring unanswered. Elizabeth had arrived. It was approaching the end of Ursula's journey too. "Have seldom been so tired in my life," she wrote that evening, although it did not stop her from clearing out the poultry shed before she left.

The flight home was via Fiji, Hawaii and Los Angeles before a Concorde flight from Washington, with free champagne served by a butler in the VIP lounge. At noon she settled down on the aircraft and briefly closed her eyes. She awoke over the Atlantic, having missed the take-off. Banks of primroses were out when she arrived home in Beckford. It was "lovely to be back."[11]

Chapter 21

"Through the magic door."

Correspondence between Ursula and her literary agent virtually dried up in 1977. The efficient and friendly Shaw liked her work, but was less effusive and emotional than his predecessor, and had a large number of other clients with bigger sales. Ursula's duties as deputy chairman of the magistrates were even more onerous than those as chairman of the juvenile bench, and as a consequence she produced little as an author in the year after her return from New Zealand. The only piece that Shaw is known to have received, *In the Middle of the Wood*, was in fact an affectionate piece of whimsy almost certainly based on Lt. Col. Richard Burlingham, chairman of Evesham magistrates and of much else. A group of children spy the fictional Colonel – "chairman of this and that" – burying a body in old pyjamas, which on exhumation they discover is his old teddy bear. The author's love of nature – the thrushes singing, pussy willows in the ditch, the hills purple and soft – is expressed distinctively through adolescent eyes. What other writer would dare compare a lovely evening to "a great plate of nice stuff to eat"?

> You think you can't eat it all now so there'll be some for presently, but there isn't any presently. And sure enough, in the morning it usually rains, and spring is quite ordinary again.

Perhaps it was this idiosyncratic style that persuaded editors Graham Barrett and Michael Morpurgo to publish the story as the first in a collection that also included pieces by Philippa Pearce, Roald Dahl, Ted Hughes, Saki, Robert Graves and Somerset Maugham.[1]

At the start of 1978 Shaw was delighted to hear that Ursula was working hard. What arrived, however, was a new version of *An Author in the Garden*. Despite his enthusiasm for "lovely characters" like the vicar's wife and the exotic Miss Flyweed who turns into her fictional characters, it was returned with little encouragement by Hamish Hamilton, Brockhampton, Dent, and Allen & Unwin. By the time the author heard of further rejection from Macmillan, in November, nearly two years had passed since her last major title, *Bogwoppit*, had been accepted for publication.

Following her return from the exhausting world tour in April 1977, Ursula had been away for several short breaks, including visits to Puffin Club colonies, but her ten-day trip to Stornaway on the Hebridean island of Lewis, in September 1978, was the first real holiday she had enjoyed since then. The time was exhilarating. She spoke at four schools, including one on the remote island of Barra to which she was taken by the Assistant Director of Education who was armed with piles of new books. She met "terrific, clever and charming" librarians, and agreed to sponsor a writing competition for children. "The Western Isles are very hungry for books and I don't think the children had met a children's writer until I went up there. They were sweet. I'm sure they thought one came from outer space," she told Webb. Looking out from the window of her hotel on Barra onto the lovely bay, with its castle on an island, and other islands beyond, she felt renewed purpose. "This part of the country has always appealed to me enormously," she wrote to Alan. "There must be something in the blood that responds or one wouldn't feel so entirely at home. … Oddly enough I don't miss Peter with nearly such poignancy up here as I have done this summer at home. There's something about the country that makes one feel comforted." She had not had leisure time for many months, she told him, but now, for half of each day she could "write and write."

Nobody, seeing Miss Amity and her little cat walking down the street to the library on a Saturday morning, would have believed that Miss Amity was a burglar.

Jeffy, the Burglar's Cat opens spiritedly, as the hero tries to reform his wicked mistress and to give back stolen goods: smuggled brandy and the proceeds of a bank robbery staged with carrots for guns. Away from the expansive horizons of the Hebrides, however, it may be that the author's imagination was once more constrained by her concerns as a magistrate, for it comes as something of a jolt when barely halfway through the story, Miss Amity and her kitten accomplice Little Lew are sent to prison for ten years. Despite their release and a riotous hijack at sea, the second half fails to match the vivacity of the first. At a second prison on an island, the reformed ex-burglar teaches others on parole to be good, aided by Little Lew wielding a cane to encourage discipline. There is even a Bishop on hand to talk about God, with particular attention given to the island's infant school. For, as the former juvenile bench chairman wrote, "The little ones are more important. Prevention is better than cure."[2]

Ursula knew that it was not one of her best books. After the negative reception given to her most recent work, she sought and was given reassurance from Shaw. "I really don't think you need have any fears about this one," he told her. Nevertheless, Birkett wanted changes, and even after most of these had been done, nearly a year after the first draft had been completed, she still turned the book down. Eventually, in August 1980, *Jeffy, the Burglar's Cat* was taken by Andersen Press, to be splendidly illustrated by David McKee. Six months later it was also broadcast over four days on

Jackanory. For once, Ursula reported, the BBC had paid "rather well."

Anthea Morton-Saner, originally O'Hea's secretary, gradually took over many of Shaw's authors at Curtis Brown. Ursula was one whose work was becoming increasingly difficult to sell, as Morton-Saner soon discovered. She recalled:

> Ursula had not kept up with changing fashion. She was not interested in doing so, because she could still tell stories to people and talked about things that children were interested in. She did not keep up with gizmos and she did not like ugliness. But publishers were in the modern p.c. world. ... All the school teachers and librarians said you could not have witches or magic, and religion made it difficult for English publishing. So selling her work could be a nightmare, for example *Bellabelinda and the No-Good Angel.* But I think that Harry Potter proved her right. Children want to be transported into a magic world. It's things you cannot see.[3]

Ursula had extended *Lucy Lollipop*, intended originally as a picture book, into a series of adventures for Bellabelinda, the lollipop lady with hidden powers, and Flipsy, the small, bedraggled and inexperienced guardian angel, visible only to children, whom Bellabelinda trains to look after others. Morton-Saner reacted favourably. Her daughters "particularly liked the way that each chapter is really a story in itself. ... It makes it much easier to get them to bed," she told her new client. The book really focuses on the Fogglebatch boys who, in the absence of parental supervision, use their considerable ingenuity to cause trouble – making toffee which sets fire to their house, or switching road signs to send their school bus party onto the moors. Flipsy usually comes to the rescue, as in one unintentionally memorable passage when she frees a Fogglebatch finger from a knothole by licking it "all over with her warm pink tongue." To round off their adventures to the author's satisfaction, the boys join the church choir, and Mrs Fogglebatch has the baby girl she has always wanted.[4]

In August 1980 a lengthy list of critical comments came back from Di Denney at Chatto & Windus, but as Morton-Saner noted, Ursula was not difficult to work with and like most authors was fairly accommodating to suggested changes. Time to make such changes, however, was short. Ursula continued to sit as a magistrate until April 1981, when she reached the compulsory retirement age of seventy. Formerly, rewritten passages would have been despatched within a few weeks, but now pressure of other work and the enjoyment of spending summer months in the garden, meant that they might not be looked at for months.

Meanwhile, Denney looked for an illustrator who would "not [be] too expensive but who will portray the characters well." In the past the employment of artists with a less literal style than Ursula's had made re-issues of her classics more appealing to new generations of young readers, and has given a modern look to her latest titles, even if the narrative followed a traditional pattern. Seeing her stories from a contemporary perspective had often produced illustrations that seemed to refresh the author's sensibility for the comic in the humdrum. McKee had achieved this in *Jeffy, the Burglar's Cat*, although Ursula surprisingly did not like the new cover that he did for the Puffin re-issue[5] two years later, and Mike Jackson had created excellent Parisian street scenes for *The Kidnapping of My Grandmother*, although no one liked that book's odd pea-green overlay.[6] Denney's choice for *Bellabelinda* was Glenys Ambrus. Her cartoon-like sketches, especially of the marooned school party on the moor, certainly added to the spiky humour, so one hopes she was not too inexpensive.

Ursula travelled to Chatto's London offices in April 1982 bearing posies, on this occasion made of primroses and spring blossom. *Bellabelinda and the No-Good Angel* was to appear that autumn, and had someone in the office been aware of the significance that might be attached to its publication, the visitor might have been the recipient of a small presentation, not its donor. The National Book League had informed Ursula that Lady Mary Annabel Nassau "Amabel" Williams-Ellis, sister of the socialist politician John Strachey, had the longest publishing career of any living British writer. Ursula would overtake her record with *Bellabelinda* on the basis of information the League had provided – wrongly as it happened.[7] Be that as it may, half a century had passed since the publication of *Jean-Pierre* in the autumn of 1931. Ursula herself had raised the question of literary longevity. How then, toward the end of a prodigious career, and with her fifty-eighth book about to appear in print, did she see her job as a writer? To answer the question, one must back-track a little.

Ursula had no qualms about talking to aspiring authors about the sources of her ideas, and how she got them down onto paper. Invariably, starting from her early days of storytelling with Barbara, she would describe the fight to find the time in which to write and the struggle to start. "How often I have envied the men writers I know, with devoted wives at hand to feed them, make their beds, answer the telephone and fend off visitors." She learnt not to waste a minute. She had trained herself to write in trains, hotel bedrooms, against conversations, record players and the television, but mostly, in winter, on kitchen tables. Every time Peter went through, he asked how she was getting on and whether she wanted a cup of tea. "And if I ask him not to, he is so hurt that it is worse than being interrupted."

She often likened herself to a hen – what was inside, had to come out, she would say. Nevertheless, however much she had been longing for a free afternoon on which to get going, beginning a new book was "sheer hell." She would "tidy the room … wash up after lunch coffee cups that can well be left till supper time, just anything to delay that moment of truth." When she got started, it took an hour "to write oneself in," so two-hour stints were better, and four hours were best, although "very exhausting." She usually wrote, very fast, in Biro; she liked the feeling of the pen on paper and fountain pens ran out too quickly. Plots formed in her head sometimes just for a few days, sometimes for months, but Ursula repeatedly described her writing as "spontaneous." The pace of handwriting matched her thoughts, she said, and the first chapter was critically important:

> [It is] the corner stone to which you return for assurance when the rest of the edifice is toppling. … You may dry up … or just hit a dull patch and you cannot see beyond it. … That is where your good beginning is so vital. … Re-reading it, you feel again the pull of the plot … you are re-infected with the urge to continue, and you know it is going to be all right if you persevere.

During the 1970s and beyond, Ursula was ready at the drop of a hatpin, it seemed, to talk in front of children, parents, amateur and professional authors, or provide articles about her own writing. Of other contemporary juvenile fiction she knew little. "Because it is so easy to unconsciously borrow another person's ideas, I never read a modern children's book today," she said.[8] So the prospect of addressing an audience of academics was daunting. In 1969 Sidney Robbins, an English lecturer at St Luke's College, Exeter, had inaugurated an annual conference to bring teachers and authors of children's books into direct contact with each other. Following his death, a colleague invited Ursula to speak at the fourth Exeter Conference in August 1972.[9] She accepted with some trepidation. "Exeter doesn't half loom and has done all year," she told Jaques. Webb urged her not to go. In the meantime, she had a trial run in Cheltenham.

The subject that she chose was 'Children's Literature Today and Yesterday', but if the audience of trainee teachers expected to hear a writer's views on contemporary fiction, or even extracts from the latest books being read at bedtime, they would have been disappointed. The speaker was "not unduly impressed" by those modern American books formerly on her sons' bookshelves that had spectacular illustration but shallow storylines. Books from the Soviet Union, presumably sent by Alan, were tendentious and tedious. Those apart, her references were all to the Classics of her own childhood, to long-dead authors, great writers like Twain, Scott, Stevenson, and many like Mrs Molesworth and Manville Fenn of whom her listeners had probably never heard.

The lecture was significant in that it was probably the first time that Ursula had tried to summarise intellectually a relationship with her young readers that she had always taken for granted. From a picture of children in pre-history gathered around a tribal storyteller, to one of young viewers around a television set, she traced an instinct to escape from one world into another. Children's imagination, she argued, was "more vivid, because it is less disciplined than ours." Illustration could work in the same way.

> I often wonder whether many of the slick, sophisticated illustrations today really appeal. … As children we used to love to 'get into' the pictures … to wander along the streets and to look into the gardens and the houses. … We

Setting up Guide camp in 1927.

One of Ursula's few surviving landscape sketches – Annecy, spring 1928.

Ursula began a series of humorous pictorial sketchbooks on her hiking trip with Alan through the Black Forest in 1932. Here, in a detail from one of the sixty four pages, the diary is discovered by the youth hostel leader.

Scenes from the 1934 Swiss sketchbook: Barbara and Perrelet paint Ursula's portrait, and breakfast – always one of Ursula's favourite times – while staying at a chalet during a climbing expedition.

Cut-outs for Ursula's early books, Jean-Pierre, *top left*, and a more developed style *below* for *Adventures of Anne*.

Below right, one of the dramatic lino-cuts for *Grandfather*, this one for the story *Climbers*.

Left: Ursula (mounted) and Barbara with their pony Puss. *Above: Kelpie* (1934) finds a happy home with two girls who call him Puck.

Left: Ursula's drawings of the milkman's splayed horse in *Grumpa* (1955) and, *below*, for *Golden Horse with a Silver Tail* (1957).

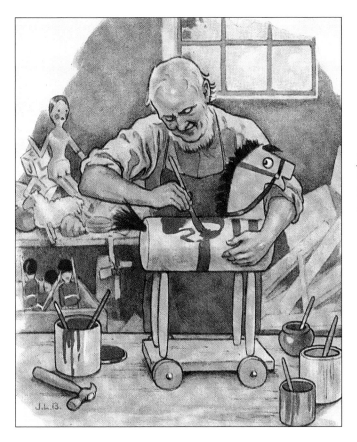

Joyce Brisley's original illustration for *Adventures of the Little Wooden Horse*.

Below: L.E. Bradley, "Bookseller, Stationer, News Agent and Fancy Repository" with a special line in little wooden horses, seen hanging under the canopy. As a girl, Ursula passed the shop every day.

Scissor-cuts for *The Good Little Christmas Tree* (1943) and, *below, The House of Happiness* (1946).

One four-year-old watched her make them on the kitchen table. "Tic-tic-tic and there was a little boy, tic-tic-tic and there was a Christmas tree. She … just cut them out freehand."

Life drawing classes at Winchester gave Ursula a life-long skill in sketching figures, which she could exploit in exaggerated poses for comic effect.

Above: She and Peter struggle to light a camp fire on their honeymoon, from Ursula's sketchbook (1935).

Below: Grumpa tries to dig his way out of the garden shed (1955).

More conventional drawings, still full of energy, for *The Binklebys at Home* (*left*, 1951) and *Secrets of the Wood* (*below*, 1955).

Cats: Gobbolino as he first appeared in the 1942 original, and *below*, in much spikier, convincing shape as Ursula drew him for Kaye Webb's 1965 Puffin edition.

And mice: Apart from the Puffin edition with new drawings of Gobbolino, *O for a Mouseless House* (1964) was the last of Ursula's books to contain her own illustrations. Here, the Church mice seem to twitch as they sleep.

named [the children] in the pictures – that's me, that's you. That's my pony, that's yours.

Best remembered books were those read when very young. "I think of a mind as a piece of blotting paper. The first words … are so clear you can read them backwards and quite often when the sheet is covered with other blottings … you can still see the original two or three words coming through."

It was more difficult, Ursula recognised, for parents to guide children's reading than it had been in the days of moralising Victorian literature, but she quoted with approval the practice at "a local Preparatory school" (her sons') to ensure that every boy read "a worthwhile type of book" each evening. For younger children, however, she extolled the value of reading aloud, and in a final flourish, that might not have appealed to her more proletarian student audience, criticised some aspects of television and radio for the young.

We have allowed the … privilege of parents … to be usurped by radio aunties and uncles now called baldly by their Christian names so that the intimate atmosphere has completely disappeared. I would like *Listen with Mother* to be called *Listen to Mother* and a break in broadcasting for fifteen minutes made accordingly.

She invited questions.[10]

Ursula described what followed as the college lecturers and students "performing the current psychiatrical hysterectomies on children's books, subjects and authors." The audience was more interested in social than literary questions. In answer to one, Ursula said that she wrote to please herself without thinking of its effect on anyone. "Hmm, rather irresponsible," said the teacher beside her. "Irresponsible?" came the response: "All right, put all your theories and your analysis and your definitions into action and just see what a rotten story you would write. I couldn't attempt to teach your children. You stick to your job and I'll stick to mine," Ursula said, or at least so she told Jaques. The young man reportedly took it "quite well." Was this to be a foretaste of Exeter?

When August came, Ursula was ready for a fight. She talked about her childhood. She talked about the quality of vocabulary in children's literature, the joy of discovering a new word like syllabub. "Had Enid Blyton been a master of the English language as she was a master of storytelling, she might have been the Shakespeare of the juvenile shelf. Hey, Noddy, Noddy." But Ursula talked mostly as if giving an extended response to her earlier interrogators. They seemed still to be there. "Behind us is the tick-tock, tick-tock reminder of what we ought to be writing, or ought not to be writing." Such people were telling writers they "should write about the backstreet children, the underprivileged … violent … racially isolated … backward children." "Not," they would say, "about talking animals or anything that can be translated as segregational, or ixie-pixies or funny bunnies or boarding schools." And God was "quite unprintable unless he is given an outlandish name and reached by way of a never never land or a wardrobe door."

She recalled the Cheltenham argument, and the response that she wished she had given: "I might more truthfully have replied that in fact I write for the forgotten child in myself, the child that I hope I shall never quite forget, and never too consciously remember." Decisions by adults governed a child's life, she told the Exeter conference, so "the role of fiction [is] to provide an escape from this necessary domination into a land of his own choice." At the same time, the author would "introduce him to emotions he may not yet have recognised in his life and to involvement in a vicarious courage he may not himself possess."

Ursula rejected the idea that children demanded fiction set in an environment similar to their own. "As children we ourselves loved to read about rich children with ponies, since we were hard up," Ursula said. She argued that the average child found the view over the next hill, or the next rooftop more exciting than what went on at home, how Pinocchio struck out on his adventures, how Babar and Celeste had engagements beyond the palace walls, and Richard Scary took his characters all over the world. Libraries, book groups, paperbacks, television, academics and conferences such as the one she was attending, put pressure on children to enter into literary imagination on adult terms. Instead, Ursula offered her own vision:

> As writers and educationalists our role is to play the Pied Piper and pipe the children up the mountain and through the magic door and to leave them there inside the enchanted country. The grown-ups can only follow so far, or the glamour goes.[11]

Her remarks would not have commanded universal approval. The gathering of solitary authors, unconcerned how teachers responded to their books, and of teachers bringing their experience of large mixed-ability classes, could end in acrimony, particularly, as the commentator Elaine Moss observed, when involving an "author who claimed he was 'writing for himself.'[12] Exeter lecturer Geoff Fox, a veteran of the conferences recalled that authors often spoke about writing for the children in themselves. "That period was something of a golden age, as people called it at the time, but I can understand those who felt that it needed to be broadened out," he said. Nevertheless, his recollection was that the spirit of the conference resembled that of a present day literary festival. "It was almost a surprise for those in attendance to discover that writers were real people, very much as children are with authors on school visits today, and there was much reverential lionising going on," he said.

Whatever the mood of the hall that day, Ursula "just survived," but her reception cannot have been uniformly hostile for she offered to give her collection of rare old books to the children's literature centre that the college hoped to create. The offer appears not to have been taken up because of a lack of suitable accommodation, but she did make a financial donation.[13]

Her gesture did not represent a change of heart. She told writers' groups the following year not to be "misled" by librarians telling them what to write about. "The best children's books come straight from the writer's heart and go straight into the hearts of children. They are created, not contrived," she said.

> If I were a child today and realised all the fuss and concern there is at present over children's books … what children ought to read, what children ought not to read, I would be outraged. This is our country, I would say. Go back to your own world. Keep out of ours.

A more direct attack on Ursula's work from the academic world was yet to come. In *Reading into Racism*, published in 1985, Gillian Klein claimed that black people were "degraded in a particularly pernicious way" in *The Nine Lives of Island Mackenzie*. "The theme harks back to Robinson Crusoe and so do the racist biases," Klein argued. She took issue with the description of the indigenous islanders not as people but as "savages," not allowed to express themselves except by inarticulate noises. Klein quotes a passage in which they "began to shriek and jabber … stamping on the flower beds with their wide flat feet. … Then, as nothing happened, down on their hands and knees went the whole party, snuffling and pointing at the footprints." Klein concluded: "As an example of the dehumanizing and degrading of an – albeit imaginary – group of people, this account of their behaviour when they come across that epitome of the English civilization, Miss Pettifer's garden, would be hard to beat."[15]

The book, first published in 1959, caught Klein's attention because of its re-issue in 1979 followed by a paperback edition the following year. Anyone with the time to go through all of its author's works, and with the desire to find corroborating evidence, could however find numerous examples to support a prosecution case of racial prejudice and social stereotyping. The further back the researcher dug, the more frequently the incriminating details would be found. *The Backwards Boy* of 1928 includes dancing "niggers," while the episode about a circus pony in *Adventures of Anne* of 1935 might be given a double sentence for featuring gypsies "who look so dirty" and a heroine who dresses as a golliwog. Gypsies appear regularly in the early novels, usually in the role of petty criminals, owners of mistreated horses, or itinerants likely to light a fire in a barn, although individuals like Tammas in *Kelpie*, or families, as in *Dumpling*, are given the chance to mend their ways. The otherwise unobjectionable gypsy event suggested in Ursula's book of children's parties includes a game "Move along please" involving gypsies and policemen. By the 1960s gypsies appearing in her stories have apparently cleaned up their criminal tendencies but not their living conditions, as seen in *O for a Mouseless House* and *Mog*.

Would Klein have been happier with references to natives in *The Cruise of the Happy-Go-Gay*, people whose chief has been to the Houses of Parliament and who live appropriately on the Paradox Islands? "How do you know they are *savages*?" said Aunt Hegarty. "Natives have just as clear an idea of property as anyone."

Ursula was not oblivious of the growing tide of social criticism that was affecting juvenile fiction, including her own. The description of savages' "woolly heads" and "garish ornaments" dropped the adjectives in the paperback edition of *The Nine Lives of Island Mackenzie* after an objection by an editor at Transworld. Klein and Ursula could not have been further apart in their experience of racial issues. Klein, an anti-apartheid campaigner, left South Africa after the Sharpeville shooting in which sixty-nine people died. She later set up the Inner London Education Authority's Centre for Urban Educational Studies. Ursula had little contact with black people, and seldom wrote about them. An exception was the short story *Up Top*, written for the "backward readers" collection, *Hurricanes*, about a Jamaican boy feeling isolated and lonely as he rides around London on the top deck of a bus. Then from the top of the Post Office Tower he feels the world under his feet and as if "everything belonged to me."

The story, about fitting in, finding one's place and making the best of it, seems to represent the author's views. She was no multi-culturalist. In a rare statement of anything that might be considered political, she wrote to Alan in 1975 about how much England had changed since the war.

> 'I have increasingly desired that each country should be essentially itself, and very national, but with an active tolerance for every other country. ... I do not want to find a little England anywhere abroad and ... I hate the hotchpotch of a kind of international free state.'

It would be surprising, however, if her views did not change a little in response to issues being raised at the time, just as her understanding of and sympathy for the underprivileged changed as a result of her experiences as a school governor and magistrate. Ursula might not have had any time for a new "progressive" publication with "Guidelines to be used in the production of anti-racist and non-racist books,"[16] but without the polemic of which it was a part, it was less likely that in the same year she would have written the line toward the end of *Jeffy, the Burglar's Cat* about an island community with "all kinds of people ... old, young, black, white, yellow, pinkish, darkish, bearded, clean-shaven, men and women, boys, girls and babies."

Someone asked Peter if he had ever read Karl Marx. "No," he answered, "too small print."[17] Politics remained almost a closed book also for his wife. It simply took place outside the domestic world of family and childhood, almost an irrelevance, it seemed, compared with more lasting personal and spiritual values. "If you can't help the world, help your neighbour," Ursula said.[18] She followed the news headlines and expressed distress at reports of disasters, but no one interviewed for this book could remember her ever talking politics. After being taken to hear Mrs Thatcher speak in Bath, her comment was on how much she enjoyed walking along the town's Regency roads.[19]

Political statements occur very rarely in her writing – private and published – and can sometimes seem, in retrospect, somewhat naive. An encounter with a hunger march through the streets of London during the Great Depression passed by without remark, but Ursula noted in her diary that her Brownies were making blankets for their children and that they "knitted wishes into the rug we are making for the unemployed." During a hiking holiday through the Black Forest in 1932, Ursula kept a delightful sketchbook, filled with comic observations, such as the legs of Dachshunds growing longer as they approached the French border. Communists and Nazis, whom she and Alan encountered repeatedly, were drawn and noted without comment, facetious or otherwise, except that the discipline at a boys' camp, presumably the Hitler Youth, seemed "rather severe." The frightened talk of older Germans about a younger generation being brought up to fight another war had nevertheless alarmed Ursula. The following year, a week after the election that brought Hitler to power, she noted in her diary that the Nazis were "all for blood and war" and despaired that differences could not be settled except "by primitive tooth and claw killing." The sentiment, neither profound nor ridiculous, seems unremarkable for a twenty-one-year-old woman at the time. More unconventional, to say the least, was a comment, written forty-five years later for *The Lady* magazine. Near the end of an article about the comforting attributes of cuddly toys, she wrote: "Who can say what lasting influence the loved ones have over their owners' lives? Would Hitler's megalomania have been less if his early years had known the comfort of a Fluff?"[20]

Although Ursula usually voted Conservative, it would be wrong to call her conservative, liberal or socialist because of the definitions of those terms by political parties. Traditional, compassionate, egalitarian might be more appropriate. Occasionally her unpublished writing touches hesitantly upon political topics. A story written for her Brownies, around 1927, described a Christmas banned in Russia, "buried under the inches of Soviet mud that hid all that the country once held sacred." She later scored out the sentence. In contrast, a satirical fragment, *The Hen and the Egg*, written "for amusement only," seems to dismiss the folly of rivalry between communism and capitalism as a couple on the planet Ultimus devour the chicken sent by rocket from Great Britain and the egg from the Soviet Union. It is not known when the piece was composed – probably well before 1960 when the fictional couple are set to blast off into space. One can be more precise about a poem with a similar theme, written less than a fortnight after the General Assembly of the United Nations met in London and adopted its first resolution – on the elimination of atomic and other weapons of mass destruction. Although the verse was untitled and remained unpublished, its author thought enough about it to draft it three times and date it February 5, 1946:

> Once in a fairy tale we heard
> That every thousand years a bird
> Perches on a certain peak
> To nest awhile and wipe his beak.
> And when, or so the prophets say
> The peak itself is rubbed away
> That space of time shall prove to be
> One second in eternity.
> So if atomic power be hurled
> Against the peak, and if the world
> Be waste, that bird will come anon
> To rest upon her skeleton
> And wipe his beak, and then they say
> The world itself is rubbed away
> That space of time shall only be
> Two seconds in eternity.
> But in his toil he makes a pause
> To raise a fragment in his claws
> That in some far off sphere shall be
> A keystone to posterity.
> And when new life has taken hold
> Upon that world built on the old
> Perchance such men may worthier be
> To justify eternity.[21]

While Ursula's interest in politics was superficial, her faith was not. Its practice was evident as secretary of the Parochial Church Council, with gifts of carpets and embroidered kneelers, and as the devoted provider of posies for children to take home on Mothering Sunday long after most had stopped going to church. Some who saw her toward the end of her life, always in the same pew, dozing, occasionally snoring through services, who observed her preference for traditional services using the Book of Common Prayer and her dislike of the ordination of women priests, might have concluded that her religion was a matter of custom, the done thing. It was true that she enjoyed playing the role of benefactor and as an unofficial welcoming party for each new incumbent. "She was an icon in the village," said one. "She knew we were coming and invited us to lunch, then was always very welcoming as soon as we came through the door," said another, whose family continued to visit long after leaving the parish. But to assume that her religious observance was merely habitual would ignore the depth of an instinctive faith. When one of her nine godchildren – with most of whom she maintained a lifetime correspondence – was confirmed, she wrote urging her to find her own religious beliefs, but added, "Public worship, often boring, depressing and inconvenient, is still the best way of paying a fair debt."[22]

Ursula had been brought up to believe "utterly" in the power of good and evil. It was not an intellectual judgement. When James, the most literary of her sons, wrote a clever poem about the origins of faith, she answered with her own view of the creation: "I'm dumb on the alphabet CAT cat / Let's call it all God and leave it at that." Unlike Barbara with her desire for unfettered artistic expression, or Alan with his intellectual restlessness, Ursula had largely retained the metaphysical outlook with which she had viewed the world in adolescence; one supported by its special trinity of God and nature and human kindness. "The Saints are so busy in the town. It is only in the mountain that they can listen to the prayers of old men," she wrote in *Grandfather* published in February 1933. It was by chance, forty years later in February 1973, that she gave a talk in the pretty village of Ashton under Hill in which she said: "It is sad to think that both love and kindness flourish less where numbers are greatest. … Here in the countryside it is easier to live kindly, loving God and one's neighbour." Kindness, she said, "is the working sister of love as Martha was working sister to Mary. Both are indispensable to the other. People starved of love and kindness are far more deeply deprived than many who lack enough food or warm clothes."[23] The choice about how to act lay within each individual. A friend, who had been sleepless with worry for someone close to her, was told:

> We were born onto a chessboard with the free will to walk on black or white squares. Without that there would be no challenge – no game, no value of life. … We ARE our brother's keeper, and we must care terribly what happens to anyone … less lucky than us.[24]

It is hardly surprising that such a deeply-held, instinctive and mystical faith should have been reflected in Ursula's books, from the angels that keep Jean-Pierre safe to the last that she wrote. Indeed, one of the problems that Ursula's agents faced from the 1970s onwards was the difficulty of placing stories that regularly featured young people who attended church or Sunday school, and who were on familiar terms with the local vicar. Of Ursula's last eight published novels, six include vicars or bishops. *O for a Mouseless House* seems to celebrate the rich vocabulary of vestments and the image of an empty building "full of love and worship." Yet if one accepts the context in which they are placed, the religious background of her writing was never obtrusive, or the moral obviously preached. Ursula was too good a writer for that, and could even get away with the occasional mention of God:

Prayer for a Happy Family

God bless Mum and Dad and Baby
God bless me and sister Sue,
God bless Auntie Bloss, and maybe
Bless my Uncle Ernest too.
God bless Granma, God bless Grandy,
God bless cousins Dick and Dot,
God bless Marge and little Mandy,
Though you needn't bless a lot.
Bless my home and bless my teacher,
Stop her telling tales to Mum.
Bless Aunt Rose if you can reach her
Safe at rest in Kingdom Come.
Bless my family and guard them
Keep them safe and free-from-sin.
Now that's finished we'll discard them,
This is where my prayers begin:
PLEASE GOD DO LET AUNTIE BLOSS ASK GRANMA TO TELL MUM
TO MAKE DAD SAY I REALLY CAN KEEP A RABBIT.[25]

Chapter 22

——————

"Like an aged sunset seen through winter birches."[1]

More than four decades had passed since Ursula published *Gobbolino, the Witch's Cat*, nearly five since she had started writing *Adventures of the Little Wooden Horse*. From the days of Brisley's *Milly-Molly-Mandy* and Blyton's *Noddy* and *The Famous Five*, to more recent arrivals like Michael Bond's *Paddington Bear*, other authors had achieved phenomenal sales success by creating characters whose adventures could be followed in volume after volume. After so long a gap since creating her two most successful heroes, it may seem less surprising that in 1983 Ursula started writing *The Further Adventures of Gobbolino and the Little Wooden Horse* than that she did not do so much earlier.

It had been in response to George Anderson's appeal to create a series of novels that she had sent him *Malkin's Mountain* – though Ursula most probably had this and possibly the third *Toymaker* volume in mind before receiving his suggestion. She had written about the decidedly domestic world of Woppit in his mini-strip for Robin magazine for a few years, and returned to the Binklebys for life on their farm after their football pools win. Yet these were exceptions; she avoided the re-introduction of characters and resisted publishers' hints to copy the formula of a specific book to promote the success of a second. Each of her main characters, it seemed – having set out and returned home, and having undergone as widely-ranging trials of virtue and courage as their creator could invent – had done their tours of duty. Why then, after so many years living in silent contentment, did these two heroes take to the road again? It seems to have been the voices of children that called them out to play.

Apart from their popularity at bedtime, with chapters lasting just long enough for a good tucking-in, the characters of Gobbolino and the Little Wooden Horse particularly appealed to primary school teachers. Pupils could identify with the small protagonists finding their way in an adult world, then retell their adventures, draw their pictures, and even make models or puppets of their favourites. Paintings, sketchbooks and poems regularly arrived at Court Farm, or were given to the author at schools all over the country. Often, of course, the class had already finished a book by the time that a visit could be arranged. Just after Peggy Tandy's granddaughter Joanne Pearse started at a local school in 1975 her infant class read *Adventures of the Little Wooden Horse*. As Joanne's mother Elaine recalled, "Mrs John ... had stayed up late the night before and had written an extra chapter to read to the children."

Both original titles continued to do well as paperbacks, with twenty-one reprints in the 1970s alone – twelve of *Gobbolino* and nine of *Little Wooden Horse* – supported by promotions at Puffin Club events. They would also have been featured in the large book fair at Cheltenham Literature Festival in November 1980. It was the first time in its thirty-one-year history that the event had included a children's section, and Ursula was invited to open it. For twenty years, ever since the re-issue of *Adventures of the Little Wooden Horse* by Puffin, fans had asked her to do a sequel. It would hardly have been a surprise if a young member of the audience had taken the opportunity to ask what happened next. When Ursula settled down to write again after the usual flock of visitors for Christmas and the New Year, she provided the answer in a short story and sent it to Webb at *Puffin Post.* The main function of *The Last Adventure of the Little Wooden Horse* – a premature title as it turned out – is to redeem all the negative characters, culminating with the cruel farmer Max, who repents at Christmas and turns up with his former employee's missing wages.[2]

Meanwhile, it was *Gobbolino, the Witch's Cat* who was starting to receive more attention. The book's adaptation for television was an obvious topic of conversation when Morton-Saner arrived for a long holiday at Court Farm on 29 October 1982, the last day of its week-long serialisation. An audiocassette was outselling the one of *Adventures of the Little Wooden Horse*, and Ursula's agent may well have mentioned how much the affable but business-like Tony Lacey, Webb's successor at Puffin Books, was likely to welcome a further volume of *Gobbolino*. If so, mention of Tony Lacey's name might not have helped. Ursula had been under the impression that he was organising a party to be held the year earlier to celebrate her fiftieth anniversary in print, but when the invitation came, with her name added to a duplicated letter, it was to an event marking the fortieth anniversary of Puffin. She did not attend.[3]

It seems to have been a winter trip to Portugal that finally persuaded her to send Gobbolino too on a new advernture. James, who was working for Harveys of Bristol, had moved with his family to Porto. There, supported no doubt by appeals from her two grandchildren, he had suggested that it would be a pity to miss the opportunity of writing a sequel to either book. In fact farmer Max, like Malkin and Marta, had already been rehabilitated, but it remained for Sootica and the witch to earn redemption. The idea started to develop during those rainy weeks in Portugal, and on her return Ursula started to write the story that begins with a message, written on a leaf, delivered by an owl: "Please come and help me, brother! Oh, please do! Oh, do! Do!"

It was only after writing the first chapter, when she was already "in full flow," she told James, that she decided to include the Little Wooden Horse as Gobbolino's companion,[4] proof if more were needed of the writer's remarkably extempore style of composition. The two flee from hounds, fly with bats, and the little horse dodges lightning bolts with the witch on her broomstick. And along the way, they find time to clean up a church. "I don't want to be a witch any more ... just company, a little love and affection, and a nice warm cavern to live in for ever," finally confesses Gobbolino's witch. Yet *The Further Adventures*, unlike the insubstantial *Last Adventure*, and several hastily-written, hackneyed short stories about the two heroes written later for magazines,[5] is saved from undue sentimentality by the reformed, but still impudent Sootica. In her late books, the author herself is not above showing little flashes of cheekiness, like the involuntary sparks from Gobbolino's whiskers. To set up the climax, she has the witch paint a magic circle around her mountain through which only a perfectly good man can pass. Ursula was perfectly familiar with Wagner, having seen performances of *Das Rheingold* and *Die Walküre* on consecutive days when she was just twenty-two. So she cannot have been unaware of the parallel with Wotan setting a ring of fire around Brünnhilde which only the heroic Siegfried could cross. In Ursula's case, her heroes brought a priest for good measure.[6]

The contract was signed by Lacey's successor at Puffin, Elizabeth Attenborough. Ursula had sent forty-six illustrations to Puffin for the story. It was ironic that for nearly half a century, she had been drawing pictures of one of her best-known characters, at talks, often on letters sent back to young fans, but had never had them published. It was still not to be. "No, we're not dead," Attenborough told her after some delay. "It's difficult obviously for us to explain to you why we feel we must seek another illustrator for this work." There was a hint, however, in a later letter, about re-issuing the two earlier titles and the need "to bring [the illustrations] up to date." The author's sketches were eventually returned sixteen months after their submission.[7]

Did Ursula feel that her books were being looked on as old-fashioned? Of fifteen short stories that she sent to Morton-Saner over a period of two years, only four appear to have been sold. Ursula did not like to write about the unattractive side of life, with the consequence that publishers felt she had failed to move with the times. As if to answer such criticism, she responded in January 1984 by writing one of her best, funniest, most inventive books, all about a spider. A big one, naturally.

> First one leg came out of the plughole and then another, and then another and then another and then another and then another and then another and then another.

From that moment *Spid* is a glorious improvisation on the visitor's efforts to win acceptance from young Henry's family, and as touching a portrayal as one might reasonably desire of Henry's fly-eating pet. When Spid looked around from the edge of the bath, the household he saw would have been not unlike that of his author, where the cleaning lady (Mrs Gridley or Peggy Tandy) was afraid of spiders, a boy's bedroom was full of model aircraft, and a grumpy grandfather came to stay. The amiable arachnid spins threads, ropes and guitar strings to rescue people, objects and situations, winning the respect of all, even grudgingly from Aunty Bloss. Unlike everyone else, she has remained single, "but that's her affair," Spid comments somewhat primly, before disappearing back down the waste pipe to find a mate. His return is brief but proud. "This is my wife!" he announces. "And this, my pet, is Henry!"[8]

Ursula had considered for some time that she might have to leave Court Farm. She loved it dearly, but was aware that advancing age would make it more difficult to cope with running the house, and especially keeping the large garden, even with help. The question had been given a sudden urgency when in 1980 Andrew successfully applied for the position of farm manager at Overbury Estate, and for a time there was discussion that he and his family might take over Court Farm and his mother move to a smaller house. In the event it was decided that Andrew would take another estate house nearby.[9] Five years later, Ursula was again considering alternatives.

Ursula was one of the few people who travelled in her car who never became alarmed about the roadworthiness of its one-eyed driver.[10] The sight in her remaining left eye was starting to deteriorate. She had retired from the bench at the age of seventy, but the strain of continuing to look after the garden, write, inviting and cooking for an undiminished stream of guests, and a heavy schedule of personal and professional visits, sometimes led to fatigue. Such was the case in August 1983 when she was making the monthly trip to Tetbury where the now ninety-seven-year-old Tchat, her former governess, was in a nursing home. It was a hot day and Ursula dozed off at the wheel. Her Renault car rolled into a ditch, turned a somersault and landed facing the direction from which it had come, the engine still running. The windscreen was smashed and the roof crushed to within an inch of her head. Trembling, Ursula released her seat belt and emerged unhurt but considerably shaken. Not enough, however, to deter her from putting the insurance money toward buying a sporty Talbot Samba. Her former colleagues fined her £55.

In fact, considering her medical history, Ursula was in relatively robust health. Nevertheless, in 1985 she was sufficiently concerned about the future that she seriously contemplated moving to a new residential development for the elderly. She had received yet another legacy, this time from a distant Williams relative, £1,500 of which she gave to Alan. She came close to using the remainder as a deposit on a flat near Moreton-in-Marsh, but did not want to spend the capital she intended to leave her sons. Such thoughts were undoubtedly on her mind when she started writing *Grandma and the Ghowlies*, about an old woman who plans to sell her house and buy a bungalow instead. Mrs O'Pheeley who, like her creator, happens to be a keen gardener, a member of the Mothers' Union and a fluent French speaker, cannot go alone as she feels she must take with her the four "unfrightening little ghosts" and Winty the mischievous poltergeist. Indeed, when Ursula sent a signed copy of the story in Italian translation to a fan, she wrote "Me" under a picture of Grandma on the title page. Memories would naturally have seeped out of every corner of Court

Farm to accompany Ursula for the rest of her life, but any deeper significance in the story is rather to be found – as so often – in a search for homely love and security. The Ghowlies are taken at first to a residential home with children as wilfully disruptive as Winty. "Of course," its owner adds, "wouldn't you be difficult if for years … nobody had loved you?"

Whatever its social context, the book's real joy is in the character of Winty, into whose face the author had looked many times from the magistrate's bench. The ghosts' first appearance is described as "a thread of pale nothingness began to stream through the keyhole like fluff, with tufts in it from time to time, as if four or five little creatures were holding hands." Later, there is a delightful and amusing episode when they write themselves onto Mrs O'Pheeley's passport and other passengers unknowingly sit on them. But it is on Winty with "a small pair of fierce and hollow eyes" that the writer concentrates her imagination, even though she cleverly delays his visible appearance until more than one-third of the way through the story. He makes hats fly and eggs explode, paper flowers are transformed into exhibition winning blooms, and Winty turns himself into a scarecrow to avoid an education service inspector. Like Marta, he is becoming "more like a human child," but even when trying to be good, the peevish poltergeist scares off the others ghosts because he is so hungry to earn all the praise and affection for himself. Magistrates, probation officers, social services, adoption services and the ubiquitous clergyman play their parts, before the idea of the bungalow is abandoned and Grandma and her Ghowlies are happily reunited at the old home.[11]

Morton-Saner, to whom it was dedicated, sold the work fairly quickly to Klaus Flugge at Andersen, and there followed a debate, just like one in the book itself, about whether the spirits were to be called Ghowlies, Ghoulies, Gowlies, Ghosts, Ghosties or Ghostings.[12] The ghosts appear to have caused something of a problem too for the illustrator Susan Varley, at least as far as the author was concerned. The figures look like deflated balloons and Ursula lamented of the international prize-winning artist that "she cannot draw … the ghosts I've … imagined, but that's quite easy to understand. I do think an artist should be accorded a certain amount of licence, and it isn't easy to get perfect accord."[13]

––––––––––––

With Andrew planning to move back to Worcestershire with his wife Elizabeth, Ursula said she was considering letting them take over the lease at Court Farm and renting another property on the Overbury Estate. She decided, in the event, not to do so; Elizabeth said later that she thought her mother-in-law had had no real intention of leaving the house, although in the light of later events she might not be considered an entirely impartial witness. Ursula was "Queen Bee of Beckford" – a phrase which implies the devotion of those around her as well as a dedication to social responsibilities – and a move would almost certainly have meant finding a home in one of the other estate villages ringing Bredon Hill. The two women had previously got on well. Ursula and Peter had been financially generous to Elizabeth and their generosity was appreciated. Peter hinted that help given for school fees might also be used for a new dress; her mother-in-law "did not hoard money – she said it would give us fun." For her part, Ursula recognised that Elizabeth was a strong character and when Andrew married she worried whether he would compare his wife's way of running a household with the way she ran Court Farm. She decided her fears were unfounded.[14] Nevertheless, the strength of the relationship between the two women had not been tested by propinquity.

Ursula had always been strong-willed and said what she thought. As she grew older, the habit grew stronger. "Now listen to me," she would interrupt if she felt excluded from conversation. Someone she thought tiresome might be silenced by *le mot juste*, possibly apposite but which the more polite would leave unsaid. Notes to villagers could be brusque. A Christmas card from an admirer brought an immediate response that she did not much like it. Basil Jenkyns, who came as vicar in 1989, called her "Joe Blunt." "She was not always politic, and it often got her into real scrapes," he said.

If Ursula appeared regal to some within the village of Beckford, then the dining room and the kitchen of Court Farm were the court and the throne room. There she was accustomed to be in control – no matter who was in attendance. The kitchen table, as James described it, "was the anvil on which our parents shaped … our behaviour and manners. When it came to grand-parenting, however, they seemed to forget that these values and disciplines were no longer their responsibility. This led to some disagreements, especially with our wives who not unnaturally felt a little raw about it."

Grandchildren sometimes, to their great surprise, found themselves at the centre of upsets. Until they reached storytelling age, Ursula had relatively little interest in toddlers. As a young woman, she longed for motherhood, but thought less about the babies that were a necessary part of its realisation. Diaries of visits to New Zealand show how she hated baby-minding. When she was nearly sixty, she had described her oldest two grandchildren, Ben and Sophie, as "the most companionable." The others, all aged below five, "I'd go miles to see behind bars or in a zoo, but I get rather bored with them before they are independent, although they are very forgiving and affectionate, and don't seem to mind my telling them how tiresome they are." Now in her seventies, her attitude had not changed. "I always feel on a wavelength with any age of child, not that I want an awful lot of their company before about eight."[16]

Ben was destined to become the innocent harbinger of future upsets when, some time in the early 1970s, Andrew and Elizabeth brought him and his sisters Sophie and

Kate on a visit to Court Farm. All were on best behaviour, but at teatime Ben helped himself to a biscuit without asking permission. Memories differ at this point – Peter may have slapped his hand, he or Ursula may have shouted at him – but all three youngsters were reduced to tears.

Others had similar experiences, which caused them greater surprise for the fact that time spent with Ursula was otherwise remembered with such pleasure. Alan had spent years in Iceland, then in Denmark, where he now lived with his second wife Erkel and their three children. The long period of separation from his sister Ursula meant that the two boys and a girl were rather older by the time they got to know her, but from the age of sixteen Ella Moray Williams started to receive frequent affectionate letters from her English aunt. One summer she came to stay at Court Farm. Ursula talked about their Scottish ancestry, took her to see churches, and introduced her to friends. Ella was full of admiration for her hostess and all went well until she wandered into the kitchen. "Get out, get out," Ursula shouted. She had, as usual, put great energy into entertaining her visitor, but when children or others left the table, she demanded time to recharge her batteries. A line had been crossed.

Ella's elder brother Nicholas also transgressed when he made the mistake of pouring his own milk at breakfast. This, he was told sharply, was not done. He too recalled visits with great fondness, not least for the indulgence with which he, Ella and his younger brother Alex were allowed to play with hockey sticks on the immaculate lawn, irrespective of the damage they might do to the grass and surrounding flowerbeds. Then, without preamble and with no prior discussion of any related matter, Ursula turned to him and said, "I'm not going to leave you anything, you know."[17] Such scenes seem trivial. Certainly they were remembered by the young people concerned not just for the vehemence of expression, but for the lack of warning that preceded them, like thunder on a sunny day. On parents, however, such scenes could have a greater effect.

Ursula had worked hard to finish *Grandma and the Ghowlies* in order to use an advance toward the cost of Robin and his family coming from New Zealand for an extended stay. That they spent less time than planned at Court Farm was due to another kitchen drama. Robin's daughter Elizabeth vividly remembers the mostly happy holiday, sharing the old nursery and its "gorgeous" dapple-grey rocking horse with thinning long silver hair with brother Peter and sister Suzy. There were Sunday surprises, little dolls or knick-knacks left under pillows, and story times during which "Granny" told them about a Court Farm ghost – one of the Ghowlies no doubt. As a consequence, one night the young trio awoke in terror and banged on the nearest door. It was Ursula's bedroom. "We were all three helped into her enormous feather-filled bed," Elizabeth recalled, "then Granny went to the dresser and popped a barley sugar in each of our mouths. The duvet was canary yellow, and the pillows stacked up behind us, so we felt that we were in a huge cloud."

Almost as frightening to young girls as the imaginary ghost, however, was the sudden transformation of their very tangible grandmother into another form. On this occasion Elizabeth and Suzy had been excused at the end of dinner, but went back into the farmhouse kitchen after realising they had left their dolls behind. It was as if they had strayed into a forbidden part of the castle. "We were greeted with a completely furious Granny who was utterly irate that we'd come back again. She yelled 'Get out! Get out! Get out!' I recall having that feeling that even as an eight-year-old I did not think it was in any way justified," Elizabeth said. The episode seems not to have spoilt the children's holiday, but their parents' reaction to such incidents was unsurprising. Within a week of arriving, Robin telephoned his brother Hugh to say that he and his mother had "fallen out," and that he could not bear to stay at Court Farm any longer. As a result, the family went to stay with Hugh and his wife Susan near Oxford.[18]

Andrew's appointment as farm manager of Overbury Estate coincided with his mother's seventieth birthday. She was doubly delighted by his appointment to a position he had long hoped for and which meant that he could call on her every day. "I can sit-in or cook for them when necessary and we have a casual and happy relationship with no demands on one another, which seems to work all right," Ursula wrote. Such an arrangement was less congenial to Andrew's wife Elizabeth. Two years later Ursula told Alan how she was watching her family with concern during "a period … when affection becomes irritation." By October 1984 Andrew and Elizabeth had separated prompting Hugh to write to his mother about pressure on them "from family and friends" to stay together when it was better that they should part.[19]

Ursula had not heard from Vifill for three years when in 1982 he wrote to say he and his wife had been divorced. Alan's marriage and later divorce from his first Icelandic wife, Annelise, seem to have passed without notice. The divorces, however, of Ursula's eldest two sons – for Hugh's marriage was also later dissolved – came as massive shocks to values in which she had trusted all her life, and which she had tried to instil in others. Her reaction was instructive.

Godchildren and grandchildren received gentle advice or admonitions about relationships, or wrote to her knowing their own uncertainties would be listened to with sympathy and in complete confidence. "Obviously I'm for marriage because I think it's a challenge and I enjoyed it so much," she wrote to a godson and his partner. "I find religion a salutary discipline for what would otherwise be a slap-happy relationship. … I'm metaphorically knocking your heads quite kindly together." Nevertheless, she went on, "I've shocked so many of my contemporaries when they deplore the lack of religion in your age group by saying 'They're so happy they don't need God.'"[20] A granddaughter who had been living with a boyfriend had such regard for Ursula's moral authority that she wrote at length to explain her situation.

"Grandma was fairly broad-minded ... and although deeply religious she was accepting of changes in behaviour. She never lectured or appeared to disapprove, and was always approachable," she said.[21]

The awkward collision of social change with a deeply-rooted faith in traditional standards and behaviour was unwelcome, but its impact was reduced by pragmatism and compassion. Such had been the case, long before any marital difficulties had arisen in her own family, when Ursula had resigned from the Mothers' Union from the late 1950s until 1962, because she could not accept its exclusion of divorced women. Both Andrew and Hugh's marital breakdowns were deeply distressing. "I hate the modern trend," she said of the former; the latter was "a horrible shock."[22] But events had to be faced in a practical way. This included remaining on friendly terms with the ex-wives, while welcoming two additional daughters-in-law into the fold. "Ros is such a sweet girl," she said to Elizabeth of Andrew's later partner after their separation. When Hugh remarried, she thought to tell his first wife how much she liked the second. Neither spouse was grateful for the information, even if they understood that such remarks were the product of naivety rather than attempted put-downs. Perhaps Ursula liked to inform them how congenial she could be to all. Perhaps she simply assumed that everyone saw the world as she did.

———————

Despite the difficulty of finding publishers for new short stories, sales of Ursula's books were doing well at the end of 1985. Children's television producer Anne Wood accepted *The Noise of the Great Dark* to be narrated by Brian Blessed in the Channel 4 series *Pob's Programme*. Benjy, for his fifth birthday, watches the sun rise over the hill, "shouting and singing and shining and calling 'Whee-eee-ee'." The poetic story, just five hundred words long and composed perhaps with grandson Ben in mind, has something of the lilting gentleness of the *Teletubbies*, the hugely successful series with which Wood was later to earn international fame and a considerable fortune. Wood also took a copy of *The Good Little Christmas Tree* – in which Prince William had acted at his nursery school – to the Cannes Festival, hoping that a team of puppet-makers would be interested in co-producing a film.[23] Nothing came of that idea, but Ursula meanwhile was busy on a new book. In June, she delivered *Paddy on the Island* to Morton-Saner at her London office, together with a large bundle of asparagus freshly cut from the Court Farm garden.

The artist chosen by Andersen Press was the Norwegian Tor Morisse. He had illustrated *The Good Little Christmas Tree* in a Swedish anthology and loved the story so much that he wrote to one of her publishers who forwarded his letter, written on a large sheet of art paper with cartoons of himself and his studio in the woods. A few months later, at Ursula's invitation, the small, bearded artist, looking rather like a happy troll, was settling down to enjoy a whisky on her terrace.

Paddy, the nine-year-old hero, seizes his opportunity to fend for himself by renting a desert island for a year, to which he is magically transported from the local estate agency. Paddy is given three wishes, which in turn pass to others whom he wishes onto the island, and there follows a parade of familiar characters, Girl Guides, a talking cat and a great-grandma who is "the best storyteller in the world," but anxious to get home to cooking, gardening and the church bazaar. Constantly sustained by enough food to satisfy a dozen children's parties, the youngsters defy pirates, escape from a cavern and brave a forest fire, although Paddy, rather improbably, longs to return to do well in his exams. The language is rich and adventurous: phosphorescence – a word for young readers to roll around the tongue like sherbet – flickers on the waves, while thick clouds "hung like velvet curtains." At the end of Paddy's stay, with all his wishes exhausted, the original possessor of the island asks how Paddy has fared. When Ursula finished the book, the only one dedicated to all four sons, she was seventy-five and must have wondered if it would be the last she would ever write. It did in fact prove to be the last of her novels to be published. In this context its ending raises an intriguing question. Is it merely fanciful to suppose that the author was also addressing herself, as Prospero-like she contemplated laying aside her powers? As it happens, Ursula had not long before written a mini-story about shipwrecked circus animals, *The Singing Island*, which has its own echo of the "isle full of noises." Are Paddy's thoughts about how he has used his magical gift autobiographical, or merely concerned with a boy's rite of passage toward manhood? Whatever the case, Ursula would surely have responded in a similar way to the question about whether it had all been worthwhile. Yes, Paddy answers after a little hesitation, and goes home to rejoin his family.[24]

Chapter 23

——————

"And once forever belied the fears
That morning laughter must end in tears."[1]

Ursula Moray Williams, *Hullabaloo!* In *Hullabaloo!*
Ed. Barbara Willard, Hamish Hamilton (1969)

Ursula sat up in bed in Tewkesbury hospital and fought for the right word, for any words. For once in her life, they would not come, and she got angry with herself. The reaction was as much a matter of self-therapy as of natural annoyance. Her lips moved, her face contorted, then at last the sound came.

"Bugger," she cried, and felt better.[2]

The years 1987 and 1988 had been busy but relatively uneventful, except for the finalisation of Andrew's divorce. Ursula had not been writing, hoping instead that her agent would succeed in publishing an anthology of short stories written over many years, or to place them individually in collections. Her most popular titles continued to sell well, with translations in many European and other languages, and *Paddy on the Island* would shortly become her latest title adapted for BBC television, with Matthew Devitt following actors including Rodney Bewes, Patrick Troughton, Bernard Cribbins, Prunella Scales, Phyllida Law and Judi Dench as narrators of her stories. An idea for a new book had started to take shape in the spring of 1988, but it had come "at the wrong moment." The burden of maintaining the garden and keeping up with commitments in Beckford meant it had to be put aside. Ursula was depressed, suffering withdrawal symptoms no doubt, but as she told her "dearest Kaye, we have to adapt, adapt, adapt."

That autumn a local newspaper reporter was struck by the "sprightly, cheerful woman" with "enormous energy" whom she found entertaining a lively party from the local mothers and toddlers group, but Ursula's reluctance to travel and postponement of further writing suggest she was already suffering health problems which were related to her cancer operation. Certainly by April 1989 she had been feeling "rotten" for some time, as a result of which she was twice admitted to hospital, emerging in September feeling "pretty limp." Then, just after Christmas, she suffered a stroke. For the third time in her life, Ursula came close to what might have been her death, and, as after cancer and her serious car crash, for the third time responded with resilience that others found extraordinary. Essential to quick recovery, she decided, was resolve, and that was greatly helped when necessary by bad temper.

"Give me the b… b…" she told a visitor.

"The bottle?" she asked.

Ursula shook her head. "The b… b…"

"The book?"

"No, the b… b… bloody glass." She was on the mend.[3]

It was not so much the extent of her recovery as the spirit behind it that was to be seen on Bredon Hill one Sunday morning in June 1990. Andrew and two friends watched as Ursula did up six zips on a multi-piece leather suit, then helped her with the heavy helmet. In front of her, its wings twitching slightly in the breeze, was what her son likened to a flying motorcycle, his microlight aircraft, which had been brought in pieces by trailer and assembled where it stood. Andrew had just obtained his licence and his mother was to have the pleasure of becoming one of his first passengers. "You are stuffed into a seat which would be a close fit for one," she wrote, "but no, the pilot comes too." Over the roar of the engine, Andrew gave a last minute reminder for Ursula not to put her feet on the fibreglass floor. It might break and cause a crash, if she did, he had helpfully explained. "Finally, up you go. Glorious!!!" The flight, up to 10,000 feet, with the Avon showing below like a twisted ribbon, was "better than Concorde," she declared, but without the Champagne. The feeling was so exhilarating that she persuaded the new vicar to follow her example. He was less enthusiastic. "It was a horrendous experience for me," he reported. "We went over the Cotswolds and I learnt to pray." Ursula, however, went on to clock-up a total of more than five hours in the air, including her seventh and last trip, at the age of ninety-one, to see the sun go down over the Malvern Hills.[4]

As Ursula turned eighty, her letters were again as full of activity as they had been after retirement from the bench ten years earlier. She wrote of a "very social" January, followed by nights at the theatre and concerts, organising a crazy tea party, planting trees and bushes, and dividing the snowdrops "to stretch their cramped toes." When Morisse returned for a holiday with his family, the party visited a Cotswolds' tourist attraction where the artist's young son was thrilled to go down its giant slide – and amazed to see a shrieking eighty-year-old Englishwoman come plunging down behind him. Ursula picked flowers from which she created thirty-five posies for church visitors from Dudley, and after refuse collectors had mistakenly carted off Overbury church's banners, Ursula helped make thirty new ones. She held a large dinner party for the new vicar and described the menu in detail the following morning: cheese tartlets, roast lamb with crab apple jelly, caramel pudding, coffee meringues. She was then expecting guests for tea and closed her letter with an apology as there was baking to be done.

Literary engagements had also resumed with a trip to Puffin's fiftieth anniversary party at the Victoria and Albert Museum, talks in Oxford, and again at the

Cheltenham Festival of Literature. Webb, now confined to a wheelchair, had also attended the festival, and came later to Court Farm with Morton-Saner for supper and talk by the fire. In fact the agent had an additional reason for the visit, for she brought with her the manuscript of Ursula's last projected novel, *Lord Polidore's Parrot*. It never flew.

The subject was unknowingly prompted by a schoolboy fan Matthew Eve who, in the summer of 1987, started writing long illustrated letters describing among other things the antics of his pet parakeet Percy. Ursula had a plot in mind when she wrote to Webb in the spring of 1988 and started work the following winter, but there were difficulties from the outset. The new book was "struggling to get past the road block." Ursula was "battling" with a story which was giving her "a little trouble." She put it aside after a few unsatisfactory months' work, intending to resume writing at the start of 1990. Because of her stroke, it was not, in fact, until a year after that date that she looked at the manuscript again. "I <u>think</u> I am past the point of no return, in that I shan't scrap it, but may re-write the first part," she told her granddaughter Alex in February 1991. Days later she wrote to a friend that she was finding it "not quite so easy when there's so much time, probably because I've always had to write with so little time. However, I'm pressing on and trying to remember that I had just the same difficulty with the Little Wooden Horse." By May it had been completed and Morisse was keen to illustrate it, but the author knew it was not quite as good as it should be and within a week of finishing the first draft was already talking about revisions. A month later she was wondering whether it would ever be published, and by the end of the year, faced with suggestions for extensive changes, was wondering whether to rewrite the entire book.

The central idea is promising. The old Lord is extremely rude to his parrot, and one day, out of annoyance with each other, they change places, having arranged that both will change back again at precisely the same second. Chaos ensues, as the pair cannot agree about the timing of their return transformation. One half of the book tells Lord Polidore's version of what happens, the other sees events from the parrot's point of view. Ursula obviously thought the idea a good one: "Don't spread the plot around or someone else may pinch it before mine is published," she told Alex. In one of the best episodes, the transmogrified aristocrat takes flight to an island inhabited by identical birds who all confusingly repeat his claim, parrot-fashion, to be the real Lord Polidore. At times the story creates the old-world charm of a lost era, among gentlemen's clubs and ladies serving tea and plum cake dipped in sherry, just sufficiently removed from everyday reality to make a virtue of the author's unfashionable view of the world. Unfortunately, the relentlessly upper class settings – cricket and hunting, the House of Lords and a Royal garden party – were unlikely to appeal to contemporary readers or savvy publishers. Nor was the problem of having a parrot transformed into a lord describing a lord transformed into a parrot claiming still to be a lord entirely overcome. And to Morton-Saner, it appeared that the once bubbling stream had lost its sparkle.

"Knock-knock-knock-knock," went the opening of *Grandma and the Ghowlies*. Nobody was there. Her last published novel opened: "Paddy was buying an island. He had money (a few pounds), he had plans, he had great determination. He was nine years old." Compare these must-read-on first lines with: "I am a grey polly parrot, and my name is Alice. I belong to a noble lord called Polidore. He tells me that at school they used to call him Polly." Morton-Saner had recognised immediately that the story did not reach the standard of its predecessors. "We were always trying to find ways of re-jigging it," she said.[5]

Sadly, as another might have observed, this was a dead parrot. The extensive rewrite was never undertaken. The story remains of interest, however, not least for the views expressed by Polly parrot, learnt no doubt from his vigorous eighty-year-old author. Infuriated by Lord P's indolence, the bird exclaims, "If I were an old gentleman, I wouldn't waste my time going to sleep with all the world going on outside me. I'd spend more time in London and the House of Lords, I'd open this bazaar and that bazaar, and play cricket, and give garden parties and have all the estate workers to tea and a lovely Christmas tree, and make everybody fond of me, and they'd give me nuts, no, not nuts, but cigars and bottles of nice drink, and I'd race my car, and make my chauffeur hurry-hurry-hurry instead of driving along so slowly and sadly."[6]

Ursula was not for the slow lane yet, but apart from a few minor short stories, her professional writing career was over, sixty years after it began. How then might it be assessed?

In an entry for the *Oxford Dictionary of National Biography*, Belinda Copson described Ursula's best-loved books as "full of old fashioned adventure, loyalty, fun and kindness" and identified as a feature of her work the "sentient toys" like the Little Wooden Horse and the doll-child Marta, which identify with human needs and emotions. As the former may have been influenced by older models, such as Pinocchio, so later writers of the 1950s and 1960s, like Joan G. Robinson with her *Teddy Robinson* adventures, and Modwena Sedgwick, creator of the *Galldora* rag doll stories, owed something to the brave little horse, she concluded.

Hobbie, Woppit, Little Wo, Boss and Dingbatt might be added to Copson's list, but the cast of animals conjured by Ursula onto her stage would be longer: real horses, goats and geese, fantastical birds, mice, a tiger, a crocodile, a spider, the indefinable Pettabomination, Moonball and Bogwoppit, and numerous cats of varying degrees of felinity. Only in *High Adventure* does a real cat appear, in a supporting role, for as Eileen Colwell realised after asking Ursula to contribute to a collection of pet stories, she would not normally choose such a hero. "I quite understand your doubt about a story of a <u>real</u> cat," Colwell told her, "you are so happy and inspired with fantasy."[8] The choice of characters, from the natural world and that of the imagination, seems to preserve the distinction made by a child, the former borrowed from the practical, regulated territory of the farm, the latter from the home or the natural world in which fantasy is unconstrained.

The American commentator Joanne Lewis Sears thus concluded that "the majority of Williams's stories employ fantasy rooted in everyday reality." An obituary in *The Times* noted the "simplicity and toughness of narrative such as is present in folk tales ... permits the sleight of hand whereby ... bits of wood mounted on four unreliable wheels can undertake astonishingly convincing journeyings." Julia Eccleshare in *The Guardian* wrote: "Throughout her writing, Williams showed a pleasing love of adventure and a delight in the unexpected. She knew what made a good story whatever the setting." Nicholas Tucker in *The Independent* wrote of the "style, pace and humour" of her work, which left "a fine legacy of storytelling" that remained "essentially moralistic but also fun."[9]

Elizabeth Hammill, Collection Director of Seven Stories, the Centre for Children's Books in Newcastle upon Tyne where most of Ursula's archives are stored, described her as "a classic storyteller [whose] friendly, conversational voice with its poetic overtones offers an irresistible invitation to young readers to adventure out into the unknown world beyond home."[10] Margery Fisher had written of the ideal children's story in her influential book *Intent Upon Reading*, saying it must be "written from the heart and from ... some memory of and contact with childhood. It must appeal directly to the imagination of the reader, must create a unique world into which the child will go willingly and actively." She included *Hobbie*, *The Moonball*, *The Noble Hawks* and *Beware of this Animal* on her recommended reading list, but praised most extensively *Adventures of the Little Wooden Horse*. "Wise, mature, richly written," it helped younger children, when they "must get on their tricycles and venture out to see what the world is like," she wrote.[11]

One such venturer was the young Nick Park, the future creator of *Wallace and Gromit*, who heard *Adventures of the Little Wooden Horse* serialised on *Jackanory*. It was also one of the first books he read. "I couldn't put it down," he said. "The story was compelling, charming and inspirational and it was one of the biggest influences on me and my love of storytelling."[12] Author Margaret Mahy remembered finding the title in her school library in New Zealand with *The Nine Lives of Island Mackenzie*. "She had such good stories to tell. She shared the imaginative pre-occupations of her readers, and the stories were told in language accessible to middle-school children," Mahy recalled.[13] Anne Wood was another great fan. As a TV producer in her *pre-Teletubbies* days, she had wanted to make a short film of *The Good Little Christmas Tree* but could not get sufficient commercial support. When she later moved to a house close to Ursula's, she became a friend as well as an admirer and recognised the spirit of her fictional heroes in their creator.

The Little Wooden Horse was one of the greatest children's books ever written and it came from the heart of Ursula, who faced life with the same joy, faith, courage and sense of humour as her most endearing characters ... Hers was not the easy path but a beautiful one, centred on the imaginative life that begins in childhood and is a constant inspiration.[14]

A book-loving blogger from Devon added his or her own tribute: the Little Wooden Horse "had been one of those favourite stories read aloud at Going Home Time in Miss Butteriss' class ... before we all said The Lord's Prayer and put our chairs up on the tables." Ursula would have approved.

Unsurprisingly, assessments of Ursula's work concentrate on this and other best-known titles such as *Gobbolino the Witch's Cat* and the Toymaker series. But the range of work is considerable. Ursula wrote more books about real horses than wooden ones, and more with children as main characters than with animals real or fantastical. Many others are about adults, although they are usually reassuringly wise and silly at the same time. Sears recognised this breadth of output, "in so many modes, and to such varied age levels, that her work occupies no fixed niche in the history of children's literature." A consequence, perhaps, is unevenness. Plots may be "inconsistent, even incoherent" but "never fail to engage. Her prose is graceful, lively, surefooted. Her simple forthright values and amusingly unrepentant protagonists please children far removed from the sunshine world she once shared with her twin sister."[15] Winifred Whitehead detected uncertainties in the more complex plots, and "some stereotyping" in the minor characters, but praised the "witty and satirical undertones" of the writing. Occasionally Ursula's books achieved "a haunting power and a delightfully sharp and witty observation of the foibles of mankind."[16]

Whitehead called the earlier stories old-fashioned, an epithet that others applied more widely to Ursula's work. "She never pursued spurious social relevance," was the curious caption in her obituary in *The Times*, which described a writer "known for her unashamedly old-fashioned and simple tales that recalled an idyllic upbringing." Writing about the 1960s, John Rowe Townsend described a period when "children were expected to face in fiction the harsh realities of divorce, illness and death as well as war and holocaust. The happy two-parent white family ceased to be the fictional norm. Not only were there one-parent families and broken homes; parents slid rapidly down the moral slope."[17] Nevertheless, Ursula was still one of the authors recommended in the Cox Report published in 1989 on the teaching of English in primary schools. Twenty years later, Dame Jacqueline Wilson described herself as "pretty strict and old-fashioned" even though her fictional teenagers stayed out late and drank alcohol. "It seems so sad that girls feel embarrassed if they want to play with dolls past the age of six," she said.[18]

Ursula's best books survived because she knew what it was like to be a child. "All that book-writing is like a lovely cloud I lived in," she told a friend.[19] In a sense, she never escaped entirely from a childhood lived through her own memories, and the imagination of those who listened to her stories. Morton-Saner put this into context:

> Today's child can be cynical. I don't think she took that into account. She was writing for children that she knew about. She was never starry-eyed about them, but was very wise, and the characters have life because of the sort of person she was.[20]

Here surely is the key to understanding her books, one more easily discovered by someone like Morton-Saner who knew her as a writer and as a friend. Such a bulky mass of work cannot be crammed into one category of juvenile fiction, but it closely corresponds to the determining features of the author's own life. Ideas of faith, hope and home dominated the parallel worlds of fact and fiction. The faith was instinctive, in the goodness of God, in the natural wonders of His creation, in the spirit of man no matter what the outward appearance of a Malkin or a young miscreant. The hope of self-realisation, of improvement in the life of others, was not, however, to be achieved without effort. Earlier generations of the family had travelled the world to find it. For Ursula it was represented in the ideals of the Girl Guides, by the challenge of growing up in a strange, uncomfortable house, in early trips abroad, or in the quests of heroes – outward-bound like her sons sent to adventure camps, or like those in the pages of her books. "A child needs happy endings," as one analyst of juvenile fiction wrote, "and those victories which result from positive action by the hero and the forces of good are likely to be much more powerful and convincing than those that just happen."[21]

Ursula and her characters travelled in hope. The journey itself was the process by which they came to know themselves. Pluck and moral courage were their watchwords on the road. Her pilgrims, like the one who had sent them forth, hid a steely determination beneath their soft exteriors. When others in the great, wild world failed to behave well, they reacted with pragmatism, for their own characters and beliefs remained constant. Then, leaving trials and travails outside, they returned to security and enduring love at home, and to kindness in the community around it. Such qualities never changed. It was, in a sense, a world that was always old-fashioned. It was preserved in memory in a form that was by no means unrealistic, but untainted by the contradictions and uncertainties of adulthood. Life was a fairly simple story, simply told, particularly in short episodes in that dreamy time before actual sleep. Ursula would no more have been capable of writing an adult novel than of comprehending politics, or the complexities of arranging a mortgage, or things which took place beyond the strictly regulated order of the kitchen and the nursery trimmed with beautiful pictures. Hers instead was the vision of St Augustine, a writer to whom she had increasingly turned, whose invitation to restless hearts was to return home from wandering, to find their rest in God. Whether the destination was to the arms of an Almighty or simply to a mortal loving embrace, here was a message that would transcend mere fashion.

Ursula grew older gracefully and gratefully, without imposing on others the indignities that she had seen in the declining years of Mabel, Moray, Jo, Ella and others. As early as 1970 she and Peter had been planning for an old age that would not pass on to others the duties of care that she had reluctantly taken upon herself for her parents. They joined Mutual Households, an association offering private rooms and communal facilities in country houses. "We're determined not to be a burden to our children," she explained. "I'm sure we'll hate it but better than having the family worried or responsible when one knows what it means."[22] She remained just as determined as years passed. "When the time comes for me to give up my independence, I will make the best of it, and go cheerfully into a retirement home and make myself happy there," she told a local Evergreen Club. "I shan't go to my family because … it is too great a strain to put on the next generation. … I am determined that the nurses shall not find it a depressing task to look after me. I shall listen to their life histories and their love affairs, and try not to offload my own small afflictions on anybody." Even in increasing older age, as sensibilities declined, Ursula regarded it a privilege "to be allowed to be kind, and loving and useful." That included listening tolerantly to the young and trying not to criticise. "Let's stick to our morals and principles, because they expect it of us," she told her elderly listeners, "but don't let us show horrors or no understanding of the … pressures they are under." Ursula called her talk "On a happy old age."[23] As in her books, the words of the author coincided with her practice.

Old age was still for living, a cause for celebration not for sadness or regret. In her final years, her eyesight almost gone, Ursula would write out little verses for her nurse with the aid of a ruler. A favourite ran:

There was a man and he was mad,
He thought he died before he had.
And this sad thought his life so saddened,
That when he died he thought he hadn't.

After abandoning work on *Lord Polidore's Parrot*, Ursula lived for another fifteen years that, by comparison with most people of her age, were exceptionally busy. Alan, whom Ursula continued to help financially but with whom relations were never very close, died after a fall in 1996. In the same year, James's wife Rosemary died of cancer. At the funeral, Ursula noted her first great-grandson, aged two, "chirruped merrily and made one think it may be death, but Harry is life beginning again."[25] In 2003 Hugh died. When Andrew brought the terrible news, his mother decided they should take a bottle to the top of Bredon Hill and drink to his memory. A plane passed overhead as they emptied their glasses. Despite her apparent calm, however, others noticed a change: the normally upright figure slumped for a time, diminished by a distress that was not outwardly displayed. She pulled herself together and did not cry.[26]

Ursula's church work went on unabated. Hobby horses, fluffy mice and owls were produced for bazaars; little wooden horses made by a village craftsman – paid it seems in apple pies – were furnished with colourful felt saddles and bridles. Her recall of the past remained vivid. One of the best things about having been an author, she told an aspiring writer, was that "you are unconsciously making an encyclopaedia of your mind and collecting information that need never be wasted." Recent events, however, were more easily forgotten. Invited guests sometimes arrived to find that they were unexpected at the appointed hour, but were fed lavishly anyway. One day she fed delivery men thinking friends had failed to arrive for the lunch she had prepared then re-made the meal when they came, as previously arranged, for dinner.[27]

In 2001 Ursula was still managing to write six hundred letters a year, but the sight in her remaining eye was failing, and by the following spring doctors had told her that she was likely to go blind within six months. "At least this means there's good time to make further arrangements – isn't that fortunate? … Don't worry about me because I am very cheerful," she wrote to a relative. "Isn't it a nuisance!" she told another. "But I can cope and I'll always love your letters." In 2003 she wrote one of her very last letters to Peggy's daughter, sent via Andrew. The words, barely decipherable, written against a ruler, say: "Dearest Elaine, I do love your letters. So – do write again." Some friends did not know why they had stopped receiving letters. Others wrote, but stopped doing so when they received no reply, and only learnt the reason later.[28]

More than her blindness, she regretted going deaf. Of the gifts of sight and hearing, the latter was the more precious, she told visitors, for its increasing loss had meant she was no longer able to join in with conversations. Visits to restaurants were abandoned because she could not hear voices over background noise and clatter. At home, even her large, old hearing aid became ineffective. She had declined use of a more modern model, but Andrew came up with a solution. Remembering those flights in his microlight that she had until recently enjoyed, he clipped together pilot's headphones with high amplification. Through them they talked and he read stories. He chose her own, picking favourites from the shelves and early titles that she had long forgotten. So she listened to her own words, following her heroes' adventures with the attention that she had herself commanded among her young audiences many years before, thinking perhaps of the events that had inspired them.

Ursula had left Court Farm in October 1998 and moved to a bungalow close to Andrew in the neighbouring village of Conderton. Most of her furniture was sold. Her collection of manuscripts and many letters were given to Seven Stories, the Centre for Children's Books, in Newcastle upon Tyne. Andrew came daily; a nurse,

Wendy Porteus, three times a day. "She never lost that inner sparkle, that sense of excitement," she said. "She treated me like the daughter that she told me she would have loved to have had, and I would have loved to have had her as my mother." Friends called often, and stayed long. Neighbour Ted McWhirter left delivery of her parish magazine until the end of his round because he knew he would not leave without a sherry or two, while Ursula talked about Stoneham and old times. Old habits died hard. When he heard her alarm buzzing and ran next door to see what was wrong, she tried to insist that he should have a quick one before calling the ambulance. But Ursula's condition was cause for concern. On another occasion a fork pushed into a toaster fused the lights. And when she started to wander in slippers along the road through the village, it seemed time to look for a place in a nursing home. "If Andrew thinks it's right, I'm happy to go," she said. In August 2006 she moved to Tewkesbury Care Home.

On 13 October, with her usual meticulous concern for orderliness, Ursula went through her will. There were legacies of a few hundred pounds each to Erkel, Rita, and the church of St John the Baptist at Beckford, and smaller gifts to each of her eleven godchildren, with less than £14,000 shared by her three sons and Hugh's two children. The rewards of industry had been spent on living. Four days later, aged ninety-five, she died.

The church was packed, with extra seats down the aisles, for the service to celebrate Ursula's life. Several of those who came were dear friends made in the previous few weeks. Richard Calver played Bach and Fauré on the organ, her nurse Wendy Porteus sang. Hugh's son Jeremy read from the opening chapter of *Gobbolino*, the first of his grandmother's books that he remembered, and Andrew's daughter Kate from *Elaine of La Signe*. Later Andrew placed a memorial plaque on the ancient stone wall of the graveyard, beside that for Peggy Tandy. But as Ursula's long aversion to attending funerals has already been noted, this story will not take its leave of her there, but a few days before, in her small room at Tewkesbury. The sister of Andrew's partner Ros Long died ten days before Ursula herself. "I'm so sorry to hear about your sister," Ursula said, and although now extremely weak herself, reached for and held her visitor's hand. "It was very supportive and kind, and we didn't need to discuss it," she remembered. "Right at the end, she was thinking about someone else."

Anne Liversidge had met Ursula only once before when she made a special trip to the nursing home with her fiancé, Hugh's son Jeremy, knowing it was likely to be the last time she would see her. Ursula listened to their talk then interrupted without preamble to say she was going to tell them a story. Immediately her voice became animated by the rhythm of the prose, and changed with the inflections of each character as she recited *Albert and the Lion*, pausing only a couple of times to recall the next line. Then it was their turn, she insisted, and giggled as they told a short limerick and an equally silly joke. They stayed an hour, talking about their journey, about the pleasant flowers in the room, but mostly about the travelling that the two had done since meeting Ursula the previous year. Ursula was lying down, too weak to rise, and it was uncertain as they spoke whether she could hear every word, or whether she was simply accommodating herself to what lay ahead, and settling down with contemplations of the past. "Oh, what fun," she said. "What fun."[29]

Notes

The following abbreviations are used:

7S: Seven Stories, the Centre for Children's Books, Newcastle upon Tyne
AM-S: Anthea Morton-Saner
BMW: Barbara Moray Williams
BU: Bristol University, Department of Arts and Social Sciences
FJ: Faith Jaques
JO'H: Juliet O'Hea
KW: Kaye Webb
PD: Private documents (used where necessary to avoid ambiguity)
RU: Reading University, Museum of English Rural Life, Special Collections
SU: Stanley Unwin
UMW: Ursula Moray Williams

Chapter One

1. UMW, *A castle for John-Peter*, Harrap, 1941, 17.
2. UMW diary 1932 lists books that she had read by that date. In *Desert Island*, 2002, PD, she cited Florence Hodgson Burnett's *The Secret Garden* as her favourite in early childhood.
3. UMW described North Stoneham House and its grounds extensively. See *I lived in this house*, 04/02/12 7S, which appeared in part in *Puffin Post*, vol. 3, no. 3, and UMW, *'Something about the author'*, in *Contemporary authors autobiography series*, vol. 9, Gale, 1990. Information is taken also from Alan's unpublished *Barbara Arnason as a young girl*; George Prosser, *Select Illustrations of Hampshire 1833*; Harold Barstow, *Recollections of North Stoneham*, 2000 and *Recollections of North Stoneham and Chilworth Manors*, 2001, privately published; from Willis-Fleming estate rent rolls; site visits; interviews with David Tew, Ralph Hallett, Douglas Bunce and Jean Burgess. The traction engine was called, appropriately, Little Fearnot.
4. *British Red Cross Journal*, October 1922, 117.

Chapter Two

1. Mary Louisa Molesworth, *Christmas-Tree Land*, Macmillan, 1884.
2. UMW, *Something …, op cit*, 237. BMW to Alan, 11 March 1968.
3. Hampshire Red Cross annual reports 1919–44. Moray is acknowledged as A. Moray-Williams by W.G. Sinclair Snow in *Arthur John Maclean, Bishop of Moray, Primus*, privately published, 1950. His death notice in *The Times* 27 October 1959, preserved the hyphen. Such social appropriations were not unknown. Robert Stephenson Smyth Powell, whose scouting ideals Moray admired, had adopted his father's name in calling himself Robert Baden-Powell.
4. *Stratford Herald* and *Stratford Chronicle* 25 March 1887.
5. Alderminster school records, Warwickshire Record Office. UMW to Alan, undated 1987, 16 May 1995.

6. C.G. Falkner, *History of Weymouth College to 1901*, privately published, 1934, 232–45. *Clavinian*, November 1901, May 1902.

7. Roy Wake and Pennie Denton, *Bedales School*, Haggerston Press, 1993, 39, 52–6.

8. SU, *The truth about a publisher*, Allen & Unwin, 1960, 17–20.

9. I. Margesson and A. Jonson, *Report of the First Year's Work at Sesame House*. Child Life. 1900, Vol. 2, No. 8, 252–254.

10. SU, *op cit*, 25; UMW, *Something …, op cit*, 237.

11. SU, *op cit*, 25; 1901 census.

12. *Bedales Record*, 1906–7, 55–6. Information elsewhere is drawn extensively from the *Bedales Record* and *Bedales Chronicle*, and Wake and Denton, *op cit*. Many former pupils wrote about the school in memoirs.

13. Mabel's diary quoting Granville Stanley Hall, *Adolescence*, Appleton, 1905.

14. UMW, *Something …, op cit*, 235.

15. Grace Stalley to Sidney Unwin, 5 December 1912. Myfanwy Thomas to UMW, 18 November 1991.

16. UMW diary, 13 March 1933.

17. UMW, *Something …, op cit*, 235.

18. UMW, *Memories*, PD; *Something …, op cit*, 235–6; Diary, 13 March 1933.

19. Geoffrey Trease, *Tales out of school*, 2nd edn, Heinemann, 1964, 124–6, states that writers of girls' stories tend to invent twins as convenient playmates.

20. Frances Partridge, *Memories*, Gollancz, 1981, 46–8.

21. Betty Wardle, *Lincroft School*, Petersfield Area Historic Society Bulletin vol. 3, no. 3, 1986, 6, and PD. It was part of the Parents' National Educational Union founded by Fröbel supporter Charlotte Mason. See Colin Palmer, *Charlotte Mason*, PNEU, 2006. UMW diary, 16 January 1933.

22. Alan, *Barbara Árnason … op cit*.

23. UMW, *The Forgotten Child*, 04/02/17, 7S, written for 1972 Exeter conference, 7. UMW, *Children's Literature Today and Yesterday*, talk to Cheltenham Teacher Training College, early 1972, PD. See also UMW, *Writing for Children*, 04/02/06, 7S, written for talks in October 1973.

24. UMW, *The Magic Casement* in Eileen Colwell (ed.), *The Magic Umbrella*, Bodley Head, 1976. Hendon library, December 1938.

25. Wake & Denton, *op cit*, 67–70.

26. *Reports by the Joint War Committee and the Joint War Finance Committee of the British Red Cross Society on Voluntary Aid*, 1921; *Red Cross Work in Hampshire 1914–1919*, Balfour Red Cross Museum, Petersfield.

27. Wake & Denton, *op cit*, 66–7, 217. Laurin Zilliacus, 'Personal impressions as boy and master' in John Haden Badley, *Bedales: A Pioneer School*, Methuen, 1923, 165–75. *Bedales Record* 1919–20, 10–12. Grace Stalley to Sidney Unwin, 6 March 1913.

28. *Bedales Record*, 1918–19, 1; Moray told SU he expected his job to end in July 1919, 28 April 1919, RU. *Red Cross Work …, op cit*. Hampshire Red Cross annual report December 1919, 99.

29. *British Red Cross Journal* October 1922, 117.

30. Willis Fleming estate records.

Chapter Three

1. He became chairman of Sun Alliance. Daughter Shirley Bulpitt to author.
2. UMW, *Something ...*, *op cit*, 236. Bedales also had an early school scout patrol, organised by Badley's deputy, Oswald Powell, second cousin of Robert Baden-Powell. Moray visited their camps to judge tent-pitching, signalling and first aid. Jill Thompson-Lewis (Oswald's granddaughter) to author. *Bedales Record* 1915–16, 64.
3. Elaine Moss, *Ursula Moray Williams and Adventures of the Little Wooden Horse*, in *Signal: Approaches to children's books*, May 1971, 58.
4. *The Bookseller*, 22 December 1938; UMW, *The Twins and Their Ponies*, Harrap, 1936, 30–1, 55, 73; *Hobbie*, Brockhampton, 1958.
5. Louise Reynolds to author.
6. UMW, *Something ... op cit*, 239–40; Douglas Bunce to author.
7. UMW, *I lived ...*, *op cit*, 15–16.
8. Douglas Bunce to author.
9. UMW, *The Secrets of the Wood*, Harrap, 1955, 45.
10. UMW, *I lived ...* 16; *Something ...* 239–40.
11. UMW, *Something ...* 240.
12. Harold Barstow, 2000, *op cit*, 42–3.
13. UMW, *I lived ...*, 3–4; UMW, *Christmas in the 1920s*, 04/02/14, 5, 7S; *Something ...*, 239. David Tew to UMW, 18 December 1977, to Harold Barstow, 8 October 2001, and to author.
14. UMW, *Something ...*, 237. See Chapter 8.
15. UMW, *For USA*, 04/02/28, 7S, 2.
16. UMW, *Writing for Children*, *op cit*, 11–13.
17. UMW, *Christmas ...*, *op cit*, 2–5.
18. Alan, *Barbara Árnason ...*, *op cit*.
19. UMW, *St George and the Dragon*, c.1927, PD.
20. UMW, *A First Class Parcel and other stories*, 1926–7, PD.
21. UMW *Puffin passport*, 04/08/01, 7S.
22. UMW, *Something ...*, *op. cit.* 238.
23. UMW, *Guide Camp Diary*, 29 July to 6 August, 1927, PD.
24. UMW to David Unwin, 2 February 1972.
25. *Partners in Progress*, privately published for diamond jubilee of George G. Harrap & Co., 1961, 21–2.
26. SU, *The Truth about Publishing*, 8th edition, Allen & Unwin, 1976, 220. A comparable income in 2009 would be nearly £560,000.
27. SU, ... *Publisher, op cit*, 136.
28. Rose Kerr, (ed.) Alix Liddell, *Story of the Girl Guides 1908–1938*, Girl Guides Association, 1976, 68. Write the words backwards.
29. UMW, *Something ...*, *op cit.*, 240.
30. SU ... *op cit.*, *Publisher*, 23.; UMW to Matthew Eve, undated, PD.

Chapter Four

1. "The Lilies-of-the-Valley." UMW, *Annecy diary*, PD.
2. "Give us this day our daily bread."
3   UMW, *Something ...*, *op cit.*, 240.
4. David Tew, Douglas Bunce, Erkel Moray Williams to author.

5. David Tew to author. UMW, *I lived* … 4.

6. Moray to SU, 27 December 1925, RU. Erkel Moray Williams to author.

7. The fees were paid from London, possibly by Moray's sister Kathleen. George Chesterton, *Malvern College 125 years*, Malvern Publishing, 1990, 70; Ralph Blumenau, *A history of Malvern College*, St. Martin's, 1965, 109–11. Alan to UMW, 19 December, probably 1990.

8. Jean Burgess (née Gemmell) to author, March 2008. The school is now the Tourist Information Office in the splendid red and cream Victorian Gothic Guildhall. The art college has moved next door.

10. UMW, *I lived …*, 4.

11. John Greenwood diary.

12. UMW, Autobiographical draft, PD.

13. UMW to FJ, 18 June 1970.

14. He described himself as an Imperialist, letter to SU, 4 August 1916, RU.

15. SU to UMW, 3 September 1931, RU. UMW to Mary Unwin 14 October 1968; to Ruth Unwin 29 December 1971, to David Unwin 2 February 1972. UMW reading list, PD. David Unwin to author. Reviews are taken from the *TLS* 26 November 1931, 9 March, 18 May 1933 and 22 November 1934; *Manchester Guardian* 13 July 1933, 6 December 1934; *Current Literature* March 1933; *Morning Post* 17 February 1933; *New York Times* 9 June 1935.

Chapter Five

1. UMW, *Jean-Pierre*, A&C Black, 1931, 30–2.

2. UMW, *The Pettabomination*, Denis Archer, 1933.

3. *Partners in Progress, op cit*, 21–2; George Harrap and M.E. Montgomery to Girl Guides' Association, 28 January 1932, Harrap archive.

4. Membership grew from 589,505 to 605,557 from 1931 to 1934. Girl Guide Association archives.

5. Moray's maternal uncle, Arthur John Maclean, was Bishop of Moray, Ross and Caithness, and in 1935 was to become Primus (Head) of the Church of Scotland. The coincidence of Moray as his nephew's name was accidental. Moray assisted in a biography of his uncle, and Inge Gosney, who stayed at North Stoneham for a year, informed the author that Moray had told her (wrongly) that his father was a bishop. There is no evidence, however, of any contact between the two.

6. Newspaper reports from Bristol, Glasgow, Dunfermline, Ipswich and Pretoria, PD.

7. UMW, *The Autumn Sweepers*, A&C Black, 1933, 8–9.

8. UMW diary, 7 March 1933.

9. *The Pettabomination* was an exception for he feared it would be so difficult to place that any condition might put off a publisher.

10. UMW, *Grandfather*, Allen & Unwin, 1933, 19–20, 43–7.

11. Guðbjörg Kristjánsdóttir ed., *Barbara Moray Williams Árnason*, Reykjavik 1996, 25–6; RCA Registry information from Neil Parkinson and Stephen Govier.

12. Conrad Southey Jahn's family anglicised their surname in 1919. For a time Ursula called him Conrad, but he disliked that Germanic name, and preferred "Peter." To avoid confusion, the latter is used throughout.

13. Philip Unwin, *The Publishing Unwins*, Heinemann, 1972, 27; UMW, *Something …, op cit.*, 241; David Unwin to author.

14. UMW, *Kelpie the Gipsies' Pony*, Harrap, 1934. On style and incidents, 9-27, 86, 96, 147–56, 175, 203 et seq, 219, 231.

15. *Evening Standard*, 18 April 1934.

Chapter Six

1. UMW, *Pretenders' Island*, Harrap, 1940, 29, 37, 52, 74, 167, 184.
2. Allen & Unwin archives, RU.
3. *Sunday Times*, 4 August 1935
4. Royalty statements, PD.
5. UMW, Autobiographical notes, PD.
6. UMW, *Something …*, 241.
7. UMW, Information about the Perrelet family from diaries and letters supplied by Alain Perrelet. UMW, *The Outlaws*, in *The Noel Streatfeild Summer Holiday* Book, Dent, 1973.
8. Philip Unwin, *op cit*, 19.
9. Jean Burgess to author.
10. "L'après-midi, tous étant partis, je suis comme dans le château de la Bell au Bois dormant … où je vis l'atmosphère de Shakespeare, le songe d'un jour de printemps, avec le silence et, seul bruit, le ramage des oiseaux qui sont partout. L'abandon de ce vieux manoir ruiné, entouré de végétation envahissante. … Les eaux grasse reflètent les grandes arbres et les verts variés du lac ont une grande beauté; en peignant cette solitude est exquise. … Un poisson sort de l'eau pour gober un moustique … Des coucous dans le lointain font leur cri interrogateur, et tout près de moi, le gargouillement des canards sauvages (… couvertes de nénuphars) qui font miroiter leur plumage coloré."
11. UMW, *Adventures of Anne*, Harrap, 1935, 11, 82.
12. Dated December 1926, it was probably among the first stories sent to Harrap the following year. See Chapter Three.
13. *TLS* 21 November 1936; *Manchester Guardian* 27 November 1936. Paul Harrap to Michael Shaw, 4 August 1978, Harrap archives.
14. UMW, *Anders & Marta*, Harrap, 1935, 95.
15. *Hampshire Chronicle* and *Hampshire Advertiser*, 5 October 1935.
16. UMW, *Out of the Shadows* in *Hurricanes* 4, Hamilton, 1971, 12.
17. *Partners …, op cit*, 21.
18. David Tew to author.

Chapter Seven

1. Andrew John to author.
2. UMW, *La Forclaz, June 1936*, PD.
3. UMW, *Something …*, 241.
4. UMW, *The Twins ..*, 45.
5. UMW, *Sandy-on-the-Shore*, Harrap, 1936, 62, 66, 81, 141, 188. *TLS* 5 December 1936.
6. *Bournemouth Times*, 10 December 1937.
7. *Daily Telegraph*, 4 December 1937.
8. UMW, *Elaine of La Signe*, Harrap, 1937, 94.
9. *Barbara Moray …, op cit*, 25–41, 80-3; Alan, *Barbara Árnason …*; *Hampshire Chronicle*, and *Hampshire Observer*, 27 February 1937. UMW, *Something …*, 241.
10. Alan to SU, 8 January 1947, RU.
11. Alan to SU, 8 October and 8 November; SU to Alan, 12 October and 17 November, all 1936, RU.
12. Adrian Bell, *Only for three months*, Mousehold, 1996, 48–67.

13. *Annual report*, King's College, Cambridge, 1997, 74–5; archivist Patricia McGuire to author; Alan, PD. Additional information from David Unwin, James John.
14. Norman Rosser, Malvern College archivist, to author.
15. R.C. Sherriff, *No leading lady, an autobiography*, Gollancz, 1968, 208–12.
16. Mabel Williams 1967 diary, PD.
17. George Harrap to UMW, 29 July 1937, PD.

Chapter Eight

1. Moss, *Ursula Moray Williams, op cit*, 56–61. Republished in Moss, *Part of the pattern*, Bodley Head, 1986, 53–7.
2. UMW in Anne Wood ed, *Books for your children*, vol. 12, no. 2, Winter 1976, 5. Pinocchio is misspelt throughout as Pinnochio.
3. UMW, *A spontaneous affair*, written for education department of Victoria, Australia, 1978, 04/02/27, 7S.
4. *The Magic Casement, op cit*, 1938, 2.
5. UMW to Faith Jaques, 24 September 1970. Timaru Herald, 16 December 1976. Wood *op cit*.
6. Wood …, *op cit*.
7. *Ibid*.
8. UMW, *Adventures of the Little Wooden Horse*, 1938, 9, 12–13, 128–131, 203.
9. Moss, *op cit*, 60.
10. Wood, *op cit*.
11. UMW to Clive Pearce, 3 November 1997, PD.
12. Photograph, Petersfield Museum, 7/203.
13. George Harrap to UMW, 29 July 1938, PD.
14. *Daily Telegraph*, 9 December; *Sunday Times*, 16 October and 4 December; *TLS*, 5 November; *The Times*, 7 December; *News Chronicle*, 16 December; *Yorkshire Post*, 30 November; *Christian Science Monitor*, 5 December; *The Bookseller*, 22 December. All 1938.
15. Hutchinson to UMW, 25 February 1939, PD.
16. Frank Frazier to UMW, 30 June 1939, PD.
17. Moss, *op cit*, 61.
18. UMW, Lands End sketchbook, PD.
19. Hamish Hamilton republished a shorter version for its Reindeer series in 1963, entitled *Peter on the Road*.
20. *The Observer*, 13 August; *Yorkshire Post*, 26 July; *TLS*, 18 November; *The Lady*, 14 September, all 1939.
21. Harrap publicity leaflet 1939, PD.
22. *Magic Casement, op cit*.
23. UMW to David Tew, 6 January 1978.
24. UMW, *Adventures of Puffin*, 1939, 7, 9, 198.25.　　*Sunday Times*, 26 November 1939; *The Observer*, 4 February 1940; *Yorkshire Post*, 29 November 1939.
26. Alan Moray Williams, *Ours not to reason why*, F. Muller, 1948, 106, 147.
27. UMW, *Wartime memories*, PD.

Chapter Nine

1. Stephen Flower, *Raiders Overhead*, privately published, 1993.
2. Esher South ARP wardens, Surrey Record Office, 4463/1/2.

3. Bob Ogley, *Surrey at War 1939-1945*, Froglets Publications, 1995.

4. UMW to Evelyn Unwin, 25 April, 4 and 8 May 1940.

5. Ogley, *op cit*.

6. Hawker company records, RAF museum, Hendon. Paul Gallico, *The Hurricane Story*, Michael Joseph, 1959.

7. Bert Tagg in John Fozard ed, *Sydney Camm and the Hurricane*, Airlife, 1991, 145. Paul Langton, Stephen Webbe to author.

8. Malcolm Peebles, *The Claygate Book*, privately published, 1983, 90–1.

9. Winston Ramsey ed, *The Blitz – then and now*, vol. 1, Battle of Britain Prints, 1987; Gallico, *op cit*, 96; sister-in-law Beatrice Paine to author.

10. RAF records, RAF Cranwell.

11. John Hook, *We died and never knew – the fatal civilian casualties 1939–1945* vol. 1, privately published, 1998, 93. UMW, *Wartime memories*, PD.

12. The CornerCot story reflects a contemporary argument between Ursula and Peter about distinguishing the sounds of explosions and of gunfire. Peter's ARP superintendent was "M.C.J", possibly a Mr James. Alternatively the name may be a variation of Mr John. PD.

13. SU, … *publisher*, 256–7. Sally Gritten, *The history of Puffin Books*, unpublished, 1991, 13, put the figure at 37.5%. Ian Harrap, *The House of Harrap, a personal memoir*, 7. David Unwin, *Fifty years with father*, Allen & Unwin, 1982, 96.

14. Paul Harrap to Michael Shaw, Curtis Brown, 4 August 1978, Harrap archives.

15. UMW, *A Castle for John-Peter*, Harrap, 1941, 11–12, 15–16, 94–5. Cyril enlisted as a rifleman in New Zealand in 1916 and was hospitalised in England after being wounded in the leg. He suffered ill-health thereafter. Daughter Diana Unwin to author and SU, … *publisher*, 24–5.

16. Ian Harrap, *House …*, 1; *Partners .. op cit*, 26.

17. Kaye Webb to Curtis Brown, 5 December 1963, PD.

18. A replica edition of 1981 supports this theory. Although printed on much higher grade paper than the wartime original, illustrations show slight fill-in, indicating they have been copied from the printed page, and the only coloured picture is missing.

19. Stephanie Thwaites, Curtis Brown, to author.

20. A cat "black as soot" with the ability to change character had first appeared in *Mrs Josephine Bakes Bread*, one of the plays in *The Autumn Sweepers*.

21. UMW, *Gobbolino, the Witch's Cat*, Harrap, 1942, 6, 20–5, 35, 66–71, 123–33, 192.

22. Gallico, *op cit*, 48.

23. Esher South ARP wardens, *op cit*..

Chapter Ten

1. Pat Smythe, *Jump for Joy*, Cassell, 1954, 45, 50.

2. Daughters Anita Cheney and Elaine Pearse to author. Peggy named Elaine after *Elaine of La Signe*.

3. *The Citizen*, 6 April 1942. See also http://www.bbc.co.uk/ww2peopleswar/stories http://www.bbc.co.uk/ww2peopleswar/categories/c54691/ and search 'Gloster'

4. Barbara Phipps to author. UMW, *Something …, op cit*, 242–3; UMW to Eugenie Unwin, 25 September 1943.

5. Jill Harris (née Cotton), Doreen Buckley (née Newbury), Barbara Phipps to author.

6. UMW to Eugenie Unwin, 25 September 1943.

7. Jill Harris to UMW, 28 September 1986, and to author.

8. Matthew Eve, *Children's literature during the Second World War*, doctoral dissertation, Oxford University, 1992, 257.

9. JO'H to UMW. 12 December 1963,7S. *Manchester Guardian*, 22 December 1945; Eileen Colwell, *The Magic Umbrella*, 1976, 159–60; *Sunday Telegraph*, 6 December 1992.

10. Joanna Jensen to Harrap, 30 May 1983. 7S holds extensive correspondence up to 19 December 1989.

11. Jill Harris, Andrew John to author. UMW notes, PD.

12. Michael Brodrick to author.

13. UMW to Eugenie Unwin, 25 September 1943; Andrew John, Elaine Pearse to author.

14. Joanne Lewis Sears, *Dictionary of Literary Biography*, Gale, 2005, wrongly refers to *Anders & Marta* as part of the Toymaker series. Jill Harris said her mother told her that the character and drawings of Anders in *The Three Toymakers* were based on Andrew.

15. UMW, *The Three Toymakers*, Harrap, 1945. 7, 29, 83–98, 130–40.

16. The dramatisation by Dehn was directed by Guthrie at Bradford Civic Theatre, undated letter from Harrap, 7S, UMW04/02/82.

17. George Anderson to UMW, 16 October 1945, 25 June 1946, 7S. Press listings appeared from 17 January 1946, and short reviews from February. SU to UMW, 3 June 1946, RU.

18. UMW to FJ, 8 January 1975, 7S.

19. Anderson to UMW, 10 August 1945, 7S.

21. Brian Kedward, *Angry skies across the Vale*, privately published, 1995, 274.

Chapter Eleven

1. UMW to Alan, undated, after Barbara's death in January 1976.

2. www.uboat.net/allies/merchants/3374.html.

3. Vifill Magnússon to author.

4. Kedward, *op cit*, 284–5.

5. UMW to Alan, 14 January 1979. Erkel Williams to author.

6. Nikolaus Pevsner & David Lloyd, *The Buildings of England, Hampshire and the Isle of Wight*, Penguin, 1967; Lord Cottesloe to author.

7. British Red Cross Journal, October 1922, 117. Diary entry 10 March 1933.

8. Lord Malmesbury, Lord Cottesloe to author.

9. Hampshire Red Cross report March 1942–January 1944, 7–8. UMW to Alan, 20 May 1993. BMW to Alan, 11 March 1968.10.   UMW to Alan, 9 January and 8 November 1987, 20 May and 18 September 1993, and undated.

11. Alan, *Russian made easy*, Sunday Pictorial, 1943, preface; *Ours not to reason why*, F. Muller, 1948, 10, 146, says Kingsley Martin, editor of the New Statesman, would not help. Alan to Chatto, 26 December 1939; John McDougall of Chatto to Alan, 12 February 1940, RU. Chatto and Sassoon declined.

12. *Russian ..., op cit*, preface.

13. SU to AMW, 25 January, 7 June, 12 November, 8 December 1943; Alan to SU, 3 January, 24 August 1943, 17 September, 2 November 1945, RU.

14. Alan, *Children of the Century*, F. Muller, 1947, 46.

15. UMW visitors' book. Evelyn Rattray to Alan, 31 December 1967.

16. BMW to Alan, 2 January 1960, 31 January 1965; UMW to Alan, 18 October 1979, 12 January 1984, *et al.*

17. UMW, *Something ..., op cit*, 243; Andrew John to author.

Chapter Twelve

1. Vifill to author.
2. SU to UMW, 3 June 1946; Anderson to UMW, 25 June, 8 July, 22 July 1946, 7S.
3. UMW, *Malkin's Mountain*, Harrap, 1948, 7, 45, 54, 82, 101–2, 137.
4. Anderson to UMW, 22 July, 2 September 1946, 28 April 1947; A.J. White to UMW, 28 April 1947, 7S. UMW royalty statements, PD.
5. Anderson to UMW, 2 September 1946, 7S.
6. UMW workbook, PD.
7. Andrew to author. Met Office website www.metofficegov.uk.
8. In *Something ...*, *op cit*, written over forty years later, Ursula wrongly refers to the boat as *Gulfoss*, and confuses other details. Her contemporaneous diary is more reliable.
9. UMW diary 23 July to 15 September 1947, PD; *Something ...*, *op cit*, 243–4; *Golden Horse with a Silver Tail*, Hamilton, 1957, 5. Andrew John to author.
10. *The Binklebys at Home*, *Jockin the Jester*, and *Goodbody's Puppet Show* continued this trend.
11. Eleanor Holland-Martin to UMW, 28 September 1947, 7S. UMW, *The Story of Laughing Dandino* Harrap, 1948, 7, 37, 87–8.
12. SU to UMW, 16 January 1948; Harrap to UMW 22 January, 16 March, 4 October 1948, *et al*, 7S.
13. Arthur Watkins, Stewart James to author.
14. George Anderson to UMW, 31 October; R.O. Anderson to UMW, 15 November 1949, 7S.

Chapter Thirteen

1. UMW to Ruth Taylor, 10 October 1949; Ruth Taylor to author.
2. Amanda Bunbury, Bridget Cooper, Anita Cheney, Doreen Harris, Sue John, Barbara Phipps to author.
3. Laurence Cotterell (Harrap) to UMW, 4 October 1948; George Anderson to UMW, 31 October 1949, PD.
4. SU to UMW, 14 December 1949, 7S. JO'H to SU, 22 December 1949, PD. Juliet O'Hea to SU, 22 December 1949, private papers. Unfortunately, fire destroyed all Curtis Brown archives, including all letters from UMW.
5. UMW, diary, January-February 1933, PD.
6. Geoffrey Trease, *The Revolution in Children's Literature* in *The Thorny Paradise*, ed. Edward Blishen, Kestrel, 1975, 13–24.
7. Dame Jacqueline Wilson to author; *The Guardian*, 24 February 2007.
8. *Manchester Guardian*, 5 September 1949; Andrew John to author.
9. Quoted by JO'H to UMW, 14 April 1950, 7S.
10. JO'H to UMW, 25 May 1950, 7S. See Chatto & Windus archive, RU, for correspondence between UMW, BMW, JO'H and Smallwood.
11. UMW, *Jockin the Jester*, Chatto & Windus, 1951, 239.
12. Smallwood to UMW, 10 October 1951, RU. Streatfeild is quoted by JO'H to UMW, 14 October 1952, 7S. Gwendolen Freeman, TLS, 23 November 1951, 756.
13. UMW workbook, PD; JO'H to UMW, 20 November 1950, 8 October 1951, 7S.
14. JO'H to UMW, 19 July, 8 October 1951, 17 January, 8 February 1952, 7S.
15. The dust-jacket says five thousand pounds.
16. Talk to Cheltenham College, November 1967, *Funny Books* ms, 8, 7S.
17. UMW, *The Binklebys on the Farm*, Harrap, 1953, 7, 13–18, 21–37, 64, 69–87, 102, 110–17, 128.

18. Stewart James, Barbara Marsh, Philip Smith, Anita Cheney to author. Moray was elected a Fellow of the Society of Antiquaries of London on 1 May 1952. His citation mentioned his work in Hampshire, and on Bredon Hill. His excavations are mentioned in R. H. Lloyd, *The Villages of Bredon Hill*. He deposited the finds at Overbury estate's private museum, of which, erroneously known as "Professor Moray Williams," he was curator. Dagny Holland-Martin, Elizabeth Stirling Lee to author.

19. JO'H to UMW, 19 November 1952, 7S.

20. UMW workbook, PD.

21. Hulton Press archive, 7S, including Morris to UMW, 22 August 1952, 24 February, 10 March 1953. On end of series, JO'H to UMW, 8 September 1961, and Rosemary Garland to UMW, 12 September 1961, 7S.

22. JO'H to UMW 19 October 1955, 7S. On Morris, see Sally Morris and Jan Hallwood, *Living with Eagles*, 1998. Other information from Steve Holland. On Mr Whoppit, see Pat Rush, *High-speed Ted*, in *Teddy Bear Stories for grown-ups*, compiled by Catherine Taylor, Michael O'Mara, 1993, 125–7.

23. Wharmby to UMW, 31 July 1953, 7S.

24. JO'H to UMW, 21 August; Snow to UMW, 15 September 1953, 7S.

25. UMW, *Grumpa*, Brockhampton, 1955. Phyllis Hostler, *TLS*, 1 July 1955, 17.

26. JO'H to UMW 11 November 1953, 23 February 1954, Snow to UMW, 14 January 1954, 7S.

27. Mabel to Alan, 14 February; Moray to Alan, 6 March 1954, PD. Her death certificate listed Paget's disease of the bone.

28. UMW to BMW, 10 March 1974, PD; to FJ, 24 September 1970, 7S; to Alan, 21 November 1991, PD.

29. UMW, On a happy old age, 4–5, 7S.

Chapter Fourteen

1. UMW diary. "Once I am up and talking, the words flow and I am happy," she wrote after the visit to Chandlers Ford school.

2. Jessie and Maurice Chambers, Barbara Harris, Sheila Weir, Anita Cheney, Rosalyn Deakin to author.

3. Twelve letters to UMW, 1977–88, 7S.

4. Lady Caroline Eyres Monsell, wife of Evesham MP Sir Bolton Eyres Monsell, was "the leading spirit of the movement," *Evesham Journal*, 25 April 1931.

5. JO'H to UMW, 19 October, 4 and 21 November 1955, 7S.

6. UMW, *Goodbody's Puppet Show*, Hamilton, 1956, chapters 10, 13.

7. Doreen Harris, Martin Buckley, Jessie Alexander, Doreen Buckley, Bridget Cooper, Barbara Phipps, Barbara Marsh, Stewart James to author.

8. Andrea Morton-Saner to author. JO'H to UMW, 9 November 1955, 7S.

9. Stephen and Roger Tandy, Elaine Pearse, Anita Cheney, to author.

10. UMW to FJ, 11 and 23 November 1970, 7S.

11. James, Alain Perrelet, Bridget Cooper, Anita Cheney, Roger Tandy, Paul Hemelryk, Elizabeth John to author.

12. James, Andrew, Anita Tandy, Sue John, Elizabeth John to author.

13. JO'H to UMW, 5 January, 14 March, 10, 19 and 25 July 1956, 7S. UMW, *The Noble Hawks*, 1959, 224.

14. Ursula-watchers can spot the usual fingerprints left at the scene – Hugh of Beckford,

references to Worcestershire, Winchester, Iceland and St David's where the John family watched peregrines flying around the headland.

15. UMW, *The Forgotten Child, op cit.*

16. UMW, *Hobbie*, 1958, 14, 32, 109, 124. JO'H to UMW, 6 November, 4 December 1956.

17. UMW, *diary*, PD. Lynette Turberville Smith to author. During the trip, Philip called on a publisher and discovered *The Kon-Tiki Story*, which became a world best-seller. Philip Unwin, *op cit*, 144–5.

18. Commander George Murray Levick. See www.bses.org.uk.

19. *Gloucestershire Echo*, 25 March 1963.

20. UMW, *Jockin …, op cit.*, 138.

21. Norma's husband is inconsistently called Clifford 22–5, 128–36, and Stan 48–56, 122.

22. The undated story, later marked "for amusement only," is set in the future in 1960 and 1965, so it is reasonable to suppose it was written in the 1950s. 7S.

23. UMW, *The Moonball*, Hamilton, 1958, 28, 41, 45–6, 81, 89–90, 92–3,123–4, 137–8. The courtroom description exactly matches the former Evesham magistrates' court, now Wychavon district council offices.

24. Andrew to UMW, 28 December 1957, PD; JOH to UMW, 30 January, 3 February 1958, 7S.

25. The description of natives as "savages" later led to charges of racism. See Chapter 22.

26. UMW, *The Nine Lives of Island Mackenzie*, Chatto & Windus, 1959, 9–10, 22, 59–64, 80, 94–8, 111–15, 121–8.

27. *The Guardian*, 4 December 1959. Streatfeild to UMW, 13 October 1959, 7S. *Elizabethan*, December 1959, 45.

28. UMW notes, visitors' book, PD. Ewart Wharmby to UMW, 11 February 1959, 7S; UMW, *Love and Kindness*, talk to Ashton-under-Hill Mothers' Union, February 1973, 7S, 5.

29. JOH to UMW, 30 June, 9 September 1959, 7S. Rita Tandy diary, 26 September 1959, PD.

Chapter Fifteen

1. He apologised twenty years later, Alan to UMW, 28 May 1980.

2. UMW, *Love ..*; *Post-operative*, PD.

3. JO'H to Smallwood, 26 September; file note 29 September 1960, RU.

4. UMW, *Johnnie Tigerskin*, Harrap, 1964, 7–8, 86. *TLS*, 26 November 1964.

5. JO'H to UMW, 16, 27 March 1962, 7S. UMW, *Beware of this animal*, Hamilton, 1963. In February 1970, Rodney Bewes, star of BBC TV's *The Likely Lads*, read an adaptation in five episodes on Jackanory. UMW, *High Adventure*, Nelson, 1965.

6. UMW, *O for a Mouseless House*, Chatto & Windus, 1964, 9, 50, 55, 88–99, 119. The church mice are white, their rivals black. See chapter 22 regarding later complaints of racial stereotyping.
   The Guardian, 4 December 1964. Streatfeild to UMW, 9 and 16 February 1964.

7. When nine years after leaving school, James became a Master of Wine, his parents showed their pride by giving him an inscribed gold watch, but Peter wrote to warn him of the dangers of being "too pleased with yourself."

8. Cheltenham College reports, PD. Robin to author, and subsequently.

9. UMW to Alan, 21 February 1965, PD. JO'H to UMW, May to November 1965, 19 December 1966, 7S.

10. UMW, *The Cruise of the Happy-Go-Gay*, Hamilton, 1967, 7, 20–9, 45–8.

11. UMW, *Writing* …,16.

12. UMW to Alan, 1 January 1967, PD.

13. In tourist industry terms, Ursula catered for 83 guest nights in 1965 and 119 the following year. UMW visitors' book.

14. UMW, *The Silver Horse*, in *Time for a Story*, compiled by Colwell, Penguin, 1967.

15. UMW, *A Crown for a Queen*, Hamilton, 1968. See chapter 17 on Shirley Hughes.

16 JO'H to UMW, 6 December 1966, 15 February 1967, 7S. The novel was later reworked as *A picnic with the aunts*. See chapter 18.

17. UMW to FJ, 14 April 1971, 7S.

18. UMW, *The Toymaker's Daughter*, Hamilton, 1968, 126.

19. UMW to Mary Unwin, 14 October 1968, PD.

20. UMW to Rayner, 1 and 17 August 1968, RU.

21. Typescripts and correspondence at 7S. O'Hea called the story, in which naughty Pedro gets a bicycle and his good sisters only dolls "very un-moral."

22. UMW to Richard Calver, 23 May 1968, UMW to Alan, undated 1968, PD. UMW, *A spontaneous* …, 2.

23. UMW, notes, PD; *Boy in a Barn*, Allen & Unwin, 1970, 9, 12, 62–4, 79–82, 100–1, 111.

Chapter Sixteen

1. John Rowe Townsend in *The Guardian*, 29 October 1979. On Webb, see Gritten, *op cit*, 18-22; Felicity Trotman in ODNB, 2004; obituaries in *The Guardian* 17 January 1996, and *The Daily Telegraph*, *The Independent*, *The Times*, 18 January 1996, *The Bookseller*, 26 January 1996. Correspondence between Webb, UMW and others, on which much information is based, is contained in the Webb archive at 7S.

2. JO'H to UMW, 13 November 1963, 7S.

3. Delyse Recording Company, DEL 194.

4. *The Times*, 13 April 1970.

5. *Puffin Post*, vol. 1, no. 1, spring 1967.

6. Gladys Williams, *Children and their books*, Duckworth, 1970, 145.

7. Webb to UMW, 8 February 1966, 7S. Eleanor Graham, *The Puffin Years*, in *Signal*, September 1973, 120.

8. Hughes to author.

9. David Lewis, *Puffin Post*, vol. 16, no. 1, spring 1982.

10. UMW to KW, 15 April 1982, 7S. The visit was in January 1971.

11. UMW, *Children's Parties (and Games for a Rainy Day)*, Corgi, 1972. Further information from Doreen and Martin Buckley, Janna and Justin Gowthorpe, Barbara Marsh, Anita Cheney, Elaine Pearse, Jeremy John, Elizabeth Stirling Lee, Mike Shaw, Sue Lindsay, Diana Birch, Lesley Slater, James John.

12. UMW to Richard Calver, 4 January 1969, PD. *Puffin Post*, vol. 3, no. 1, 1969.

13. Moss, *Many happy returns Puffin Club*, 1970, *Children's Book News*, republished in … *Pattern, op cit*, 38.

14. Chris Green, John Clark (jnr) and Susan Hetherington to author.

15. UMW Puffin passport, 7S.

16. *Puffin Post*, vol. 4, no. 1, 1970; Webb, *What sort of holidays do children really like?* In *The Observer*, colour supplement, 8 March 1970.

17. UMW to FJ, 1 March 1970, 7S.

18. UMW, *Castle Merlin*, Allen & Unwin, 1972, 90.

19. KW to UMW, 5 February, 8 and 12 May 1970, 7S.
20. UMW to FJ, 24 September 1970,7S; Sheila Weir to author. UMW notes, PD.
21. Jane Allen to UMW 1 February 1978, and Newcastle club newsletter, 7S.
22. UMW to KW, 28 January 1979, 7S.
23. Patrick Hardy to UMW, 12 November 1979, 7S.

Chapter Seventeen

1. See UMW, *For Brownies*, Harrap, 59–61, 85; *Gobbolino ...*, 1942 and 1991 reprint, 137; Norah Shaw, *Vermilion*, Methuen, 1935, 83.
2. See UMW, *Grumpa*, 12, 72-3; *Golden horse ...*1, 26; *The Binklebys at home*, Harrap, 1951, 9; *Secrets ...*, 14; *... mouseless*, 40.
3. UMW in *Partners in Progress, op cit*, 22.
4. Graham, memorandum, probably July 1958, BU. Unattributed information is based on correspondence between Graham, Clark, and Fortnum, BU.
5. Webb to Richard Hough, 5 January 1968, BU.
6. UMW to Elizabeth Attenborough, 26 March 1984 (?), BU.
7. On Soper see David Wootton, *The art of George and Eileen Soper*, Chris Beetles, 1995.
8. Cited by O'Hea to Smallwood, 2 June 1958, RU.
9. Nicholas Tucker, *The child and the book*, CUP, 1981, 49. Gabriel White, *Edward Ardizzone, Artist and Illustrator*, Bodley Head, 1979, 121–49.
10. UMW to Smallwood, 11 November 1959, RU.
11. UMW to Elaine Pearse, 20 January 1993, PD.
12. AM-S to MacRae, 2 September 1988, 7S. Gillian Tyler to UMW, undated letters c 1989/90, PD.
13. Hughes, *A Life Drawing*, Bodley Head, 2002, 122–3, and to author.
14. UMW, *Mog*, Allen & Unwin, 31–2.
15. JO'H to UMW, 20 November 1968, 7S.
16. Their correspondence 1969-74 is in the Jaques archive, 7S.
17. Douglas Martin, *The book illustrations of Faith Jaques*, in *The Private Library*, Private Libraries Association, winter 1985, 153. Hughes to author.
18. UMW to FJ, 1 August 1973, 7S.
19. FJ to UMW, undated, early August, and 13 August 1973, 7S.
20. UMW to FJ, 30 November 1973, 8 February 1974. *Grandpapa's Folly and the Woodworm-Bookworm*, Chatto & Windus, 1974, artwork, 7S.

Chapter Eighteen

1. In *The Friday Miracle*, ed. Webb, Puffin, 1969.
2. UMW to Smallwood, 30 January 1969, RU. Information is drawn widely from the Chatto & Windus archive.
3. *Puffin Post*, 1973, vol. 1, no. 3.
4. UMW, *No Ponies for Miss Pobjoy*, Chatto & Windus, 1975, 10.
5. UMW quoted in *Timaru Herald*, New Zealand, undated December 1976, PD.
6. UMW, *The Kidnapping of my Grandmother*, Heinemann, 1972, 33. *TLS*, 3 November 1972.
7. UMW to Louise Reynolds, 9 June 1974, PD; to FJ, 16 May 1973, 7S.
8. UMW, *Love ..., op cit*.
9. *Evesham Journal*, January 1972 to April 1975, with quotes from 9 June, 8 August, 31 October 1974. In 1975 Ursula stood down as juvenile chairman to become deputy

chairman of the senior bench.

10. UMW, *Love ..., op cit.*
11. In *Hullabaloo*, ed Willard, Hamilton, 1969, 206–7.
12. JO'H to UMW, 31 January, 11 February, 7 April 1972; UMW to FJ, 14 April, 10 December 1971, 7S. UMW to Richard Calver, 16 September, 11 December 1971, PD.
13. UMW, *Tiger Nanny*, Brockhampton, 1973, 76. 116–20.
14. UMW to Rita Tandy, 30 December 1973, PD. UMW to FJ, 8 February 1974, 7S.

Chapter Nineteen

1. Richard Calver to author, and UMW letters to him, PD.
2. UMW to Richard Calver, 4 February 1974.
3. UMW to FJ, 14 March 1974, 7S.

Chapter Twenty

1. Unattributed information is taken from UMW correspondence with JO'H and FJ, 1974–5, at 7S.
2. UMW to KW, 21 October 1974.3. BMW to Alan, 5 March 1962, 6 December 1963, 31 January 1965, 12 August 1970, PD.
4. Guðbjörg Kristjánsdóttir ed., *Barbara Moray Williams Árnason*, 1996, 80-94.
5. UMW to Alan, 14 January 1976; Hugh John to UMW, 17 January 1976, PD. Vifill Árnason, James John to author.
6. UMW to Vifill and Ágústa Sigfusdottir, 31 December 1975, 31 January 1976, PD.
7. Shaw to UMW, 1 and 25 June, 2 September 1976, 7S; Birkett to UMW, 23 September 1976, PD.
8. UMW, *Bogwoppit*, Hamilton, 1978, 10, 37, 50.
9. *TLS*, 7 July 1978, 765.
10. Hughes to UMW, 2 January 1980, 7S. Nicholas and Ann Clark, Sheila Weir to author.
11. UMW diary, 1976–7, PD.

Chapter Twenty-One

1. UMW, *In the Middle of the Wood*, in The Story-Teller 2, Ward Lock, 1979, 7–16.
2. UMW, *Jeffy, the Burglar's Cat*, Andersen, 1981, 7, 75, 135.
3. AM-S to UMW, 1 May 1979, 10 January, 27 August 1980, 7S. UMW to Alan, 2 February 1982, PD. AM-S to author.
4. UMW, *Bellabelinda and the No-Good Angel*, Chatto & Windus, 1982, 37–47, 99–104, 122, 143.
5. Tom Lacy at Puffin strongly disagreed in his letter to UMW, 2 December 1982, 7S.
6. JO'H to UMW, 23 June 1972, 7S.
7. Letter to UMW, 9 October 1980, 7S. Williams-Ellis published a play *The sea-power of England* in 1913, nine years earlier than the first publication date given by the League.
8. UMW, *Writing ...,* and *... spontaneous ..., op cit.*
9. David Rees to UMW, 21 December 1971, 7S.
10. UMW, *Children's Literature ..., op cit*, PD.
11. UMW, *The Forgotten ..., op cit.*, 7S.
12. Moss, in *The Signal Approach to Children's Books*, ed Nancy Chambers, Kestrel, 1980, 51.
13. UMW to Richard Calver, 9 September 1972, PD. Frederick Smith to UMW, 9 September, 5 November 1972, 8 July 1973, 7S.
14. UMW, *Writing ...,* 7–8. 11.

15. UMW, ...*Mackenzie*, 105. Gillian Klein, *Reading into racism*, Routledge & Kegan Paul, 1985, 51.

16. *Children's Book Bulletin*, 1979, no 1, 7.

17. UMW, *Children's Literature ...*, *op cit*.

18. UMW to Alan, 14 June 1972, PD.

19. UMW to Rita Tandy, 25 October 1993, PD.

20. UMW, *The Loved Ones*, in *The Lady*, 1 June 1978.

21. UMW, *The Christmas story*, probably 1927; *Once in a fairy tale*, 1946, PD. *The hen and the Egg*, 7S.

22. The Rev. Basil Jenkyns, The Rev. Horace Phillips, Sandra Andrews, Dennis Oxley, Anita Cheney, Donald Cooper to author. UMW to Diana Birch, 3 July 1966, to Margaret Burton, December 1992, to Alexandra John, 8 March 1993, PD.

23. UMW, *Love* ...

24. UMW to Mimi Tait, 21 March 1984, PD.

25. In Kaye Webb ed., *Family Tree*, Hamilton, 1994, 33.

Chapter Twenty-Two

1. UMW, *Boy in a barn*, *op cit*, 137.

2. *Puffin Post*, December 1981.

3. UMW to Alan, 9 January 1981, PD. UMW to KW, 2 November 1980; KW to UMW, 6 January, 5 November 1981, 7S.

4. James John to author.

5. *Gobbolino's Halloween* 1983, *Christmas in the Forest* 1984, *A carol for Gobbolino* 1985, *Gobbolino goes to school* ?1995 typescripts at 7S.

6. *The Further Adventures of Gobbolino and the Little Wooden Horse*, Puffin, 1984. Diary , 8 May 1933, PD. There are references to "Valkyries" in The Line, Puffin, 1973, 106 and *No Ponies ...* 15.

7. Attenborough to UMW, 16 November, 7 December 1983, 19 February 1985, 7S.

8. UMW, *Spid*, Andersen, 1985, 7, 131, 138.

9. UMW to Alan, 2 August, 23 August 1980, PD.

10. To overcome infirmity, she developed the technique of revving the engine to its maximum in first gear, then slamming it into fourth. Andrew John to author.

11. UMW, *Grandma and the Ghowlies*, Andersen, 1986, 8, 10, 53, 111.

12. AM-S to UMW, June to August 1985, 7S.

13. UMW to Elaine Pearse, 26 April 1986, PD.

14. Elizabeth John to author. UMW to Alan, 2 August 1980, PD.

15. Jeremy John, Doreen Buckley, Ros Long, Andrew John, Jenkyns to author.

16. UMW to FJ, 1 March 1971, 7S. to Alan, 8 January 1985, PD.

17. Ella Moray Williams, Nicholas Moray Williams to author. Alan, like his father, passed the name Moray to his children.

18. Elizabeth Beckett (née John), Robin John, Sue John to author.

19. UMW to Richard Calver, 30 December 1981; to Alan, 12 January 1984; Hugh to UMW, 21 October 1984, PD.

21. Sophie Richmond (née John) to author.

22. UMW to Diana Unwin, 19 November 1985; to Ágústa Sigfusdottir, 18 June 1990, PD.

23. UMW to Elaine Pearse, undated December 1985, PD. AM-S to UMW, 15 April 1986, 7S.

24. UMW, *Paddy on the Island*, Andersen, 1987, 21, 48, 55, 86, 148–50. *The Singing Island*, ts, 7S. AM-S to UMW, 18 February 1983, 7S.

Chapter Twenty-Three

1. UMW, *Hullabaloo!*, *op cit.*
2. Bruce Woodward, Andrew John to author.
3. Rosamund Long, Andrew John to author. UMW to Alan, 25 January 1990; Rita Griffin diary, PD.
4. Basil Jenkyns to author. UMW to KW 29 June, 2 October 1990, 7S.
5. AM-S to author. 7S holds an annotated typescript and pencil sketches by Morisse.
6. UMW, *Lord Polidore's Parrot*, unpublished, 5, 7S.
7. Belinda Copson, Ursula Moray Williams, ODNB, and to author.
8. Colwell to UMW, 15 January 1991, 7S. Ursula had owned cats, but although respecting their independence, was not in her later life particularly fond of them. She reluctantly adopted a stray in the 1970s, which stayed twelve years. Andrew and James John to author.
9. Sears, *Dictionary ... , op cit. The Times*, 27 December 2006. *The Guardian*, 15 November, 2006. *The Independent*, 7 November 2006.
11. Margery Fisher, *Intent upon reading*, Brockhampton, 1964, 18, 41–2, 240, 342.
12. Nick Park to author.
13. Margaret Mahy to author.
14. Anne Wood to author.
15. Sears, *op cit.*
16. Winifred Whitehead, in *Twentieth Century Children's Writers*, St. James, 3rd edition, 1989, 696–8.
17. John Rowe Townsend, *Written for Children*, Bodley Head, 1990, 171–2.
18. *Daily Telegraph*, 3 March 2008.
19. UMW to Matthew Eve, 24 December 2003.
20. AM-S to author.
21. Gladys Williams, *op cit.*, 45.
22. UMW to FJ, 24 September 1970, 7S.
23. UMW, *On a happy old age*, 7S.
24. Wendy Porteus to author.
25. UMW to Elaine Pearse, undated December 1996, PD.
26. Rosamund Long to author.
27. UMW to Clive Pearce, 14 January 1998. Margaret Burton, Elaine Pearse, Bridget Cooper, Paul Hemelryk, Pat Leahy, Dennis Oxley to author.
28. UMW to Ágústa Sigfusdottir, March 2002; to Diana Unwin, April 2002; to Elaine Pearse, undated, probably 2003. Elizabeth Matte to author.
29. Bridget Cooper, Sheila Weir, Andrew and James John, Ted McWhirter, Doreen Buckley, Jeremy John.

Bibliography

Principal published works by Ursula Moray Williams.
Those marked * are illustrated by the author.

1931 *Jean-Pierre (A&C Black).
1932 *For Brownies: Stories and games for the pack and everybody else (Harrap).
1933 *Grandfather (Allen & Unwin).
1933 *The Pettabomination (Denis Archer).
1933 *The Autumn Sweepers and other Plays for Children (A&C Black).
1934 *Kelpie the Gipsies' Pony (Harrap).
1934 *More for Brownies (Harrap).
1935 *Anders & Marta (Harrap).
1935 *Adventures of Anne (Harrap).
1936 *Tales for the Sixes and Sevens (Harrap).
1936 *Sandy-on-the-Shore (Harrap).
1936 *The Twins and Their Ponies (Harrap).
1937 The Adventures of Boss and Dingbatt (photographs by Conrad Southey John) (Harrap).
1937 *Elaine of La Signe (Harrap).
1937 *Dumpling (Harrap).
1938 Adventures of the Little Wooden Horse (Harrap).
1939 Peter and the Wanderlust (later as Peter on the Road) (Harrap).
1939 Adventures of Puffin (Harrap).
1940 Pretenders' Island (Harrap).
1941 A Castle for John-Peter (Harrap).
1942 *Gobbolino, the Witch's Cat (Harrap).
1943 *The Good Little Christmas Tree (Harrap).
1946 *The Three Toymakers (Harrap).
1946 *The House of Happiness (Harrap).
1948 *Malkin's Mountain (Harrap).
1948 *The Story of Laughing Dandino (Harrap).
1951 *The Binklebys at Home (Harrap).
1951 Jockin the Jester (Chatto & Windus).
1953 *The Binklebys on the Farm (Harrap).
1955 *Grumpa (Brockhampton).
1955 *The Secrets of the Wood (Harrap).
1956 *Goodbody's Puppet Show (Hamilton).
1957 *Golden Horse with a Silver Tail (Hamilton).
1958 *Hobbie (Brockhampton).
1958 *The Moonball (Hamilton).
1959 The Noble Hawks (published in the US as The Earl's Falconer) (Hamilton).
1959 The Nine Lives of Island Mackenzie (Chatto & Windus).

1963 *Beware of This Animal* (Hamilton).

1964 *Johnnie Tigerskin* (Harrap).

1964 **O for a Mouseless House* (Chatto & Windus).

1965 *High Adventure* (Nelson).

1967 *The Cruise of the Happy-Go-Gay* (Hamilton).

1968 *A Crown for a Queen* (Hamilton).

1968 *The Toymaker's Daughter* (Hamilton).

1969 *Mog* (Allen & Unwin).

1970 *Boy in a Barn* (Allen & Unwin).

1970 *Johnnie Golightly and his Crocodile* (Chatto & Windus).

1971 *Hurricanes* (4 volumes of short stories for backward readers) (Chatto & Windus).

1972 *A Picnic with the Aunts* (Chatto & Windus).

1972 *Castle Merlin* (Allen & Unwin).

1972 *The Kidnapping of My Grandmother* (Heinemann).

1972 *Children's Parties (and Games for a Rainy Day)* (Corgi).

1973 *Tiger Nanny* (Brockhampton).

1973 *The Line* (Puffin).

1974 *Granpapa's Folly and the Woodworm-Bookworm* (Chatto & Windus).

1975 *No Ponies for Miss Pobjoy* (Chatto & Windus).

1978 *Bogwoppit* (Hamilton).

1981 *Jeffy, The Burglar's Cat* (Andersen).

1982 *Bellabelinda and the No-Good Angel* (Chatto & Windus).

1984 *The Further Adventures of Gobbolino and the Little Wooden Horse* (Puffin).

1985 *Spid* (Andersen).

1986 *Grandma and the Ghowlies* (Andersen).

1987 *Paddy on the Island* (Andersen).

1935 *Vermilion* by Norah G. Shaw (UMW as illustrator), Methuen.

The Pettabomination, *The Good Little Christmas Tree* and *The House of Happiness* also appeared as plays. Another 24 short stories were published in anthologies. Unpublished works, manuscripts of many of which were bequeathed to Seven Stories, The Centre for Children's Books, Newcastle upon Tyne, include another 5 plays, 35 short stories, poetry, and 4 longer works later abandoned.

Unpublished material

Autobiographical articles, manuscripts and correspondence held at Seven Stories, Newcastle upon Tyne.
Personal diaries, letters and photographs retained by John family.

Biographical

Winifred Whitehead (ed.), *Twentieth-Century Children's Writers* (St James, 1989).
Colwell, Eileen (ed.), *The Magic Umbrella* (Bodley Head, 1976).
Contemporary authors autobiography series, vol. 9 (Gale, 1990).
Sears, Joanne Lewis, in *Dictionary of Literary Biography* (Gale, 2005).

Family

Kristjánsdóttir, Guðbjörg (ed.), *Barbara Moray Williams Árnason* (Reykjavik 1996).

Unwin, David, *Fifty Years with Father: A Relationship* (Allen & Unwin, 1982).

Unwin, Philip, *The Publishing Unwins* (Heinemann, 1972).

Unwin, Rayner, *George Allen & Unwin: A Remembrancer* (privately published, 1999).

Unwin, Stanley (ed.), The work of V.A.D., London 1 during the war (Allen & Unwin, 1920).

    – *The Truth about Publishing* (Allen & Unwin, 1976).

    – *The Truth about a Publisher* (Allen & Unwin, 1982).

Williams, Alan Moray, *Russian Made Easy* (Sunday Pictorial, 1943).

    – *The Malachite casket, Tales from the Urals* (trans.) (Hutchinson, 1944).

    – *The road to the west, sixty Soviet war poems* (trans. with Vivian de Sola Pinto) (F. Muller, 1945).

    – *Children of the Century* (F. Muller, 1947).

    – *Ours not to reason why* (ed), (F. Muller, 1948).

    – *Autumn in Copenhagen* (as Robert the Rhymer) (privately published, 1963).

Williams, Barbara Moray (illustrator) in Marzials, Ada, *Fireside Stories* (Harrap, 1935).

    – Bellhouse, Lucy Wilered, *The Coming of George* (Harrap, 1937).

Topography and historical context

Bakes, Anne, *The Parish of North Stoneham and Bassett* (privately published, 1996).

Barstow, Harold, *Recollections of North Stoneham* (privately published, 2000).

    – *Recollections of North Stoneham and Chilworth Manors* (privately published, 2001).

Bell, Adrian, *Only for three months: the Basque children in exile* (Mousehold, 1996).

Costello, John, *Mask of Treachery* (Collins, 1988).

Farnham, Des & Dine, Derek, *Petersfield Remembered* (Hampshire Library, 1982).

Fozard, John (ed.), *Sydney Camm and the Hurricane* (Airlife, 1991).

Gallico, Paul, *The Hurricane Story* (Michael Joseph, 1959).

Hook, John, *We died and never knew – the fatal civilian casualties 1939 – 1945* (privately published, 1998).

Kincaid, Dave, *Horn Park* (Lewisham Local Studies, privately published, 1999).

Lloyd, F.H.M., *Hurricane, The story of a great fighter* (privately published, 1945).

Mallinson, Howard, *Hinchley Wood: the origins of a 1930s settlement* (privately published, 2003).

Ogley, Bob, *Surrey at War 1939–1945* (Froglets Publications, 1995).

Peebles, Malcolm, *The Claygate Book* (privately published, 1983).

Pevsner, Nikolaus & Lloyd, David, *The Buildings of England, Hampshire and the Isle of Wight* (Penguin, 1967).

Prosser, George, *Select illustrations of Hampshire*, (J&A Arch, 1833).

Ramsey, Winston G., *The Blitz Then and Now* (Battle of Britain Prints, 1987).

Rhind, Neil, *Blackheath Village and Environs* (privately published, 1976).

Rivaz, Richard, *Tail Gunner* (Jarrold's, 1943).

Runyan, Timothy & Copes, Jan, *To Die Gallantly: The Battle of the Atlantic* (Westview, 1994).

Thomas, Helen, *World without End* (Heinemann, 1931).

Education

Archives of the Froebel Educational Institute at Roehampton University

The Bedales Record & *Bedales Chronicle*, Bedales School

Allen, Marjory, *Memoirs of an Uneducated Lady* (Thames and Hudson, 1975).

Badley, John Haden, *Education after the war* (OUP, 1917).

    – *Memories and reflections* (Allen & Unwin, 1955).

    – *Bedales: A Pioneer School* (Methuen, 1923).

Best, Robert, *A Short Life and A Gay One, Frank Best* (unpublished: Bedales archives, c.1918).

Blumenau, Ralph, *A history of Malvern College* (Macmillan, 1965).

Brehony, Kevin (ed.), *The origins of nursery education* (Routledge, 2001).

Chesterton, George, *Malvern College 125 years* (Malvern College, 1990).

Falkner, C.G., *History of Weymouth College to 1901* (privately published, c.1934).

Frankenburg, Charis U., *Not old, Madam, Vintage* (Galaxy, 1975).

Grant Watson, E.L., *But to what purpose* (Cresset, 1946).

Hardie, Avril, *Boys and Girls* (Bedales, 1998).

Henderson, James, *Irregularly Bold: A Study of Bedales School* (Deutsch, 1978).

Lawrence, Evelyn (ed.), *Friedrich Froebel and English Education* (University of London, 1952).

Liebschner, Joachim, *Foundations of Progressive Education, The History of The National Froebel Society* (Lutterworth, 1991).

Palmer, Colin, *Charlotte Mason, Her Life Philosophy and Legacy* (PNEU, 2006).

Partridge, Frances, *Memories* (Gollancz, 1981).

Sanders, George, *Memoirs of a Professional Cad* (Scarecrow, 1992).

Selwyn-Clarke, Selwyn, *Footprints* (Sino-American Publishing, 1975).

Stewart, W.A.C., *The Educational Innovators, Volume 2: Progressive Schools 1881–1967* (Macmillan, 2000).

Unwin, William Jordan (ed.), *The Educator; or, Home, the school, and the teacher, with the proceedings of the Congregational board of education,*(Congregational Board of Education, 1851–64).

Wake, Roy & Denton, Pennie, *Bedales School* (Haggerston Press, 1993).

Organisations affecting early years

Baden-Powell, Robert, *Brownies or Blue Birds* (Arthur Pearson, 1921).

Balfour, E & Cullen, M.F., *The Story of the Hampshire County Branch of the British Red Cross*, (Red Cross, 1994).

Jeffery, David, *The History of Petersfield and Sheet Scouts and Guides* (unpublished, 2007).

Kerr, Rose & Liddell, Alix, *Story of the Girl Guides* (Girl Guide Association, 1976).

Liddell, Alix, *The true Book about Girl Guides* (Muller, 1956).

British Red Cross, *Reports by the Joint War Committee and the Joint War Finance Committee of the British Red Cross on Voluntary Aid* (HMSO, 1921).

Teal, Jim, *Baden-Powell* (Hutchinson, 1989).

Wood, Emily, *The Red Cross Story* (Dorling Kindersley, 1995).

Later years

Lord Chancellor's Office, *Handbook for newly appointed Justices of the Peace* (Lord Chancellor's Office, 1974).

Jenkyns, Basil, *Hotter under the Collar* (privately published, 2003).

Kedward, Brian, *Angry skies across the Vale* (privately published, 1995).

Moyse, Cordelia, *125 years: The Mothers' Union 1876–2001* (Mothers' Union, 2001).

Smythe, Pat, *Jump for Joy* (Cassell, 1954).

Literary

Correspondence of Allen & Unwin, A&C Black and Chatto & Windus at Museum of Rural Life, Reading University.

Penguin Books archive at Department of Arts and Social Sciences, Bristol University.

Butler, Dorothy, *Five to Eight* (Bodley Head, 1986).

Fisher, Margery, *Intent Upon Reading* (Brockhampton, 1964).

Grove, Valerie, *So Much to Tell* (Viking, 2010).

Gritten, Sally, *The History of Puffin Books* (unpublished, 1991).

Harrap, George G & Co., *Partners in Progress* (privately published, 1961).

Harrap, Ian G., *The House of Harrap*, (privately published, c.1974)

Hughes, Shirley, *A Life Drawing* (Bodley Head, 2002).

Hunt, Peter (ed.), *Children's Literature: An Illustrated History* (OUP, 1995).

Klein, Gillian, *Reading into racism: bias in children's literature and learning materials* (Routledge & Kegan Paul, 1985).

Martin, Douglas, 'The book illustrations of Faith Jaques', in *The Private Library*, vol. 7(4), winter 1985.

    – *The Telling Line* (Julia MacRae, 1989).

Morris, Sally & Hallwood, Jan, *Living with Eagles: Marcus Morris, priest and publisher* (Lutterworth, 1998).

Moss, Elaine, 'Ursula Moray Williams and Adventures of the Little Wooden Horse', in Nancy Chambers (ed.), *The Signal Approach to Children's Books*, (Kestrel, 1980).

    – *Part of the Pattern: A Personal Journey through the World of Children's Books, 1960–1985* (Bodley Head, 1986).

Mumby, F.A. & Stallybrass, Frances, *From Swan Sonnenschein to George Allen & Unwin Ltd* (Allen & Unwin, 1955).

Peppin, Brigid & Micklethwait, Lucy, *Dictionary of British Book Illustrators* (Murray, 1983).

Powling, Chris, *Shirley Hughes* (Evans, 1999).

Rush, Pat, 'High Speed Ted', in Catherine Taylor (ed.), *Teddy Bear stories for grown ups*, (Michael O'Mara, 1993).

Sherriff, Robert Cedric, *No leading lady* (Gollancz, 1968).

Townsend, John Rowe, *Written for Children* (Bodley Head, 1990).

Trease, Geoffrey, *Tales out of school* (Heinemann, 1964).

    – *The Revolution in Children's Literature*, in Edward Blishen (ed.), *The Thorny Paradise* (Kestrel, 1975).

Tucker, Nicholas, *The Child and the Book* (CUP, 1981).

Vernon, M.D., *Backwardness in reading* (CUP 1957).

Watson, Victor (ed.), *The Cambridge Guide to Children's Books in English* (CUP, 2001).

White, Gabriel, *Edward Ardizzone* (Bodley Head, 1979).

Williams, Gladys, *Children and their books*, (Duckworth, 1970).

Wootton, David, *The Art of George and Eileen Soper* (Chris Beetles, 1995).
Aiken, Joan 137

Index